An Introduction to
Survey Research
and Data Analysis

An Introduction to
Survey Research
and Data Analysis

Second Edition

Herbert F. Weisberg
THE OHIO STATE UNIVERSITY

Jon A. Krosnick
THE OHIO STATE UNIVERSITY

Bruce D. Bowen
KAISER FOUNDATION HEALTH PLAN, INC.

Scott, Foresman/Little, Brown Series in Political Science
SCOTT, FORESMAN AND COMPANY
Glenview, Illinois   Boston   London

LIBRARY OF CONGRESS
Library of Congress Cataloging-in-Publication Data

Weisberg, Herbert F.
   An introduction to survey research and data analysis / Herbert F.
Weisberg, Jon A. Krosnick, Bruce D. Bowen.—2nd ed.
         p.   cm.
   Bibliography: p.
   Includes index.
   ISBN 0–673–39764–5
      1. Social surveys.   2. Social sciences—Statistical methods.
   I. Krosnick, Jon A.   II. Bowen, Bruce D.   III. Title.
   HN29.W399 1989   88–18473
   300'.72—dc19   CIP

   2 3 4 5 6 7 8 9 10-KPF-94 93 92 91 90 89

Printed in the United States of America

Preface

As survey results and statistical analysis are used increasingly in social science courses, beginning students inevitably ask two questions: (1) Why should we believe the results of surveys based on relatively few interviews? (2) How do we make sense of the statistical results? This book is designed to answer those two questions. Part I describes how surveys are conducted. Part II explains how survey data are analyzed. Part III gives some further guidelines about how to write, read, and evaluate reports of surveys. This book was written because we consider survey research and data analysis to be essential parts of social science research and because we feel that these topics can and must be communicated to nonspecialists.

Additionally, we regard training in analytical thinking to be an important part of a liberal education. Such training, with its emphasis on explanation, causal processes, and empirical evidence, is critically important in social science research. It is also a welcome departure for many students from shallow stereotypes of the attitudes of social groups and from glib generalizations about the impact of public policy on popular attitudes.

Admittedly, there are differences of opinion within the field about the emphasis to be given to three matters treated here: (1) interval statistics versus ordinal statistics, (2) the role of statistical inference, and (3) the importance of hypothesis testing. We have our own positions on these issues in our research, but we have chosen to emphasize here the approach we consider most useful pedagogically: understanding tables thoroughly before moving to interval statistics; downplaying statistical inference, especially for large surveys; and emphasizing relationships more than hypothesis testing. Because these issues are controversial, we have attempted to explain both sides when possible.

The practice of survey research has changed considerably over the twelve years since the first edition of this book was published. Telephone interviewing has become more prevalent than face-to-face interviewing. Experiments have changed some of the conventional wisdom about how to word survey questions. The computer card technology described in the first edition has become passé. The importance of statistical inference procedures and regression analysis in survey analysis has increased. And there is more self-conscious concern about ethical problems inherent in survey research. We have shifted our emphasis on several topics to incorporate these changes in this edition.

We would like to express our appreciation to several people and organizations that have affected our thinking and work on this project. Our approaches to survey research and data analysis have been strongly influenced by the Political Behavior Program, the Center for Political Studies, and the Survey Research Center of the University of Michigan's Institute for Social Research. Additionally, the National Election Study data used in this book were provided by the Inter-University Consortium for Political and Social Research, which bears no responsibility for the interpretations. Richard Niemi, George Rabinowitz, Robert Bates, and Gerald Finch gave us valuable comments on the first edition, as have Larry M. Bartels, Edward G. Carmines, Michael Margolis, and Steven T. Seitz on the second edition. D.K. and N.A. constantly reminded us of the frailities of survey data. We owe a special debt to two editors: John Covell at Scott, Foresman, who has given us considerable encouragement in revising this book, and Dick Lamb, who played a major role in helping us work on the first edition when he was with W. H. Freeman and Company. We are grateful for the assistance of Thomas Little and John Felice. Finally, we give our thanks to the several institutions that have provided us with atmospheres in which we could work on this project: the University of Michigan, the Ohio State University, Arizona State University, the Inter-University Consortium for Political and Social Research summer program, and Blue Cross of California.

Contents

An Introduction to Survey Research and Data Analysis

Introduction

Every day we are all constantly bombarded by surveys:

- The morning paper headline says that the president's public approval rating is at its high for the year.
- The sports page reports which team was voted number one in the nation in this week's United Press International poll of coaches.
- On the bottom of its editorial page, *USA Today* has the pictures of seven typical Americans along with quotes from them on their topic of the day.
- On the way to work, you hear on the radio that according to government statistics the unemployment rate fell 0.3 percent last month.
- Walking by a newsstand, you notice a magazine whose cover trumpets a story: "What Features Americans Want in Their Homes."
- At lunch you debate with a friend which players to vote for this year for the baseball All Star teams.
- On the way home from work, you hear last week's top forty countdown for songs on the radio.
- The radio news headline on the hour is that government statistics show an increase of 3 percent in the robbery rate last month.
- The day's mail includes a questionnaire from your congressman, asking you to express your opinion on a variety of national issues.

- As you decide where to go to dinner, you look back at last month's *Wichita Monthly* magazine, which included a report of readers' votes for the best and worst restaurants of Wichita.
- The television evening news begins with a story indicating that a preliminary poll shows the president's veto of an important bill will be overridden in the Senate tomorrow.
- The television news devotes three minutes to a congressional committee hearing on a bill to ban the reporting of election exit polls before the polling places close.
- You sit down after dinner to watch your favorite television show, and when it is not on, you remember that it was canceled because of low ratings.
- You switch channels and watch the *People's Choice Awards* to see who the public voted as their favorite movie, actor, and actress of last year.
- Just as you get comfortable, the phone rings and someone asks you a series of questions about your favorite brands of sweaters.

All of the above examples are based on surveys, some of which are high quality and some of which are not. As surveys and polls increasingly dominate our society, it becomes important to be able to differentiate the good polls, the bad polls, and the ugly ones.

In this book, we will describe how surveys are conducted and analyzed. We hope this will be useful to three types of readers:

- The person who plans to design and conduct a survey
- The person who wishes to analyze survey data that someone else has collected
- The citizen who reads or hears poll results and wishes to decide which to take seriously.

The book is divided into three parts. The first part introduces the design of surveys, describing the steps from sampling and question writing through interviewing and coding. The second part explains the analysis of surveys, from simple procedures such as frequency distributions and cross-tabulations through more complicated techniques such as control tables and correlation and regression. The final part of the book summarizes the material presented in the two parts of the book, discusses how to read and write reports of survey results, and considers the ethics of survey research.

Survey Design

1

The Nature of Survey Research

What are surveys used for? What can they measure? What kinds of questions can they be used to answer? We address these preliminary topics in this chapter in order to describe the modern polling industry.

It is impossible to determine when the first survey was conducted. There are several biblical accounts, beginning with a census taken after Moses ascended Mount Sinai. Later, the Romans took censuses to prepare for taxation. There were other early censuses, including the Domesday Book, a listing of all landowners in England in 1086. During the late nineteenth century and early twentieth century, some polls were conducted by independent individuals and government agencies in England and the United States to study social conditions and the nature of poverty. Shortly thereafter, newspapers and political parties began conducting surveys in America.

By the 1920s, researchers were beginning to employ surveys as we know them today. The magazine *Literary Digest* conducted surveys to predict the outcomes of many early twentieth century presidential elections. These polls predicted the outcomes of the 1928 and 1932 elections correctly, though their prediction in 1936 was a failure. George Gallup began his political polling in the mid-1930s, as did several university researchers. Many of them worked for the federal government during World War II, measuring public attitudes on food rationing, price controls, and foreign policy as well as studying the attitudes of soldiers. After the war these researchers returned to universities to establish some of the major academic social science research organizations.

Today, survey research is a booming business. Surveys are sponsored by a wide variety of individuals and organizations. Some are sponsored by government agencies such as the Census Bureau. Others are sponsored by the media: newspapers, magazines, and television stations. Still others are sponsored by political candidates running for public office. Companies that manufacture and distribute consumer products or services—including airlines, dog food manufacturers, and phonograph record companies—are also sponsors of surveys. And finally, many surveys are sponsored by researchers at colleges and universities across the country. In total, these sponsors spend millions of dollars each year on surveys.

Surveys are conducted by hundreds of organizations throughout the world. Some are conducted by private research firms that are in business solely to conduct surveys for their clients. You have probably heard of some of these companies, including the Gallup Organization, which conducts surveys for *Newsweek* magazine; Yankelovich Clancy Shulman, which conducts surveys for *Time* magazine; and Louis Harris and Associates, which conducts surveys for the National Public Radio network. Others are conducted by research organizations that are parts of firms (including the major television networks, Procter & Gamble, and Quaker Oats), advertising agencies (such as Ted Bates and Associates and the Leo Burnett Company), and private consulting companies (such as Response Analysis and Westat). In total, these companies employ many thousands of people across the country in one phase or another of survey research.

As a result of the work that these individuals do, surveys are prominent aspects of contemporary life. Most people see the results of surveys in newspapers or magazines or hear about them on radio or television. Most often, these surveys gauge public attitudes on social and political issues. Surveys done by advertising agencies usually measure purchasing behavior, purchasing intentions for the near future, attitudes toward consumer products, and people's reasons for liking or disliking particular products. People who work in marketing departments of large manufacturing and distribution companies make extensive use of surveys when deciding which products to make and sell and which ideas for products not to pursue. Consulting companies that are hired by large corporations measure employees' attitudes about their jobs and workplaces, their communication patterns, and their usual ways of doing their work in order to advise these firms on how to improve employee satisfaction and productivity.

On page 7, you will see an example of a typical newspaper report of a poll. The poll was conducted by Media General along with the Associated Press, and the article summarizes the results from questions relating to fear of crime. This article illustrates how the news media conduct polls to report, an increasingly common practice.

USES OF SURVEYS

Why have surveys become so important? Increasingly, our modern society requires data, and data that are useful for answering many important questions can be gathered by interviewing people. Surveys have been put to use in a number of important contexts.

Political Polls

We are all familiar with polls conducted to predict who will win an upcoming election. A generation ago newspaper articles about who was ahead in a political race relied on speculation by political experts. A political reporter, a political scientist, or a politician would have been asked to say which candidate was leading in the race. The experts were rarely identified in the articles, so readers were not able to evaluate the credibility of the predictions. As polling techniques were refined, it became clear that the best way to gauge public sentiment about an election was to ask people directly, and so polls have largely replaced political experts as the means for predicting election outcomes.

Surveys now have tremendous impact on political candidates' planning of campaign strategy. In the present age of television politics, many presidential candidates hire polling companies to track public opinion about them and about their opponents. These data are used to determine whether to make certain public appearances, whom to associate with publicly, what to say, what not to say, and so on.

Pollsters are also now accepted members of a president's team of advisers. Just as ancient kings kept court magicians around in case they needed special assistance, modern presidents retain pollsters. Thus, Jimmy Carter's key advisers included pollster Pat Caddell, and Ronald Reagan's presidential advisers included pollster Richard Wirthlin. These pollsters are consulted on a variety of matters, from the content of presidential speeches to policy decisions. In general, they advise the president on how to sell his ideas to the public.

GUNS DON'T HELP PEOPLE FEEL SAFER

NEW YORK (AP)— People who keep guns for protection are no more likely to feel safe at home than those who don't have guns, according to a Media General— Associated Press poll.

In fact, gun owners are slightly less likely to feel secure from crime.

But whether they keep guns or not, 70 percent of Americans think people should have the right to shoot intruders, even if they're unsure the person is armed, according to the poll.

Three in 10 Americans keep guns in their homes for security reasons, according to the nationwide telephone poll of 1,251 adult Americans.

Asked whether they generally feel their home is secure from crime, 70 percent of the gun owners and 75 percent of those who don't have guns said yes.

OVERALL, 73 percent of respondents said they felt their homes were safe.

Black and white respondents had significantly different feelings of security. Among blacks, 57 percent felt their homes were secure against crime, and 64 percent felt safe on their streets at night. Among whites, three-quarters felt their homes were secure against crime, and 80 percent felt safe on their streets at night.

Blacks also had less confidence than whites in the protection they received from local police. A total of 39 percent of black respondents thought the police in their communities did a good job against crime, compared with 61 percent of white respondents who said police did a good job.

GUN OWNERS also were less likely to have confidence in the ability of local police to protect them, the poll said. While 54 percent of gun owners thought local police were doing a good job, 61 percent of those who don't have guns felt that way.

Overall, 59 percent said police were doing a good job, 31 percent said they were doing a fair job, 8 percent said police were doing a poor job, and 2 percent didn't know or didn't answer.

The vast majority of gun owners believed they have the right to shoot intruders, even if they're unsure an intruder is armed. Although fewer people who don't keep guns felt that way, a majority also thought people should have the right to shoot intruders.

PEOPLE WHO live in rural areas are far more likely to keep guns for security than those who live in suburbs or cities. Forty-one percent of those from rural areas had guns, compared with about one-quarter of suburban and urban dwellers.

Rural residents were no more likely to feel secure against crime at home than urban or suburban respondents. However, rural and suburban respondents were more likely to feel their communities were safe than urban respondents.

Suburban respondents also had more confidence in local police than either rural or urban respondents.

SOURCE: Columbus Dispatch, Feb. 2, 1987. Reprinted with permission of The Associated Press.

Surveys in Court

In addition to their political uses, surveys have often been used as evidence in courts of law. Take, for example, trademark infringement lawsuits. If one company has a trademark on its product and another company makes a similar product, the first company may sue the second for infringing on its trademark. One question courts wish to answer in such cases is whether the public is confusing the second product with the first. This is a question that can best be answered through surveys.

For example, in 1964, the Zippo® lighter company accused the Rogers lighter company of infringing on Zippo®'s patent rights. Rogers had been manufacturing a lighter that looked almost identical to the Zippo® lighter, and Zippo® claimed that consumers were confused about which lighter was which. They commissioned surveys in which national samples of American adults were asked to name the company that manufactured various lighters that they were shown during the interview. A large number of respondents incorrectly identified the Rogers lighter as a Zippo®, even though the Rogers brand name was stamped on the bottom. This evidence convinced the judge that consumers were confused about which product was which.

Another example involved the Dallas Cap and Emblem Company, which put National Football League emblems on products they sold. The NFL sued claiming trademark violation. They used a survey to show that 80 percent of the public associated the emblems with the NFL and that 64 percent thought they were official NFL products.

The courts were slow to admit survey evidence. In the 1930s, the courts viewed such evidence as hearsay and hence inadmissible, particularly since those interviewed could not be cross-examined in court. By the 1950s, some courts held that surveys were not hearsay since they were not being used to prove the truth of what the respondents said. Meanwhile, other courts were accepting surveys as evidence of "present state of mind, attitude, or belief," which is a recognized exception to the hearsay rule. Survey evidence in trademark cases is still often challenged on the basis of the quality of the survey, but surveys are now recognized as appropriate means of testing trademark violation.

Surveys have been admitted in court in many areas beyond trademark cases. When federal regulatory commissions have charged that advertising creates a false impression in consumers' minds, surveys have been used to show the actual effects of the ads. For example, when the Federal Trade Commission charged that Hi-C® fruit drink ads led consumers to believe that Hi-C® contained more vitamin C than orange juice does, the manufacturer of Hi-C® won its case by submitting a survey showing that consumers did not draw that conclusion. As another example, some defendants in criminal cases seek to move their trial from one community to another because extensive pretrial publicity makes it impossible to empanel a jury that has not heard about the case. Defense lawyers in these cases frequently submit survey evidence documenting the extent of public knowledge about the case in the community.

Government Surveys

Surveys are also often used by the government to compile statistics. The most famous government survey in the United States is the one taken every ten years by the Bureau of the Census to determine the population of the country. Interviewers fan out across the country and knock on doors in order to find out how many people live in each house and apartment. That information is used to determine the population of each city, county, and state; several important political decisions are made on that basis. For example, some states gain representation and other states lose representation in the House of Representatives every decade on the basis of the census's determination of their population. Similarly, census results are used to divide each state into districts of equal population for election of representatives to Congress. Allocation of federal funds to cities is based on their population, so the population census affects the revenue of cities as well.

The use of surveys by the United States government goes far beyond the census. Many government agencies are charged with gathering statistics, and surveys are used as part of their effort. For example, the 1965 Voting Rights Act was designed to remove barriers to voting by blacks and other minorities. As part of the administration of that act, the Bureau of the Census conducts a survey after each presidential election, asking people whether or not they were registered and whether or not they voted. Statistics are compiled by state, race, ethnicity, sex, and other demographics in order to monitor compliance with the Voting Rights Act.

Every month the Labor Department publishes statistics about the level of unemployment in the United States. They might report that the unemployment rate is 7.2 percent, up 0.3 percent since the previous month. Have you ever wondered about the basis of those statistics?

It turns out that the Labor Department conducts monthly surveys, asking people whether or not they were employed during the past month. If they were employed, they are asked further questions about how many hours they worked per week. If they were not employed, they are asked whether or not they sought employment—since the people who do not want a job are not counted as unemployed. It would be difficult to gauge unemployment accurately without such surveys.

As a final example of government use of surveys, consider reports of the crime rate. There are many ways to find out about the level of crime in the United States. One can collect information from police departments about the number of crimes, and the National Institute of Justice does just that. However, not all crime is reported to the authorities. As a result, the National Institute of Justice conducts regular surveys of crime victimization, asking a sample of the public whether or not they were victimized by crime in the last month. These surveys find much higher rates of certain crimes, such as robbery, than police data show. Victimless crimes, such as prostitution and drug use, are understated in the surveys, as is murder, since the victim is not available to be interviewed.

Consumer Research

Many commercial firms conduct polls, often as part of regular market opinion research. Companies use surveys to determine what new products to manufacture so that they can gain market share and to see what features are most desired for those products. Companies planning advertising campaigns often conduct surveys to determine what type of spin to put on advertising pitches in order to maximize effectiveness. Also, corporations use surveys to determine why a product is not selling well and use what they learn to redesign their product or marketing strategy.

The Nielsen and the Arbitron ratings of television viewing are especially well-known consumer surveys. Advertisers buy time on television on the basis of the number of viewers of each program as measured by these surveys. The most popular ways to determine this are by phoning people to find out what program they are currently watching, having households keep weekly diaries of their television viewing, and attaching a device to televisions in a sample of homes to keep track of when they are on. Networks use this information to determine how much to charge advertisers for each of their time blocks. Of course, when a program has too low a viewership, the network cannot charge enough for the advertising time and usually chooses to cancel the show. Thus, these surveys affect the content of television programming.

Academic Research

Surveys are also conducted regularly by researchers at universities. For example, the University of Michigan's Survey Research Center surveys about 600 American adults every month to learn about their current family financial situation; their intentions to purchase houses, cars, and major household appliances; and their savings and investment behavior. The Survey Research Center also measures people's beliefs about the future of the nation's economy. The results of these surveys are used extensively by economists and business people to forecast purchasing, saving, and other financial behavior as well as to plan manufacturing and distribution strategies.

Scholars at the University of Chicago and at the University of Michigan conduct large-scale surveys every year to measure public attitudes on controversial social and political issues. The General Social Survey, conducted by the National Opinion Research Corporation (NORC) at the University of Chicago, has monitored changing social trends since the early 1970s. The National Election Studies, surveys that are conducted by the Institute for Social Research at the University of Michigan, have tracked national political attitudes since the early 1950s. In addition to these national surveys, countless state and local polls are conducted each year by university researchers.

Media Polls

The major news media in the United States frequently conduct polls. Because of the expense involved in polling, many of these polls are joint operations of several media. Collaborators pool their questions and use the results differently according to their differing needs. Television networks generally focus more on a quick summary of public opinion that they can add to a major study, while newspapers may write two or three stories about the same poll. For example, *The New York Times* and CBS News have polled together for several years, with *The New York Times* running the interviewing operation and CBS News performing the computer analysis. The Media General–Associated Press poll in the article reprinted earlier in this chapter is another example of a media poll. In recent years, *Newsweek* and *Time* magazines have also regularly contracted for polls.

The media use polls in order to obtain novel news stories. One example is *The New York Times*/CBS News poll before Christmas 1985, in which children were asked whether or not they believed in Santa Claus. Not exactly hard news, but wonderful material for a feature story. The Media General–Associated Press poll on fear of crime similarly provided newspapers with an article on a topic that interests many readers. Before elections, media polls are used to predict results. Also, monthly media surveys can be used to trace changing support for political parties and the president over several years. Finally, exit polls conducted during elections measure the demographics, motivations, and behavior of voters.

WHAT SURVEYS CAN MEASURE

This review illustrates how polls are a prominent part of everyday life and that they have tremendous effects; it also shows that surveys are used to measure many things. Although it is difficult to fit everything a survey can measure into a few categories, most things that surveys are used to measure can be regarded as attitudes (or preferences), beliefs (including predictions and assessments of importance), or facts (including past behavioral experiences).

Attitudes and Preferences

Attitudes are likes and dislikes. In more technical terms, an attitude is a positive or negative orientation toward an object, and it can be strong or weak. Many children have strong negative attitudes toward spinach, and most Americans have strong positive attitudes toward the American flag. Most of the attitudes measured in surveys are toward people (such as people running for public office) or toward government policies (such as legalized abortion or laws to limit who can purchase handguns). Many techniques have been developed to measure how positively or negatively people feel toward attitude objects of all kinds, and they are often used in surveys.

Preferences are based on comparisons of attitudes toward different objects. For example, if people are asked if they prefer hamburgers or hot dogs, they presumably compare their attitudes toward those two foods and state which is more liked. Surveys are frequently used to obtain such preference data, whether preferences about presidential candidates or automobile makes.

The Media General – Associated Press poll reprinted above includes many attitude questions. For example, it reports that 70 percent of the public think "people should have the right to shoot intruders, even if they're unsure the person is armed." That is an attitude toward a policy. Later the article reports that 59 percent of the public felt that police were doing a good job. Again, that is an attitude, this time toward a group.

Beliefs and Predictions

Beliefs are opinions about the objective state of the world. For example, I might claim that the sky is blue today. This is a statement of a belief. Still another is "Ronald Reagan favors lowering taxes." An example of a belief in the Media General – Associated Press poll report is that 73 percent of the public felt their homes were safe from crime. Beliefs may be true or untrue; what is important is that the individual who holds a belief thinks it is true. When survey researchers measure beliefs, they are not usually interested in finding out the truth. That is, they don't conduct surveys to determine whether Ronald Reagan actually favors lowering taxes. If they wanted to learn that, there are better ways to do so. Rather, researchers usually measure beliefs in surveys because they are interested in what people think is true.

Surveys are also good at measuring *predictions* of the future. One example of a prediction is "the national unemployment rate will decrease during the next twelve months." Another example is "I expect to find a job during the next week." Or "Michael Dukakis will win the next presidential election." Like beliefs, predictions need not be true, but it can be useful to know what the public believes about the future.

Surveys are often used to measure people's beliefs about how *important* various things are. For example, academic surveys often ask the public what they believe is the most important problem facing the United States today. Surveys have also been used to measure how important parents think it is for their children to have various characteristics such as intelligence and honesty. Again, the public's assessments of importance may not be correct, but they are nevertheless useful in their own right.

Facts and Past Behavioral Experiences

Finally, surveys are often used to measure *facts*. For example, people are often asked how many years they have attended school, how many bedrooms there are in their house, how many television sets their family owns, and so on. The Media General–Associated Press poll reports that three in ten Americans keep guns in their homes. The interest here is in learning the truth about these matters, so it is important that what people tell interviewers is actually true.

One of the most common uses of surveys is to measure people's *past behavioral experiences*. The National Health Survey, conducted by the United States Census Bureau, asks people how many times they visited a doctor during the last six months, how many times they were hospitalized, and so on. In the National Crime Survey, respondents are asked to report how many times they were victims of crimes during the previous month. In many political surveys, respondents are asked for whom they voted in the last presidential election.

The distinction between beliefs and facts is not always clean-cut. Many questions about facts actually turn out to be questions about beliefs. For example, answers as to how often the person was a victim of crime in the past month depends on the person's views as to what a crime is. Even when people are asked about their ethnicity, the answers often depend on what ethnic background the people consider themselves — and that is especially the case for people of mixed ethnic heritage.[1] The problems involved in asking about beliefs and facts are somewhat different, but the differences are not as large as one might expect.

GOALS OF SURVEYS

What kinds of questions can one answer with surveys? There are four broad classes of questions that surveys are used to address:

- The prevalence of attitudes, beliefs, and behavior
- Changes in them over time
- Differences between groups of people in their attitudes, beliefs, and behavior

---

[1]See Tom Smith, "The Subjectivity of Ethnicity," in *Surveying Subjective Phenomena*, vol. 2., ed. Charles Turner and Elizabeth Martin (New York: Russell Sage, 1984).

• Causal propositions about these attitudes, beliefs, and behavior

Prevalence of Attitudes, Beliefs, and Behavior

Surveys are most often used to measure the frequency of certain attitudes, beliefs, and behavior. Thus, we use surveys to see what proportion of the public approves of the president's performance in office (an attitude), what proportion of the public feels that the Republican party is the party best able to deal with the economy (a belief), and what proportion of the public has been unemployed and looked for a job during the last month (a behavior).

If we want to ascertain the prevalence of such matters, surveys are an excellent way of measuring their occurrence. In fact, many researchers believe that the best way to find out what people like and believe is to ask them. There may be other ways to find out about behavior, but it is often difficult to determine the frequency of a behavior without asking people whether or not it is something they have done. As already pointed out, the Media General–Associated Press poll reprinted at the beginning of this chapter includes questions allowing assessment of the prevalence of attitudes, beliefs, and behavior.

Changes over Time

Measuring the prevalence of attitudes, beliefs, and behavior is generally only of limited interest. The proportions often mean little by themselves. To say, for example, that 53 percent of the public approves of the president's performance in office does not in itself tell us much. We know that a bare majority approve of his performance, but is that an improvement for him over last year's ratings or a decline? Is it better than other presidents have achieved or worse? These are *change* questions, and they are important. Thus, attitude changes are often more interesting than frequencies themselves.

Of course, the same holds for beliefs and behavior. If 33 percent of the public views the president as a conservative, an interesting question is whether that belief is stronger or weaker than it used to be— whether he is seen as moving to the right or the left. If 22 percent of high school students have used drugs in the past month, it is useful to know whether that percentage is higher or lower than previous years —whether there is an increase in drug use or whether it is tapering off. Repeated surveys are good ways for measuring change.

Subgroup Differences

Another way in which frequencies gain meaning is by comparing the attitudes, beliefs, and behavior of different *groups* of people. It is often interesting to know whether one group is more likely to hold an attitude, have a belief, or perform a behavior than another group. Are men more likely than women to approve of the president's handling of foreign affairs? Are blacks more likely than whites to feel that the president is supportive of a strong federal government? Did men vote at a higher rate than women in the last election?

There are several possible reasons to look at subgroup differences. Sometimes, researchers are interested in the attitudes, beliefs, and behavior of one group, for example the political behavior of women. Looking at a single group by itself is not very informative, since you cannot tell whether the group differs from the rest of the public. As a result, people interested in one group generally perform their research by comparing groups, as by comparing the political behavior of women with that of men.

At other times, researchers are interested in describing the demographics of an attitude, belief, or behavior. When political pollsters examine who supports the president, they are trying to discover the groups to which he appeals in order to understand the bases of his appeals. The report of the Media General – Associated Press poll draws several subgroup comparisons, such as whites feeling more secure against crimes in their homes than blacks, gun owners having less confidence in the local police than non-gun owners, and rural residents being more likely to keep guns for security than urban residents.

Assessing Causation

Surveys are also used to test causal propositions. Academic researchers are particularly interested in identifying the *causes* of social behavior. Why do some people approve of the president's performance more than others? To what extent is that approval due to the person's party ties, and to what extent is it due to other factors? Why do some people view the president as more conservative than others do? Why do some people vote in elections and others do not? Is it due to their reactions to the candidates in the particular election, or is it due to their early childhood learning about politics? These are the types of causal questions that can be addressed through surveys.

The Media General – Associated Press poll on crime considers a causal question in its opening paragraphs. The author of the article was interested in what makes people feel safe from crime in their homes, and he or she thought that owning a gun might be a factor in making people feel secure. Instead, the poll found that 70 percent of gun owners felt secure in their homes compared with 75 percent of people who did not have guns. With that finding, a plausible causal hypothesis was disproved. The article does not probe further as to the causes of feeling safe at home; instead it turns at that point to the presentation of overall frequencies and subgroup differences.

Measuring frequencies, changes, and differences in attitudes, beliefs, and behavior is fairly straightforward, but as we shall see, testing causal hypotheses is more complicated. One has to include in the survey a variety of questions that tap alternative causal logics, then analyze the data to determine which causal explanation fits better.

CHOOSING THE BEST RESEARCH DESIGN

Surveys are one way to collect information about attitudes, beliefs, and behavior, but they are not the only way. Whenever surveys are considered, it is important to realize their limitations and consider the alternatives.

Experiments

One alternative is the experiment. Experiments permit researchers to control events in a way that is not possible in a survey. For example, if the effects of a political speech are to be studied, it might be appropriate (1) to ask some questions before the speech to gauge prior attitudes, (2) to vary systematically the content of the speech that the experimental subjects hear, and then (3) to observe differences in their subsequent attitudes. Causal propositions about changes in attitude, belief, or behavior can sometimes be tested more definitively in experiments than in surveys.

However, experiments often involve highly artificial conditions. Communications may have different effects in a contrived experimental setting than they would have in more natural settings. It is often unclear what results transfer from an experimental setting with volunteer subjects to the more general population under natural conditions. As a result, surveys might be better able to monitor phenomena such as the effects of campaign communications and attitude change over long periods of time as they naturally occur.

Aggregate Data

Another important alternative to surveys is analysis of aggregate data, such as election totals or census data, which measure variables at the level of a state, a county, a city, a ward in a city, a precinct, or a census tract. Aggregate data are widely available and are useful for certain purposes. For example, following a presidential election, vote counts reveal the actual number of votes cast for each candidate and the actual turnout figures. A survey can only estimate these figures.

However, aggregate data cannot substitute for survey data for all purposes, since aggregate data are not individual-level data. Suppose we were interested in studying the voting behavior of blacks. If we examined the election returns from black precincts, we might find that 90 percent of the votes cast in those precincts were Democratic. But we still would not know exactly how blacks voted. The black precincts are probably about 90 percent black, so this may mean that all the blacks in the black precincts voted Democratic, while all the whites in those precincts voted Republican. Or it may mean that all the whites in those precincts voted Democratic along with 89 percent of the blacks, while 11 percent of the blacks voted Republican. If blacks and whites turned out to vote at different rates, then these figures could be wrong. Perhaps all whites voted Democratic, all blacks voted Republican, but very few blacks voted. Furthermore, we have no way of knowing how blacks who did not live in black precincts voted. There is always the strong possibility of failing to notice an ecological fallacy when trying to deduce individual behavior (for example, the voting behavior of individual blacks) from the behavior of aggregates (for example, precinct election returns).

When only aggregate election data are available, such as when one wishes to study the 1832 presidential election, one must make the most of it. However, if one is interested in individual attitudes, it is usually better to use survey data.

Surveys

The explanation of mass behavior often requires mass attitude data that can be obtained only by a survey. We cannot assume that people think in certain ways without asking them what they think. We cannot regard aggregate data as equivalent to individual data, nor can we use experiments as alternatives to the collection of data in the natural environment. If it is possible to ask people questions, we can gain much information about what they are thinking—and why they do things. When public attitudes and mass behavior are of interest, surveys play important roles in social science.

Of course, surveys also have their limitations. They are expensive, particularly if sophisticated procedures are implemented. Many surveys are run on a shoestring, but a large-scale national study can cost over a quarter of a million dollars. Also, people sometimes do not give truthful answers to questions. For example, more white people say they will vote for black candidates than actually do. Thus, surveys are less accurate sources of some sensitive information than are aggregate data.

Actually, surveys are often used nowadays in concert with experimental and aggregate data. In evaluation research, for example, a survey might be used to measure the crime rate and fear of crime before a new police program is instituted to fight burglary, and then another survey would be taken a few months later. The surveys help in the evaluation of the experimental program. Analysis of survey data also often makes use of aggregate data. For example, to compare attitudes of people who live in high-status areas and low-status areas, one could add to the survey data set some information about the demographic characteristics of each respondent's neighborhood.

SECONDARY ANALYSIS OF SURVEY DATA

Sometimes, researchers decide that a survey is the best way to achieve research goals but that collecting a new set of survey data is impractical. In such situations, researchers occasionally decide to analyze survey data that someone else has already collected. This is termed *secondary analysis* to distinguish it from analysis by the primary investigators, who collected the data. It is becoming common for those who design a survey to make their data available to other researchers. The expense of surveys make this important, because few investigators can afford to collect their own survey data. Making data available to other researchers means that secondary analysts can test their own hypotheses and can check the findings of the original researchers. Even researchers planning to conduct their own surveys benefit from this development. They can learn from other studies on similar topics before they conduct their own project.

There are now several major archives that store data released by primary investigators. For example, the Inter-university Consortium for Political and Social Research, based at the University of Michigan, has an extensive archive of thousands of major national surveys from the United States and many other countries. In addition to survey data, the consortium also stores data on national attributes, United States census data, and data on world-event interactions. Often within a year of a survey, universities that belong to the consortium can obtain the survey data free, and nonmember universities can purchase individual sets of data for a fee. The Gallup, Harris, and Roper polls have similar services that permit their surveys to be acquired by interested researchers. Since these archives contain data from surveys done as long as thirty years ago, they permit researchers to evaluate attitude and demographic changes over long periods. The National Science Foundation's Division of Social and Economic Science now requires data collected with its funds to be placed in an archive for the general use of the larger scientific community.

Table 1.1 lists some of the continuing surveys in the consortium's holdings. Earlier in this chapter, we described two of the major ongoing studies—the American National Election Studies and the General Social Survey. There have also been continuing studies focusing on consumer attitudes, health, nutrition, crime, employment, income, and political socialization. The Euro-Barometers have surveyed since 1975 in several Western European nations, focusing on political variables and values. In addition, there are many state polls and some local polls, including the Detroit Area Study, which has conducted surveys on different sociological and political topics in Detroit since the 1950s.

As a result of the development of such archives, secondary analysis is now very common—probably even more common than primary analysis. Most large universities have large collections of survey and other data available for secondary analysis by faculty and students.

SUMMARY

Survey research is very popular. It permits us to measure the prevalence of attitudes, beliefs, and behaviors, to study change in them over time, to examine subgroup differences, and to test causal propositions about the sources of attitudes, beliefs, and behavior. Surveys have important advantages over other research methods and are therefore a useful tool for social scientific investigations.

Table 1.1   Some Continuing Surveys Archived by the Inter—University
Consortium for Political and Social Research

ABC News/Washington Post Polls	1981–
American National Election Studies (CPS)	1948–
Chicago Council on Foreign Relations American Public Opinion & U. S. Foreign Policy	1975, 1979, 1982
Americans' Use of Time (SRC)	1965–66, 1975–76
Annual Housing Surveys (Census Bureau)	1973–
Annual Survey of Governments (Census Bureau)	1973–
British Election Study	1969–
CBS/New York Times Polls	1976–
Census of Governments (Census Bureau)	1962–
Census of Population & Housing (Census Bureau)	1790–
Consumer Attitudes & Behavior (SRC)	1953–
Current Population Surveys (Census Bureau)	1968–
Detroit Area Studies	1953–78
Euro-Barometers	1975–
European Community Study	1970–73
General Social Surveys (NORC)	1972–
German Election Studies	1961–
Health Interview Surveys (National Center for Health Statistics)	1970–
Health & Nutrition Examination Surveys (National Center for Health Statistics)	1971–
Juvenile Detection & Correction Facility Census (U. S. Dept.of Justice)	1971–
Monitoring the Future (SRC)	1976–
National Camping Market Surveys (U. S. Dept. of Agriculture)	1971, 1973, 1978
National Crime Surveys (U. S. Dept. of Justice)	1972–
National Jail Census (U. S. Dept. of Justice)	1970–
National Longitudinal Surveys of Labor Market Experience	1966–
National Surveys of Family Growth (National Center for Health Statistics)	1973–
Panel Study of Income Dynamics (SRC)	1968–
Retirement History Longitudinal Survey (Social Security Administration)	1969–
Survey of Income & Program Participation (Census Bureau)	1983–
Women in Development (Census Bureau)	1979–83
Youth Socialization Panel Survey (CPS)	1965–

Organization Abbreviations
CPS: Center for Political Studies (University of Michigan)
NORC: National Opinion Research Center (University of Chicago)
SRC: Survey Research Center (University of Michigan)

Questions

1. For the next two days keep track of all reports of polls you read or hear. Be especially sensitive to reports that do not mention polls but that contain information which could be obtained only through a survey.
2. Find a recent news story that reports a poll. Who sponsored the poll? Does it report attitudes, beliefs, behavior, or some combination of the three? What were the purposes of the poll?

2

The Survey Process

There are many steps involved in survey research. Before a survey is conducted, important decisions must be made about the objectives of the study and the design of the survey. We describe each of them in this chapter.

A STATEMENT OF OBJECTIVES

Any research study must begin with a statement of its objectives. What does one want to study? On what subject is information desired? If the goal is to test a certain proposition, the statement of objectives should state the proposition clearly and should also state how an appropriate test of the proposition could be constructed. This statement of objectives will guide the selection of respondents (the persons who are interviewed) and the writing of questions so as to guarantee that the survey design meshes with the study's objectives. The more complete the statement of objectives, the more assurance there is that the survey design can be shaped to satisfy them.

Construction of Hypotheses

In scientific research, the specific propositions to be tested are called *hypotheses*. The social sciences are most interested in testing *causal hypotheses*, propositions about the causes of phenomena. For example, researchers studying voting might expect that economic conditions influence voting behavior. We might hypothesize that a person's vote will be affected by whether that person's real income has increased or decreased during the preceding year. We might hypothesize further that people whose real income has increased will be more likely to vote for the incumbent party than will people whose real income has decreased.

Operationalization of Concepts

If hypotheses are to be stated so that they can be tested, it is necessary to understand a fundamental idea: concept operationalization. How concepts are to be *operationalized* (defined in such a way that they can be measured) must always be considered carefully. As an example, we might be interested in understanding public opinions on abortion. Cognitive dissonance theory, a theory developed by social psychologists, states that members of a group will tend to accept that group's positions on issues rather than undergo the stress of disagreeing with their own group. On the basis of this theory, we might hypothesize that Catholics oppose abortion in order to avoid conflicts with their other religious beliefs. The hypothesis specifies a relation between the person's religion and his or her views on abortion. These concepts may seem straightforward, but they require further precision before they can be tested. Who is a Catholic? A person who answers "Catholic" when asked his or her religion? A person who regularly attends mass? Or a person who believes in the teachings of the Roman Catholic Church? What do we mean by opposition to abortion—opposition to all abortions or only those for reasons other than medical ones? The concepts can be defined in many different ways, and a survey researcher must select the operational definition that provides the most meaningful test of the hypothesis.

Taking Alternative Views into Account

When testing an hypothesis, it is important to think of alternative explanations. Religion is not the only possible cause of a person's opinion of abortion. We would want to spell out in our statement of objectives other relationships to examine. In this example, we might want to test the impact of sex, education, marital status, and age on a person's opinions about abortion. If we found that older people, regardless of their religion, tend to oppose abortion more than younger people, then age rather than religion may be the most powerful determinant of views on abortion. The statement of objectives must be framed broadly enough to permit competing explanations to be tested.

The Importance of Theory

Social scientists disagree regarding how much emphasis should be placed on theory and formal methodology when designing a research project. Some argue that in order to advance social science, all research should deduce hypotheses from theories about behavior and then formally test those hypotheses. By contrast, other social scientists see no necessity to place such an emphasis on theory and formal methodology. They place their emphasis on inductively discovering relationships in the data. Many other social scientists take the middle ground between the two positions and seek to build theory from relationships found in the data. They see the importance of relating their research to preexisting theory but allow for the discovery of relationships in the data rather than limiting their studies solely to the testing of preestablished hypotheses. Although we favor the middle ground, most of the material in this book is compatible with all three approaches.

THE SURVEY-DESIGN STAGE

Once the objectives of a survey are specified, the design of the survey must be chosen. In doing so, it is essential to keep the study objectives in mind so that the data will address those objectives. It is also important to anticipate the data analysis, because a desired analysis can be performed only if appropriate design decisions are made. We shall introduce several basic design questions in this section and discuss them in more detail in later chapters.

What Population Should Be Studied?

In designing a survey, the first basic design question is what population should be described. Whose attitudes do we want to describe or generalize about? In some studies, a researcher may be interested in the entire population of a country (or for that matter, the entire population of a state or city). However, most surveys focus only on part of that population—those who are eighteen years old or older, who are citizens of that country (or residents of that state or city), and who are not institutionalized in mental hospitals or prisons. In some surveys special populations are surveyed. For example, if a researcher wanted to study the thinking of those entering the United States electorate in the next two years, the relevant population might be sixteen- and seventeen-year-olds. A study of the attitudes of college students would have the set of college students as its relevant population. The important point is that we must describe or define very carefully the population that we want to study.

Obviously, one should not choose a population that makes the basic hypotheses impossible to test. We hypothesized above that Catholics might oppose abortion in order to avoid conflict with their other religious beliefs. One might believe that only Catholics need to be interviewed in order to test this hypothesis. However, the effect of religion on opinions about abortion can be tested only by interviewing Catholics as well as non-Catholics. If members of other religions are as strongly opposed to abortion as are Catholics, then religion seems not to be an important factor in views on abortion. Researchers usually want to compare the views of different groups, so the population to be studied must include the various groups of interest.

Who Should Be Interviewed?

Once the *target population* is selected, the next study-design question is who should be interviewed. Is the target population so small and geographically concentrated that it is possible to interview everyone? Is the research so exploratory that a few in-depth interviews with an unsystematic sample would suffice? Or is a large, representative sample required?

How Many Interviews Are Necessary?

If sampling is employed, enough interviews must be taken to permit generalizing to the population of interest. Also, enough interviews are needed to allow one to study subgroups of interest. Financial limits are always present, and more interviews always cost more money. Consequently, a balance must be struck between the number of interviews desired and the limits imposed by available funds.

This is a good example of the importance of planning for data analysis when designing a survey. What if one finds after conducting a survey that too few interviews were conducted with an important type of respondent? At that point it is too late to take more interviews. It is essential to anticipate what groups will be of interest and to select a sample that will ensure their adequate coverage.

For example, we shall see in the next chapter that a sample comprising 1,500 people is sufficient for studying the voting of the American public. However, if the total sample is 1,500 one would expect to obtain only about 150 interviews with blacks. That number may be enough to permit comparisons of whites with blacks, but it is not adequate if one wishes to compare older blacks born in the South with younger blacks born in the North. There would not be enough people in these categories to sustain a meaningful analysis. If such comparisons are desired, then either the total sample size must be increased or additional interviews with blacks must be conducted. It is common to *oversample* a group in a survey so that the group can be studied in detail, although those extra interviews are dropped (or counted only partially) when the entire population is being described. Such an approach is possible only if one anticipates such needs at the study-design stage.

How Should the Data Be Collected?

There are three methods of collecting survey data. One method is to send interviewers to the homes of respondents so that they may be interviewed face to face. Interviews can be conducted over the telephone. Finally, one can give (or mail) questionnaires to respondents to fill out. Each of these data collection methods has advantages and disadvantages, and some are better suited to particular topics of study.

Are Follow-up Surveys Necessary?

Another study-design question is whether the focus of the study is on change. If so, it makes sense to interview the same people more than once to see if their attitudes, beliefs, or behavior change. In a typical *cross-section survey*, people are interviewed just once. By contrast, in a *panel study*, the same people are interviewed repeatedly. For example, the same people could be interviewed at successive presidential elections in order to assess changes in attitude and vote. Long-term panel studies are complicated by the expense and difficulty of finding respondents who have moved in intervening years, but these studies give the best evidence as to the extent of attitude change.

OVERVIEW OF THE SURVEY PROCESS

Answering the study-design questions—whether to conduct a survey, what the target population should be, whom to interview, how many interviews to take, how to collect the data, and whether to adopt a panel approach—sets the framework for the study. The full set of steps involved in conducting a survey is listed in Table 2.1. Each step has numerous potential errors associated with it, so each must be performed with care.

The survey-design process is the subject of the first part of this book. In this chapter we have traced through the early stages of the survey process: the study objectives and the study design. Chapter 3 will describe how the *sample* of people being interviewed is selected so that it is representative of a larger population. It is critical that the sample be selected so that it does not bias the results of the study. Chapter 4 will discuss how survey questions are carefully written and tested prior to the actual interviews. A questionnaire is put together after the researcher has decided on the exact question wording and the order of the

Table 2.1   The Stages of the Survey Process (Keyed to Chapters in This Book)

Stage	See Chapter
Survey Design and Data Collection	
Statement of study objectives	2
Preparation of study design	2
Sampling—choosing people to interview	3
Questionnaire construction and pretesting	4
Interviewing—data collection	5
Coding—categorizing the responses	6
Entering the data into the computer	6
Data Analysis	
Specification of hypotheses	8
Tabulation of responses	9
Building new measures	9
Hypothesis testing	10
Analysis of two-variable relationships	11, 12, 14
Use of control variables	13, 14
Reporting Results	
Writing research report	15
Reading survey reports	16

questions. Chapter 5 will present rules the interview process must follow to obtain the most complete and most accurate information. Personal interviews, phone polls, and self-administered questionnaires can all be used in surveying the public, and each has its own advantages and disadvantages. Chapter 6 shows how the verbal responses of people are then translated into numbers—called *codes*—so that a computer can be used to analyze the data.

The second part of this book turns to the analysis of data. In this phase specific hypotheses are developed. The responses to individual questions are tabulated and summarized statistically. Then the relationships between answers to different questions are analyzed and summarized statistically.

The third part of this book provides guidelines on the conduct and reporting of survey research. The reading and writing of research reports is discussed. The final chapter focuses on the ethics of survey research.

SUMMARY

Good research has clear objectives and keeps those objectives in mind when deciding how to collect the data. Hypotheses must be constructed, and the concepts must be operationalized to test between alternative explanations. Surveys are frequently an appropriate and useful means of collecting information to test one's hypotheses, though experiments and aggregate data often provide alternative data sources. Secondary analysis of existing surveys can sometimes substitute for collecting one's own survey data. If a survey is to be conducted, the researcher must decide upon the population to be studied, who should be interviewed, how many interviews to take, how the data should be collected, and whether to take follow-up surveys. Overall, a variety of survey designs can be used to accommodate different substantive needs and problems—if those problems are anticipated in the planning of the survey.

Questions

1. Say that you were concerned with the extent of violence in America and chose to study why some people approve of violence. Further, say that interracial violence was of particular concern to you and that you wanted to determine why some people approve of interracial violence while others dis-

approve. Construct a set of hypotheses regarding alternative causes of attitudes toward violence in general and interracial violence in particular. How would you define violence?

2. What research designs would be suited to testing your hypotheses? Would experiments be useful in studying attitudes toward violence? How could surveys be used? How would you define your target population for a survey? Would it be valid to interview only those who have participated in violent acts? What about interviewing only men or only city dwellers? Would you use only questions on interracial violence, or would you want to see if attitudes on interracial violence differed from attitudes on other types of violence?

3

Sampling Procedures

Many researchers who conduct surveys do so in order to understand the attitudes, behavior, or beliefs of a large group of people such as the entire population of the United States. However, it would be prohibitively expensive for every researcher to interview every one of the 220 million citizens in this country. Fortunately, accurate estimates of the nation's attitudes may be obtained by interviewing a sample of a few thousand carefully selected respondents. The technique by which survey researchers choose respondents is called sampling.

Sampling is widely used in the sciences, and an extensive body of statistical theory has been developed to guide its application. Many different sampling procedures can be used to generate samples that are representative of a population. Implementing them correctly requires strict adherence to certain logical principles. In this chapter we describe some of the sampling procedures that are frequently used in the social sciences.

SAMPLING METHODS

As described in Chapter 2, the first step is to define the relevant population. If the population we are interested in is so small that we can easily interview the entire population, we need not sample at all. For example, we could easily interview everyone on an eleven-person city council. But let us assume that the population comprises millions of people and that sampling is essential. How can we obtain a representative sample?

Once the population of interest is defined, it is necessary to determine the *sampling frame*—the list of units from which the sample will be drawn. Ideally the sampling frame would be identical to the population of interest, but often that is not possible. For example, one might want to take a sample of all eligible voters (the population of interest), but doing so from the voter registration list (the sampling frame) would lead to some problems, since the voter registration list might be old and incomplete. Similarly, one might want to take a sample of all residents of a city (the population of interest), but doing so by interviewing people who walk by a particular corner (the sampling frame) inadvertently modifies the nature of the sample. Strictly speaking, sampling can generalize only to the sampling frame from which the sample was drawn rather than to the full population, so one should try to use a sampling frame that corresponds as closely as possible to the population.

Nonprobability Sampling Methods

One important distinction to be made is between nonprobability sampling procedures and probability sampling procedures. We begin by describing some nonprobability procedures so that the advantages of probability sampling can be shown.

Typical People.   We could seek people who seem to be *typical* of the population in social and economic terms. However, there is no guarantee that people with typical social and economic characteristics have attitudes that are representative of the entire population. Indeed, such people may actually have very distinctive attitudes that are not at all like those of sizable groups in the population, so that such a sample would not be representative.

This is where probability sampling procedures come to our aid. They will permit us to select a group that is similar to the population in its composition, though of a much smaller and more manageable size. The classical procedure used for this purpose is known as *randomization*. As we shall see below, randomization is a procedure that gives everyone in the sampling frame an equal chance of being part of the sample: by doing this, randomization eliminates the possibility that any portion of the sampling frame will be overrepresented or underrepresented in the sample.

Purposive Samples.   Another nonprobability approach is to choose some cases to study purposively. In studying the elite decision makers in a community, one might get advice as to who the major decision makers are and then seek to interview them. At best the success of this procedure depends on how carefully the people are selected. Even if the people are carefully selected, however, there always remains a possibility that some key decision makers were omitted. Purposive sampling often works well, but it can be tricky and it is hard to prove that one has sampled appropriately.

Volunteer Subjects.   Another way of choosing people for a study is to ask for volunteers. Some people will volunteer to participate, and we can ascertain their attitudes, beliefs, and behavior. The problem is that people who volunteer may not be typical. Volunteers usually are more interested in the topic of the study than are the general population, so they are not representative of the larger population.

The most famous example of an interview study using volunteer subjects is the research in the 1950s by the Kinsey Institute at Indiana University on the sexual behavior of the American public. The researchers asked their respondents how many times they had engaged in a long list of sexual activities. The *Kinsey Report* showed that Americans were much more sexually active than had previously been thought. However, the use of volunteers in their study made this conclusion questionable: people who volunteered to participate in a study on their sexual practices are likely to have been more sexually liberated and more sexually active than people who were unwilling to participate in such a study. Thus, the use of volunteer subjects probably biased the results. More generally, volunteers are often likely to differ from the rest of the population, so the use of volunteers can bias a study.

Another example of volunteer subjects is the call-in poll on radio and television that asks people to phone one phone number if they want to vote yes on the issue of the day (such as whether prayer should be allowed in schools) and a different phone number if they want to vote no on that issue. The sample obtained from such a poll consists of volunteer subjects, and as such it measures the views of people who feel strongly enough to call rather than the entire audience of the station. The phone numbers to be called in such polls are often ones that the caller has to pay for calling (such as calling a 900 area code in a national poll for a charge of fifty cents), which means that only people who are willing to pay to record their views will participate. Furthermore, it is easy for an organized group to rig call-in polls by having their supporters phone one of the numbers repeatedly so that it looks like their side commands a majority. All in all, call-in polls should not be taken seriously.

Haphazard Sampling.   Another simple sampling procedure is the *haphazard sample*, in which you survey people who can be contacted easily. For example, a professor might use a questionnaire to measure the attitudes of a college class, but their attitudes may not be identical with those of the American public. Haphazard samples can sometimes generate results that are representative of the larger population of interest, if there is no source of bias. For example, the now defunct *Literary Digest* conducted some of the earliest election polls in the 1920s and 1930s. They sampled large numbers of people from telephone books and automobile registrations, and they were quite accurate in predicting the winner of presidential elections.

However, haphazard samples can also generate results that are not representative of the population. In the midst of the Great Depression, the *Digest* poll predicted a Landon victory in the 1936 election and lost its credibility when Franklin Delano Roosevelt won in a landslide. The *Digest* poll had missed the large Democratic vote of poor people who lacked phones and cars during the Depression and who had not been voting in previous elections. Unfortunately, haphazard sampling almost always yields unrepresentative samples. Consequently, this approach is rarely used today, though during presidential election campaigns one still hears of polls based on whether popcorn buyers in movie theaters choose boxes with pictures of elephants or donkeys on them.

Quota Sampling.   Another inexpensive means is quota sampling. If the census indicates that half of the country is female and 10 percent is black, then interviewers are told to obtain half of their interviews with women and one-tenth with blacks. The drawback in this approach is that the interviewers will tend to select the people they want to interview. They will tend to choose people they can find easily, people who are particularly willing to be interviewed, and people whom they do not find to be hostile or intimidating. These are usually people who are similar to the interviewers themselves. Since most interviewers are middle-class, the result is typically a middle-class bias with insufficient interviews with working-class people. Although more complex quotas could be imposed, the bias problem cannot be eliminated unless interviewers make none of the decisions regarding whom to interview.

After the *Literary Digest* debacle, the Gallup Poll became the dominant election poll. Then, in 1948, Gallup declared Dewey the president-elect, only to be embarrassed when the American public did not concur. One reason why this happened is that Gallup (and the other commercial pollsters of that era) used a quota-sampling procedure. Truman's victory that year was correctly forecast only by academic polls using more accurate sampling procedures. Today, pure quota samples are rarely used, though some commercial pollsters continue to use quota samples with careful instructions to interviewers on how to avoid a middle-class bias.

In our discussion of volunteer, haphazard, and quota samples we touched on one of the most important points in sampling: a sampling procedure must avoid bias. Clearly, all of the subgroups, classes, and races in a population must have a chance to be included in the sample. If any group is excluded from the sample, then the sample is biased, and generalizations from the sample to the population may be very inaccurate.

Probability Sampling

Today, most high-quality surveys employ probability sampling, in which the sample is drawn before the survey so that each person in the population has a known probability of being included in the sample. This eliminates the bias inherent in the other sampling procedures.

The Simple Random Sample.   One form of probability sampling is done by taking a list of the individuals in a population and randomly selecting people to be surveyed. In principle, this could be done by writing each person's name on a piece of paper, putting all the names in a hat, mixing up the names, and drawing the sample. For larger populations the random selection is performed with a computer. The result is called a *simple random sample*. This is an excellent sampling procedure. However, most probability samples do not use a straight simple random sample but instead use variants of the technique.

The Systematic Selection Procedure.   One convenient variant of the simple random sample is the *systematic selection* procedure. This procedure requires a list of everyone in the population. A random number is chosen to choose the first person to be interviewed, and then a specified number of names on the list are skipped to choose the next person, and so on. Say, for example, that you were choosing a sample of students from a university with 20,000 students and that you desired a sample of 400 (a 1-in-50 sample). You could take the student directory and randomly choose one of the first 50 students, using a published table of random numbers. If you picked the number 37, you would interview the 37th person and every 50th person following on the list: the 37th, the 87th, the 137th, the 187th, and so on. Through this procedure, you would obtain a sample of 400 people.

This procedure makes sample selection easy as long as the list corresponds exactly to the population. One would not want to sample from a student directory that lists only students who live on campus if one wanted to develop a sample of all students at a college. A second problem with this procedure is that there could be some periodicity in the list. For example, if the list was of houses, and if one chose the first house and every fifteenth house down the street, one might accidentally obtain a sample containing only houses on corners, which are sometimes more expensive than houses in the middles of blocks. Fortunately, periodicity is rarely a problem, but when using systematic sampling, it is important to be sure that there is no periodicity in the list. A third problem with systematic sampling is that elements adjacent on the list cannot be included in the same sample. Thus, if one were selecting a sample of United Nations delegations to interview, systematic sampling using an alphabetical list of member nations would preclude having interviews with all of the major powers, since Russia (the Union of Soviet Socialist Republics), Britain (the United Kingdom), and the United States would all be in the same part of the alphabet.

In spite of their advantages, simple random sampling and systematic sampling share two significant disadvantages. First, they require a listing of the entire population of interest so that random or systematic selection can be made. This is impossible for a national survey in the United States—there are no lists of all residents, citizens, or voters in this country, and no one could afford to construct such a list. Second, it is too expensive to interview a national face-to-face sample based on such sampling procedures. Most survey budgets do not allow for an interviewer to fly to Snowflake, Arizona, for only one interview and then to Casper, Wyoming, for the next interview—transportation costs for interviewers require that several interviews be physically clustered near one another.

Stratifying the Sample.   Several approaches are used to solve these problems. One is *stratifying*—dividing the population up into small, manageable chunks and randomly sampling from each chunk. If you are interested in sampling the population of the United States and know the proportion of the population living in each region, it makes sense to stratify your sample by region so that the proper proportion of interviews can be taken independently within each region. That way, you can make sure that 25 percent of the interviews are taken in the Midwest, that 30 percent are taken in small towns, and so on. Stratifying helps maximize accuracy in a sample, since it assures that certain known proportions of the population are matched in your sample. Stratifying is especially useful in increasing accuracy when two groups differ widely on the topic being studied, yet members within each group are very similar. For example, if we were interested in contrasting freshmen with seniors in terms of their views on some issue, we could obtain more accurate estimates of each group's views by sampling from them separately than if we sampled the entire college and then compared the lower-division and upper-division students in the sample. Stratifying is useful if the researcher knows what variables are worth stratifying on.

Unfortunately, stratification is often not possible because it requires knowing all population members' status on the stratifying variable prior to the sampling. This is easy to do with regions of the country, for example, but would be much harder to do with religion. There is no easy way to create separate samples of Protestants and Catholics, since there are not separate lists of all members of each religion in the nation and there is not residential segregation by religion. Incidentally, note that stratifying is not the same as quota sampling, since the interviewer is not choosing whom to interview; the selection of exact respondents is still random.

The Cluster Sample.   Another approach is to use a *cluster sample*. Since it is too expensive to take each interview in a different neighborhood, one clusters by taking several interviews in one neighborhood. This reduces interviewing costs, since the expenses of paying for interviewers' time and transportation decrease.

Regrettably, accuracy declines in cluster sampling. People who live in the same area tend to be similar, so taking several interviews in the same area yields less information than would be gained by spreading the same number of interviews across a wider area. Most survey organizations believe that some loss of accuracy is acceptable if it permits greatly decreased costs.

Paradoxically, if a cluster sample and a simple random sample *of equal cost* were taken of the same large, geographically dispersed population, the cluster sample would probably be more accurate. The reason for this is that the reduced cost per interview of the cluster sample allows the sample size to be increased sufficiently to offset the increased error from clustering. Of course, one should not go to the extreme of drawing an entire sample from only one or two clusters; as long as there are enough clusters, the error will be within reasonable bounds as well.

Multistage Sampling. Another permutation of probability sampling, *multistage area sampling* first requires sampling a set of geographical areas. Next is to sample a subset of geographical areas within each of those areas, and so on. The chances of an area being included increase with the number of people living in it.

Let's say you begin by randomly selecting 100 towns in the United States. If a particular town is selected, you next randomly choose neighborhoods—maybe one area in the northeast corner, another on the near south side, and a third in a western suburb. At the next stage, a sample of blocks would be chosen within each neighborhood, and than a sample of houses would be chosen on each block. The advantage of multistage area probability sampling is that a complete listing of the population is now unnecessary. All that is required is a list of towns, a list of neighborhoods within the towns selected, a list of blocks within the neighborhoods chosen, and a list of houses on the blocks that are chosen. The clustering inherent in this scheme means that it yields higher error than simple random samples, but this is offset by the ability to sample without a complete listing of the population and by lower costs per interview.

Summary. Typically, sampling for face-to-face interviews combines the several procedures we have mentioned above, which are listed in Table 3.1 along with their advantages and disadvantages. Using only volunteers, taking a haphazard sample, and interviewing through quota techniques are relatively cheap, but accuracy suffers. Probability sampling is required if estimates of the survey's accuracy are desired. The simple random sample is the textbook ideal, but it is expensive—its accuracy requires a listing of all elements in the population as well as interviews in widely scattered locations. Systematic sampling simplifies the sample selection, but it also requires a listing of the population and widely scattered interviews. Multistage sampling permits the listings to be made only in small areas. Clustering cuts transportation costs, though with some increase in error. Stratifying guarantees matching some population proportions to safeguard accuracy. All in all, the accuracy of a survey is significantly affected by

Table 3.1 Types of Samples

Sampling Method	Advantages	Disadvantages
Nonprobability		

Purposive sample	Cheap
	Uses best available
	  information
		No estimates of accuracy
		May miss important
		  elements

Volunteer subjects	Cooperative respondents	Not representative of population
Haphazard sample	Available sample	No necessary relation to population
Quota sampling	Willing respondents	Middleclass and other biases
Probability		

Simple random sample	Accuracy can be estimated
	Sampling error can be
	  estimated
		Expensive
		Interviews too dispersed
		  and full list required

Systematic sample	Convenience	Periodicity in list

Stratified	Guarantee adequate
	  representation of
	  groups
	Usually decreased error
		Sometimes requires
		  weighting

Cluster	Decreased cost	Increased error

Multistage	Lower cost than simple
	  random sample for
	  large populations
	Lower error than cluster
		Higher error than simple
		  random sample
		
		Higher cost than cluster

its sampling procedures, and the choice of the proper sampling technique is crucial to the success of the survey.

EXAMPLES OF SAMPLES

To illustrate how samples are actually drawn, we will give examples of different strategies you could use to draw a sample from a series of different populations.

A National Sample for Face-to-Face Interviewing

How are national samples for face-to-face interviewing drawn? Simple random sampling cannot be used because of the size and dispersion of the population, so multistage samples with clustering and stratifying are used instead. For purposes of illustration, we will describe the sampling procedures used by the University of Michigan's Survey Research Center (SRC) and by the University of Chicago's Na-

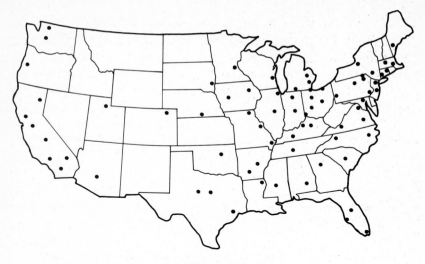

Figure 3.1
Survey Research Center Primary Sampling Units
(Adapted from Leslie Kish and Irene Hess, "The Survey Research Center's National
Sample of Dwellings," Institute for Social Research, University of Michigan, 1965.
Reprinted by permission of Leslie Kish.)

tional Opinion Research Center, which now does its sampling jointly
with the SRC.

Choosing Where to Interview.   The first stage consists of sampling a number of *primary sampling units*, or *psu's*. A *psu* is an area, a
Standard Metropolitan Statistical Area (the Census Bureau's desig-
nation for the largest cities along with the rest of their county and adjacent urban counties), a county, or a set of adjacent small counties. The
psu's are stratified by region as well as by the size of their largest cities.
The resulting sample of *psu's* might include the Syracuse area, a farm
area in eastern Kansas, and so on. The largest sixteen metropolitan
areas are typically represented in every sample, so interviews are always taken in New York City, Chicago, Los Angeles, Houston, and
other big cities. SRC and NORC choose a sample of about 100 *psu's* after each census (Figure 3.1), and use those *psu's* for as many of their
surveys as possible during the next ten years. People who live in those
psu's are hired as interviewers for that decade in order to have stable,
experienced field staffs.

For a national survey the researchers must first decide how many
interviews are to be conducted. This is usually determined by the
amount of money available, since the bigger the sample, the better.
The number of interviews to be assigned in each region of the country is

determined by the percentage of the population living in each region. A similar logic is used to determine the number of interviews to take in each psu. Next, smaller areas are chosen within each psu. If the Syracuse area is a psu, for example, then the populations of the city, the suburbs, other towns in the county, and rural townships are determined using the United States Census Bureau's data. These figures are used to estimate how many interviews should be conducted within each *sample place*. Because it contains most of the population in the psu, the city of Syracuse would most likely be chosen as one of the sample places within its county. Then, a list of blocks in the city (or other chunks in nonurban areas) is obtained. A random sample of the city blocks (or chunks) is chosen, so that interviews are taken on the 1500 block of Ontario Street, the 2400 block of Superior Avenue, and so on. List of houses or apartments on the blocks or segments in the sample are obtained, and random samples of the houses are drawn. Interviewers are then told which houses and apartments to visit. Figure 3.2 illustrates this multistage sampling procedure.

Choosing Whom to Interview.   Rather than let the interviewer make a subjective choice of respondents, objective procedures have been developed to choose the resident at each dwelling unit to be interviewed. Table 3.2 reproduces part of the *cover sheet* given to the interviewer. The interviewer checks to see whether there is more than one housing unit at the address (as when a two-story house contains two apartments). If so, extra housing units are added to the sample.

For each dwelling unit, the interviewer records the name, gender, and age of each person living in the household. The interviewer numbers these persons sequentially, using 1 for the oldest eligible male, 2 for the next oldest eligible male, and so on until all the eligible males have been numbered; the oldest eligible female is given the next number, the next oldest eligible female the next number, and so on. The interviewer then looks at a selection table to see which person to interview. In the example shown in Table 3.2, if there are one or two people over eighteen in the household, then person number 1 (the oldest male if there is one) is interviewed; if there are three or four people over eighteen, then person number 2 is interviewed; and if there are five or more people over eighteen, then person number 3 is interviewed. Different selection tables are used in different households so as to randomize the selection of individuals within households. This might result in the interviewing of the oldest male in one house, the youngest female in the next, the second oldest female in the third, and so on. This selection procedure is used rather than just interviewing whoever an-

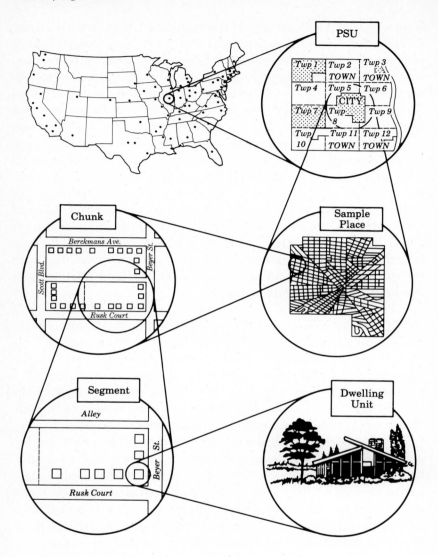

Figure 3.2
Survey Research Center Sampling Method
(From the Survey Research Center's *Interviewer's Manual*. [Ann Arbor, MI: Institute for Social Research, The University of Michigan, copyright 1969]. Reprinted by permission of the Institute for Social Research.)

swers the door in order to avoid any biases as to which types of people are most likely to be home. For example, young males tend not to be at home as much as other members of a family, but this selection procedure obtains the proper proportion of young males as designated respondents.

If the person to be interviewed is not at home when the interviewer visits, SRC interviewers make an appointment to stop back and interview the designated respondent. If that person is not at home when the interviewer stops back, the interviewer is instructed to call back two or three more times to find the designated respondent. If these attempts fail, the person is dropped from the sample. The interviewer cannot just pick someone else in the household or a neighbor. Commercial pollsters instead allow their interviewers to interview anyone who is at home or instruct their interviewers to talk to a neighbor if the designated respondent is not at home, since repeated call-backs are expensive. The quality of the data collected is unlikely to be hurt by this unless the not-at-homes differ significantly from their neighbors.

Telephone Samples

Telephone interviewing has become an important means of conducting surveys, and sampling for telephone interviewing raises unique problems.

Choosing Phone Numbers. One way to obtain a sample for phone interviews is to take a random selection of numbers in local telephone directories and phone those numbers. Unfortunately, there are two serious problems with this approach. First, some people who have phones do not list their numbers in directories. Second, phone directories are a few months out of date by the time they are published and become increasingly out of date as time passes. Because of these factors, in many localities more than 20 percent of residential phones are not listed in phone directories.

A slight modification of the use of phone directories is the *add-a-digit* approach. In this procedure, a set of random phone numbers is selected from the telephone directory (using simple random sampling or systematic sampling of every nth number in the directory) and then adding one to that number. For example, if the number 292-6446 is obtained from the directory, the value 1 is added so that the number to be dialed for the interview is 292-6447. A variant of this approach is to add a random digit from 0 to 9 to the directory number. These add-a-digit procedures make it possible to call unlisted numbers as well as

Table 3.2 Part of a Cover Sheet (Items 1–14, 16–20)

```
┌─────────────────────┐        NATIONAL ELECTION STUDY          ┌───┐      495827
│                     │   Coversheet for Listed and Selected HU │ B │       P. 27
│ FOR OFFICE USE ONLY │      Labeled Coversheet--FORM B         └───┘     Fall 1986
└─────────────────────┘
```

1. SAMPLE LABEL	2. Interviewer's Label

1a. IF YOU ALTERED ANY INFORMATION ON THE SAMPLE LABEL, INDICATE REASON FOR CHANGE:

SAMPLE LABEL IS A DESCRIPTION: IWER SUPPLIED HU STREET ADDRESS	SEGMENT FOLDER REPORTS DIFFERENT HU ADDRESS: IWER UPDATED SAMPLE LABEL & NOTIFIED SUPV	OTHER, SPECIFY: _____

3. Iwer ID ____ ____ ____ ____

4. Your Iw No. ____ ____

5. Date of Iw _____

6. Length of Iw _____ Minutes

7. Length of Pre-Edit:____MIN Post-Edit:____MIN

8. Persuasion letter requested?

[NO] [YES] --> _____
                Date Requested

9. Total Calls (Call # of Final Call) ____

10. Date of Final Call _____

11. Final Call Result Code: _____

12. THE ADDRESS OR DESCRIPTION ON THE SAMPLE LABEL ABOVE WAS FOUND TO HAVE: (CHECK ONE)

[1 HU] [2 HU's] [3 HU's] [4 HU's] [5 OR MORE HU's] --> Do not attempt any interviews. Obtain HU locations within the structure and call your supervisor.

HU 1 is uniquely described by adding to the sample address on the label the following description about the location of HU 1 in the structure:

_____

The unique and complete address or description for each of the additional HU's is (use street address/description _and_ location of HU in the structure).

		SAMPLE ID:	FORM
HU2:	_____	□□-□□-□□□□-[2]	B
HU3:	_____	□□-□□-□□□□-[3]	B
HU4:	_____	□□-□□-□□□□-[4]	B

Make out an unlabelled coversheet for each of the additional HU's. Attempt an interview at HU1 and at each of the additional HU's.

Call your supervisor later to obtain a Sample ID for each of the additional HU's. Record the ID's on the respective lines above. Enter the appropriate ID in Box O of the unlabelled coversheet(s) for each additional HU.

13. Hello, my name is _____, and I work for The University of Michigan's Survey Research Center. Here is my identification (SHOW ID). The University is conducting a study throughout the nation, asking the American people about their feelings on a variety of topics, things like feelings about the economy, the recent congressional elections, and some of the important issues facing the country these days. This address was selected as part of the study's national sample, and I would like to interview a member of this household.-->TURN TO P. 4, ITEM 16, "HOUSEHOLD LISTING"

14. CALL RECORD

CALL #	a. DATE	b. DAY OF WEEK	c. TIME AM/PM	d. MODE TEL/FTF	e. IWER ID#	f. RESULT CODE	g. COMPLETE DESCRIPTION OF CONTACT:

new numbers, though many calls are made to numbers not in service. This is still a reasonable sampling procedure, especially when studying a single community with only one telephone directory. It is feasible even when studying a single state where all the state's directories can be obtained, but it is unmanageable when conducting a national sur-

Table 3.2   Part of a Cover Sheet (Items 1–14, 16–20) (*continued*)

16(a)-(c). In order to determine who to interview, I need to know who lives here at this address--not their names, just their ages and their relationship to you and whether any of the persons is not an American citizen. Let's start with you--how old are you?
Now I'd like the sex and age and relationship to you of each of the other members of this household who are 18 years of age or older.

16(d). (IF 18 YEARS OF AGE) Was (PERSON) 18 years old on or before November 4?

16(e). Are all of these people U.S. citizens? (Who is not a U.S. Citizen?)

PERSONS 18 YEARS OLD OR OLDER	(a) Household Member's Relationship to Informant	(b) Age	(c) Sex	(d) 18 by Nov. 4? YES/NO	(e) U.S. Citizen YES/NO	(f) Eligible Person "✓"	(g) Person Number	(h) Selected Respondent "R"
M			M					
A			M					
L			M					
E			M					
S			M					
F			F					
E			F					
M			F					
A			F					
L			F					
E			F					
S			F					

17. Now I'd like the sex and age and relationship to you of each of the members of this household who are 17 years of age or younger.

	(a) Household Member	(b) Age	(c) Sex
PERSONS			
17			
YEARS			
OLD			
OR			
YOUNGER			

SELECTION TABLE A	
If the number of eligible persons is:	Interview the person numbered:
1	1
2	1
3	2
4	2
5	3
6 or more	3

18. You've said there are (REPEAT LISTING); does that include everyone living here at the present time? (IF NO, CORRECT ABOVE.) [Now I will use a selection procedure--I'm going to number the persons in this household to determine whom we need to interview--(it will take a second...)]

19. ☐ NO ELIGIBLE RESPONDENT (NO ADULTS 18 BY NOV. 4 OR NO U.S.CITIZENS)--->SEND IN COVERSHEET WITHOUT NONINTERVIEW FORM. CODE RESULT "NER".

RESPONDENT SELECTION

16f. Enter a check mark (✓) in column (f) for each person eligible for selection. Eligible persons are U.S. citizens who were 18 on or before Nov. 4. In other words, if (d) is "NO" and/or (e) is "NO", do not enter a check mark in (f).

16g. In column (g) assign a sequential number to each eligible person checked in column (f). First number checked MALES from oldest to youngest and then continue the numbering with checked FEMALES, again from oldest to youngest.

16h. Use the selection table above to select a respondent. In the first column circle the total number of eligible persons (the highest number assigned in column (g)). The corresponding number in the second column of the selection table denotes the person selected to be interviewed. Enter "R" in column (h) for this person.

20. IF NO INTERVIEW WAS OBTAINED AND THE HU IS OCCUPIED: Were you able to list all adults (18 years or older) residing in this household?

1. YES, ALL ADULTS LISTED	2. YES, PROBABLY ALL ADULTS LISTED	3. NO, ADULT LIST IS INCOMPLETE OR DK

SOURCE: Reprinted by permission of National Election Studies.

vey. Strictly speaking, this is not a probability sample, since the likelihood of each household being selected is not a known nonzero value, so it can produce biased estimates of population values.[1]

---

[1]Graham Kalton, *Introduction to Survey Sampling* (Beverly Hills: Sage, 1983), 87.

A commonly used alternative procedure is *random digit dialing* (RDD). This approach uses computers to make up phone numbers randomly. It is used in many phone polls, such as the *New York Times*/CBS News poll. In most areas of the country, many phone exchanges are not used, so completely random dialing would result in large numbers of wasted phone calls to nonexistent exchanges. As a result, RDD is generally limited to exchanges that are in use.

Phone numbers in the United States are composed of three parts. In the number (614) 292-6446, for example, 614 is the area code, 292 is the central office code, and 6446 is the suffix. It is possible to find out which central office codes are used in a particular area code, either from the local phone company or from national directories. One can then randomly choose a set of area code–central office codes and add random suffixes to them. In samples from a single community, the local phone company may be able to provide information as to the number of residential phones per central office code, and then one can stratify by central office code using that information. There are usually many unused suffixes within each central office code, so it is necessary to sample many phone numbers for each desired interview. A 5-to-1 ratio is necessary, since generally only one-fifth of the numbers turn out to be working residential phones. Phone calls are placed until the desired number of interviews is obtained. This is a probability sampling procedure, but it is inefficient because so many numbers are not working residential numbers.

A commonly used variant of this technique that involves fewer wasted calls is known as the Waksberg method. The four-digit phone number suffixes (6446 in the above example) can be thought of as having two parts: the first two numbers (64) and the last two numbers (46). Within an area code–central office code combination, randomly choose several banks of first two numbers (64 could be one). Within each of those banks, select one phone number randomly (say 46 is chosen so as to get 6446). Dial that number. If that number is not a residential number, then reject that bank and dial no more numbers from it. If that number is a residential number, get a specified number of interviews from that bank. One might keep calling numbers in that bank until, say, eight interviews are taken with working residential numbers. With this system, two-thirds of the phone calls are placed to working residential phones. This is considered a two-stage probability sampling procedure with clustering. The University of Michigan's Survey Research Center is one of the many polling operations using this method for telephone sampling.

There is tremendous diversity in the procedures used for selecting phone numbers. The Waksberg procedure is highly regarded, but it is complicated to explain. As a result, many polling companies prefer to use straight random digit dialing, since they find it easier to justify to their clients.

There are several possible outcomes of survey phone calls. There can be no answer, a busy signal, or an immediate hang-up, in which cases the number can be tried again later. On the other hand, the number is set aside if it is a disconnected number, a business, or outside of the intended geographic area, or if it does not have an eligible respondent. If the call is answered by a nonresident, one can try phoning back later to see if someone else answers, which also can be done if the person answering the phone refuses to cooperate. In addition, study directors have to decide how to handle special situations, such as answering machines and when the phone is answered by someone who does not speak English. Finally, designated respondents must be dropped if they are out of town throughout the interviewing period or too handicapped to be interviewed. Careful record keeping is required during the phone calling to keep track of what numbers to try again and to keep statistics on response rates.

When a phone number does not answer, academic polling operations tend to have interviewers call the number back repeatedly in case the people return home. Some studies show that repeated call-backs over a period of days are effective, although there is little gain after six call-backs. Commercial polling operations are more likely to substitute other numbers for numbers that do not answer. Call-backs are important if the people who are home less often differ in relevant ways from those who are home most of the time.

Screening Questions.   Some problems with phone samples can be handled by asking the person who answers the phone some screening questions. First, if one wishes to sample a particular city, the sampling procedures described above are likely to yield some calls to homes that are not in the city. Therefore, the person answering the phone must be asked whether he or she lives in the desired area rather than an adjoining suburb.

Another problem involves multiple phone lines. A family with two phone lines has twice as great a chance of being included in a sample as a family with just one line. This problem is handled by asking the respondents how many phone lines they have. Respondents with two phone lines are given a *weight* of one-half, meaning that their data are only counted for half of that of respondents with just one phone line so as to compensate for their greater chance of selection in the sampling.

Screening questions are also used to select the respondent in a household. Studies of households sometimes accept any adult who answers the phone even though that means more interviews with women and older people, but most surveys instead use random selection of respondents. Early phone researchers tried asking people for the full listing of members of the household that is obtained for face-to-face interviews (Table 3.2), but they soon found that many people would not disclose that information on the phone.

Several alternatives have been developed. One, known as the Trol-dahl-Carter-Bryant method, asks the person answering the phone how many adults are in the household and how many adult females are in the household. The interviewer then consults a chart (chosen randomly from a set of charts) to decide which person to interview. This method also encounters problems, since many people are still unwilling to cooperate with interviewers asking about the composition of the household. A less obtrusive method, the Hagen-Collier method, is randomly to ask to speak to one of four types of people—the youngest woman over eighteen, the oldest woman over that age, the youngest man over that age, or the oldest man over that age. If there is no person of the designated sex in the household, then the interviewer randomly asks to speak to either the youngest or oldest person of the opposite sex. A final system now used frequently is the *next birthday method*. The interviewer simply asks for the person in the household who will have the next birthday, and that person is the designated respondent. These last two methods both seem to get lower refusal rates than the other methods.

A Sample of Students at a University

How could you draw a sample from the population of students at a university? You could use all the students who are taking a particular course for your sample, but they would not necessarily be representative of the total population. A single course would be a haphazard sample rather than a probability sample, since students do not all have known chances of being included. A probability sample would be preferable.

For conducting a probability sample, you must first obtain a list of all the university students. An up-to-date student directory is perfect for this purpose. If you can gain access to a computerized version of that directory, you can use a computer program to draw a simple random sample. Alternatively, a systematic sample based on the student directory would give a good sample of the student body. You could stratify the sample in order to guarantee proper coverage in the freshman, sophomore, junior, and senior classes, if you can find a separate listing of each class.

In this example, the list of students (your sampling frame) must match the population of university students as closely as possible. If there is a bias in the list, certain types of students will be missing from the sample. For example, a list of students who live in the dormitories would miss students who live off campus. In this case it would be important to locate many different student lists, investigate the biases of each, and then choose the list that provides the most complete coverage.

Finally, it is important to keep in mind that the population for this study is from a single university, so the results can be generalized only to that university. One should not generalize from results on one campus to the population of college students. The university studied would constitute a haphazard sample of all universities, so generalizations should be limited to that campus.

A Sample of Residents of a City

The sampling problem is somewhat more complicated for a city. You could use a city directory for the listing of the population, but directories are always somewhat out of date by the time they are published. Similarly, if you wanted to interview voters a few months before an election, you could sample from the voter registration lists, but the voter registration lists miss people who register just before the election.

The best procedure for selecting a sample for face-to-face interviews would be the multistage approach described above. Obtain lists of neighborhoods of the city and sample those. For each neighborhood in the sample, obtain lists of blocks and sample those. Finally, list the houses and apartments in the blocks that have been chosen and randomly sample those. This procedure guarantees a high-quality sample, though it is so difficult to perform that using directories and/or registration lists is often more convenient regardless of their drawbacks.

Another possibility is conducting telephone interviews. A sample of numbers from the telephone book can be drawn, adding one to each number in order to be able to locate unlisted numbers. In many cities there are also *reverse directories*, which list houses geographically in order of their addresses and then give the corresponding phone numbers, and samples can be drawn from these reverse directories. Alternatively, the local phone company can provide a listing of residential central office codes, and a computer can be used to randomly choose central office codes and four-digit suffixes.

A Sample from a Rare Population

Sometimes a researcher is interested in a specialized population, such as of Jews or disabled people. These are fairly small groups, and it would be very expensive to phone the general population until one accumulated enough people in these groups. Membership lists of organizations are sometimes useful in locating such people, but this would still miss people who are not members of organized groups. Polling operations that regularly conduct surveys handle this problem by looking through their past surveys to locate respondents who fall into these groups and then recontacting those respondents.

Election Exit Polls

One type of poll that involves unusual sampling procedures is the survey taken by a television network on election day to predict the winners of elections as early as possible. These are generally statewide polls, since most American elections are state elections. Each network decides which states to poll. The networks generally want to give early predictions of the results in the large states, but they often are willing to ignore the small states.

In states in which they are polling, the networks draw a sample of the voting precincts. At one extreme this could be a simple random sample drawn from the list of all the voting precincts in the state, but that would allow a sample that would be too urban or too rural. At the opposite extreme the networks could construct a purposive sample of precincts with known properties (such as precincts that usually go with the election winner or a quota sample with the right proportion of black and white precincts), but such nonprobability samples can contain unsuspected biases. The actual sampling procedures generally are stratified random samples, with stratification on urban versus rural precincts and parts of the state (such as upstate versus downstate in such states as New York and Illinois). Voting patterns in the sample precincts are examined to make sure that the sample has been representative of statewide trends in the past.

In these sample precincts the networks conduct *exit polls* with voters leaving the polling places. Interviewers might be instructed to take interviews with the fifth person leaving the polls after each quarter of an hour (6:00, 6:15, 6:30, and so on). The results of these exit polls are phoned in throughout election day so that network analysts can spot trends long before the polls close. The networks use these exit polls to project election winners as well as to provide insights into the attitudes of voters.

When the polling places close, interviewers phone in the official returns for the precinct as soon as they are available. The network analysts sum up those returns for the state, which provides another means of projecting the vote in the state before the official returns for the whole state are available.

These examples of polling procedures should demonstrate that sampling is a very practical operation. Mathematical theory guides sampling, but taking a sample requires knowledge of what problems are likely to occur. The sampling procedure chosen must handle those likely problems.

PROBLEMS IN SAMPLING

The procedures for taking probability samples are complicated, but it is possible to design probability sampling procedures that do not bias the results and that keep costs reasonable. Generally, so long as (1) the interviewer cannot select the respondent, (2) the sample is large, and (3) there are enough clusters, samples will be highly representative of the population. An occasional sample may by chance be far from representative, but such a bad sample can often be detected if one checks to make sure that the sample approximately matches the percentages for each sex, race, and educational level given by the latest data from the Census Bureau. Still, some potential problems require attention.

Noncoverage Error

One of the complicating problems in sampling is noncoverage error—the omission of part of the intended population. Soldiers, students living on campuses, people living in hospitals, prisoners, and residents of Alaska and Hawaii are typically excluded from national samples, as are hoboes and others without identifying addresses. These discrepancies are unlikely to affect national results by more than 1 percent, and in some cases they are viewed as completely irrelevant, as in election surveys, since many of these groups have very low turnout rates.

The Wrong Population Is Sampled

One must always be sure that the group being sampled is drawn from the population that one wishes to generalize about. For example, one should not draw a sample of college students if one wants to generalize about all college-aged persons. A similar problem might arise if city officials were to survey swimmers at the city pool to determine whether the admission price is so high as to discourage use of the pool. The problem with sampling the swimmers is that the officials intend to make a generalization about all potential users, but those potential users who have already found the price too high will not be among the swimmers.

The Response Rate

We have already mentioned the problem that some people are never at home when the interviewer calls or visits. A related problem is that some people in a sample refuse to be interviewed because they are ill, are too busy, or simply don't trust the interviewer. Interviewers employ many kinds of persuasive arguments to get their cooperation, but in the end many people still refuse. In the 1950s response rates of about 90 percent were typical. However, today people seem less trusting of interviewers, so that response rates are in the 70 percent range.

Response rates for phone interviews are also in the range of 70 percent of the answered phones. This requires three to five call-backs at different times of the day and week to numbers that do not answer. About 5 percent of interviews are not completed because the respondent hangs up in the middle, a higher noncompletion rate than for face-to-face interviews. These response rate figures vary by area, with lower rates in large cities for both face-to-face and phone surveys.

When telephone interviewing was first being attempted, researchers were concerned because many Americans did not have telephones and would therefore be omitted from survey samples. This became a less serious problem when phone ownership in the United States reached the 90 percent level in the 1970s. Response rates in face-to-face interviews fell at that same time, making the lack of complete coverage of telephones less serious.

A national experiment by Groves and Kahn compared demographic characteristics of respondents in face-to-face interviews with those of respondents in a comparable phone interview.[2] They found telephone respondents to be younger and to have somewhat higher income and education, but the differences were not large and do not necessarily signify an unacceptable bias in phone samples. Instead, they reflect reasonable differences in getting people to be interviewed by the two different approaches. For example, young people are generally at home less and at more erratic hours than older people, so phoning back several times may be more effective at contacting them than call-back procedures for face-to-face interviews. Similarly, people with higher socioeconomic status might feel more threatened by letting interviewers into their houses. They might therefore be more likely to refuse face-to-face interviews but be more approachable by phone interviews. Thus the few demographic differences that emerge between face-to-face and phone interviews may indicate problems with face-to-face interviews as much as problems with phone coverage.

This does not mean that researchers can be entirely sanguine about the demographics of phone interviewing. As society changes, phone interviewing may not remain as successful as it was in the early 1980s. For one thing, the breakup of the American Telephone and Telegraph Company (AT&T) has meant higher phone costs for many people, which could cause poorer people to drop or lose their phone service. In fact, a 1987 survey of households with incomes under $15,000 found one-quarter without phones.[3] For another, the increasingly common practice of companies phoning people and pretending to conduct a survey as a ruse to sell them a product (known as *sugging* — selling under the guise of a survey) makes people wary of cooperating with phone surveys. More people are using telephone-answering machines to screen their phone calls, which makes it harder for polling operations to get through to their intended respondents. If these developments continue, nonresponse with telephone interviews may become so serious as to make that procedure less attractive.

---

[2]Robert M. Groves and Robert L. Kahn, *Surveys by Telephone: A National Comparison with Personal Interviews* (New York: Academic, 1979).

[3]This is based on a survey of 816 low-income households conducted by the U.S. Public Interest Research Group, as reported in "Many Poor Say Phone Too Costly," *Columbus Dispatch*, Feb. 1, 1987, 10A.

Nonresponse can be a problem, though people who refuse to respond usually do not differ much from those who do respond (other than being less cooperative). The higher the refusal rate, the more important it is to ascertain whether the refusals are concentrated among a certain group. If, for example, there is some reason to fear that Democrats are less willing to be interviewed than Republicans (and we know of no reason to believe this is happening today), then a survey's results should be adjusted to compensate for the unequal coverage. The demographics of the sample can often be compared with census data in order to determine how representative the sample is, and the data can be adjusted if need be. Usually, though, nonresponse can be ignored.

Sampling Error

A more basic type of error is sampling error—the error that arises from trying to represent a population with a sample. Inevitably, samples differ from populations. Consequently, we should not take sample results as absolutes but rather as approximations. If we find that 67 percent of a sample favors some program, we have learned that the odds are very high that the proportion favoring the program is near 67 percent.

The chances of error cannot be calculated for nonprobability samples, but they can be estimated for probability samples. Say, for example, that there are 200 people (100 women and 100 men) in a population, and we draw a sample of 50. There are many different 50-person samples that could be drawn, and not all would have the same sex ratio. Most of the samples would have sex ratios that are close to the sex ratio of the total population. We might draw an all-male sample, but that would be very unlikely.

Simple random sampling permits precision about the representativeness of the sample. If the true proportion of men is 50 percent, then a sample of 50 people would be expected to have a sex ratio (that is, would have a sex ratio most of the time) within 14 percent of that value. More precisely, given a 14 percent sampling error, 95 percent of the samples would have between 36 percent (18) and 64 percent (32) men. The 14 percent error is called sampling error and can be determined for probability samples.

To state this technically, if repeated samples of 50 were taken with replacement from a population with a 50:50 sex ratio, the percentage of males for 95 percent of the samples would be between 36 percent and

64 percent. This is known as the *95 percent confidence interval*.[4] Of course, we take only one sample, but we hope that our sample is one of the 95 percent rather than one of the 5 percent. A statistician would say that we are taking a 5 percent chance of drawing a faulty conclusion —and 95:5 isn't bad betting odds.

As an example of a simple random sample with sampling error, it is worth conducting an experiment. Starting with 200 cards, write red numbers on half and blue numbers (1-100) on the other half. Shuffle them well. Draw a card. Record its color. Put it back in the deck. Shuffle again. Draw another card. Replace it, shuffle, and draw again. Keep doing this until you have drawn 50 cards. You may begin with a run of same-color cards, but you will probably end up with approximately 25 cards of each color. Figure 3.3 shows the probability of having a given number of blue cards in your sample. Since half of the cards are blue, the most frequent result will be to have 25 blue cards; the next most frequent results will be to have 24 or 26 blue cards, and the least frequent results will be to have 0 or 50 blue cards. If you add up the probabilities of getting 18 blue cards, 19 blue cards, 20, and so on through 32 blue cards, the total should be about 95 percent.

Note that Figure 3.3 shows a normal curve. If one drew a large number of samples from the same population and calculated the mean of each sample (such as the sex ratio or the number of blue cards in the examples above), the distribution of the sample means has a normal distribution around the population mean. Values near the population mean are most likely, while values far from the population mean are unlikely. Of course, a researcher only takes one sample, but the odds are that its mean is close to the population mean. According to published tables, 95 percent of the area under the normal curve is within a known distance from its mean, and that is used to generate the sampling error range.

Of course, with unusual luck, your sample might be 50 blue cards, but that should not stop you from believing in sampling theory. Just take 99 more samples of 50 and you will find that such eccentric samples will occur in only about 5 of them. Sampling is not done by magic —mathematical theory assures that notwithstanding the chances of

---

[4]To simplify this example, we are assuming the sample is with replacement. After we draw a name, that name is thrown back into the pool so that all drawings have identical probabilities. Sampling with replacement is unusual. However, when the population of interest is large relative to the sample, the chance of drawing the same person twice is negligible, so the effect is the same as sampling with replacement.

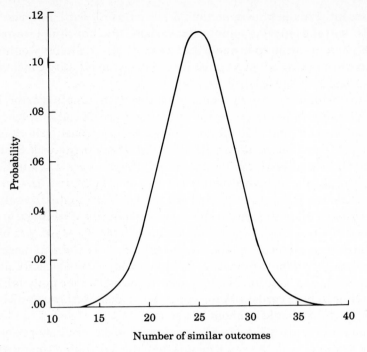

Figure 3.3
Sampling Distribution for Binomial With Fifty-Case Sample
(Based on Harry G. Romig, *50–100 Binomial Tables* [New York: Wiley Copyright
1947] p. 15. Reprinted by permission of the publisher.)

getting a bad sample now and then, almost all results will be on target.
Fortunately, researchers are not entirely at the mercy of bad samples.
If one knows from past surveys what results to expect, one does not
trust a poll that departs radically from them. Thus, if one poll predicts a
Republican landslide, while every other poll taken that year predicts a
Democratic victory, one should be suspicious of the inconsistent poll.

Sample Size.   The 14 percent sampling error in this example is
high, but we could cut it by taking a larger sample. The key ingredient
in determining the sampling error for a simple random sample is the
sample size. The more people who are interviewed, the smaller the error. Actually, quadrupling the sample cuts the error rate in half.[5] Sur-

---

[5]The sampling error is $\pm t\sqrt{p(1-p)/(N-1)}\sqrt{1-f}$, where t approaches 1.96 for the
95 percent confidence interval with large samples (at least 120 cases); f is the sampling

veys generally take more than 100 interviews, since the error rate for samples that size would be too high. But as one increases the number of interviews, one also increases the cost of the study. There is some point at which added precision is not worth the extra cost. Most national samples use about 1,500 interviews. The sampling error with that size multistage sample is generally about 3 percent. To cut a 3 percent sampling error to 1.5 percent would require not 1,500 interviews but 6,000 and the extra expense would not be justified. Elections can be safely predicted with a 3 percent to 4 percent error rate, since most are decided by at least that large a margin. We rarely need accuracy of 1 percent.

The Sampling Fraction. The sampling error is also affected by the sampling fraction—the percentage of the population that is being interviewed. When the sampling fraction is above 30 percent, enough of the population has been sampled so public attitudes are likely to be very similar to those of the sample. The sampling error then is less than it would have been for samples of the same size from a larger population. Usually, though, the sampling fraction is very small; few samples include more than 1,500 interviews even when there are millions of people in the population for national samples or hundreds of thousands in the population for surveys of major cities. Thus, the sampling fraction is typically less than 1 percent, which is too small to matter.[6]

If 1,500 interviews are needed for a representative sample of the 220

---

fraction (sample size divided by population size); p is the sample proportion; and N is the sample size. The term $\sqrt{1-f}$ is ignored when sampling with replacement. The term t is larger than 1.96 for small samples: for example, 2.01 for a sample size of 50, 2.09 for a sample of size 20, 2.26 for a sample of size 10, and 2.77 for a sample of size 5.

To illustrate the formula, let us return to the example above of selecting 50 cards from a deck of cards; however, it requires that we phrase the problem slightly differently. If we took a sample (with replacement) of 50 cards and found 25 to be blue (the proportion of blue cards, $p = 0.5$), how much confidence could we have in that number? The formula is

$$\pm\ 2.01 \sqrt{\frac{p(1-p)}{N-1}} = \pm\ 2.01 \sqrt{\frac{.5(1-.5)}{50-1}} = \pm\ 2.01 \sqrt{\frac{.25}{49}} = \pm\ .14$$

Hence, there is a 95 percent chance that the population proportion is $.5 \pm .14$, or between .36 and .64, so the number of blue cards is between $(.36 \times 50) = 18$ and $(.64 \times 50) = 32$. Note that the sampling fraction is omitted because the sampling is with replacement.

[6]The sampling error depends upon the sample size, the sampling fraction if it is large, and the amount of variation in the variable being measured. Throughout this discussion we have assumed there is some variation of the variable. If there were no variation (such as if everyone's party were the same), a sample of one would be sufficient, and there would be no error. However, most of the variables that social scientists deal with have considerable variation. The confidence interval and sampling error figures in the text assume a population proportion of 0.5, which yields the maximum error.

million residents of the United States, most people would expect that a sample of 500 or 1,000 respondents would suffice for a sample of the 9 million residents of Florida or of the 600,000 residents of San Francisco County. However, since the sampling fraction generally has little effect on the sampling error, a big change in population size does not produce a big change in needed sample size. You need as large a sample to study the attitudes of San Francisco County residents or Florida citizens as for the entire United States. If you use a smaller sample for studying a smaller area, the sampling error will be higher.

Determining Sampling Error When Stratifying and Clustering Are Used. Note that when stratifying and clustering are used, one can still determine the probability of error. Clustering increases the sampling error, but stratifying reduces it. The sampling error for such a design is greater than is the case for a simple random sample, but the multistage sample is considered preferable, since it is much less expensive than a national simple random sample. In the SRC's samples, the sampling error for typical variables is about 3 percent for a multistage stratified and clustered 1,500-person sample. That is, if they find that 67 percent of the sample favors a proposal for government medical assistance, then the true population proportion is likely to be within 3 percentage points of 67 percent. More precisely, in 95 out of every 100 samples, the sample value should be within 3 percentage points of the true population value. The odds that the true population value here is between 64 percent (67 − 3) and 70 percent (67 + 3) are 95:5.

Table 3.3 shows the sampling errors for various sizes of samples and different sampling procedures.[7] The sampling error is always lowest with simple random sampling, but the Gallup and SRC procedures are designed to provide more economical samples with sampling error still within reasonable limits. The total survey error is inevitably greater than these sampling errors, but it is impossible to estimate the magnitude of the other sources of error in a survey.

Choosing a Sample Size. How does one choose a sample size for a survey? A primary consideration is the degree of sampling error that is tolerable. If you consider a 5 percent sampling error reasonable, that suggests a particular sample size. The sampling procedure is also relevant in that the sampling error is smaller with simple random

---

[7]The sampling error in cluster samples can be much larger (three or four times these values) for geographical variables related to the clustering— such as the rural-urban variable.

Table 3.3   Maximum Sampling Error for Samples of Various Sizes

Sample Size	Sampling Procedure		
	Sample Random Sample	Gallup Poll	Survey Research Center Survey
2,000	2.2	3	3
1,500	2.6	3	—
1,000	3.2	4	4
750	3.6	5	—
700	3.8	5	5
600	4.1	5	—
500	4.5	6	6
400	5.0	6	—
300	5.8	8	8
200	7.2	9	—
100	10.3	13	14

NOTE: These are *maximum* sampling errors, since sampling errors depend on the proportion being estimated. Sampling errors are maximal in estimating proportions around 50 percent. There is less error in estimating proportions less than 30 percent or above 70 percent, particularly in estimating proportions less than 10 percent or above 90 percent. Yet, in any event, the sampling errors are not greater than those shown in the table.

SOURCES: The figures in the second column are exact binomial values. The figures in the third column are taken from *Gallup Opinion Index*, August 1987, report 263, p. 32. Reprinted by permission. The figures in the fourth column are taken from Leslie Kish, *Survey Sampling* (New York; Wiley, 1965), Table 14.1.I, p. 576; the latter figures are based on the 1963 Survey of Consumer Finances and may differ from survey to survey. Reprinted by permission of the publisher.

sampling than with some other procedures. Additionally, you should consider the sampling error for subgroups that are of particular importance. If you are primarily interested in political participation by women and how it differs from participation by men, you would look at the sampling error for women and men as subgroups. A sample of 400 gives an overall sampling error of 5 percent, but if about half the sample is female, then any conclusions about women have a sampling error of 7 percent. If you want only a 5 percent sampling error for your statements about women, you will require a sample of 800.

The other major consideration in deciding the size of the sample is the budget. More interviews cost more money, and studies conduct only as many interviews as they can afford. From this perspective, what size sampling error is tolerable depends on the purposes of the study. If you are trying to predict a landslide election, the 7 percent sampling error of a simple random sample with 200 interviews could suffice. If you are trying to predict a hard-fought election, even the 3 percent sampling error with 1,500 interviews may be too large to declare a winner, which is why polls often declare an election to be "too close to call." If you want to measure public attitudes on a matter of public policy, the 5 percent sampling error with 400 interviews might be adequate.

SUMMARY

The quality of a survey is determined largely by its sampling procedures. Nonprobability samples can give biased results. Probability samples are required for good polls. With such samples it is possible to estimate statistically the error that results from the sampling. There are other sources of errors in surveys, but sampling error is particularly important, since it can be estimated mathematically.

Questions

1. If the sampling error is 1 percent and you find that the proportion of respondents favoring government restrictions on abortion is 45 percent, the findings mean that:
   a. The true proportion is probably between 43 percent and 47 percent.
   b. The true proportion is probably between 44 percent and 46 percent.
   c. There is only a 1 percent chance that the population proportion is not 45 percent.
   d. You have made a 1 percent error in your sampling, so the true proportion is 44 percent.
2. According to your analysis of a survey, there is only 25 percent support for government health insurance among the eight Southern college-educated white respondents with income over $15,000. What do you conclude from this?
3. Sampling error is most affected by the:
   a. Proportion of the population sampled.
   b. Response rate.
   c. Number of people sampled.
   d. Size of the population.
4. Cluster sampling is used rather than simple random sampling in order to:
   a. Increase precision of surveys.
   b. Cut transportation costs.
   c. Get better estimates of attitudes in neighborhoods.
   d. Get the proper representation of different regions of the country.
5. Sampling error is caused by which of the following (circle all correct answers):
   a. Refusal of some people to be interviewed.
   b. Differences between the sampling frame and the intended population.
   c. Interviewing the wrong respondent.
   d. Trying to describe a population with only a sample.
6. The sampling error with 1,500 interviews using the Survey Research Center or Gallup sampling procedure is about _____ percent.

4

Questionnaire Construction

The preceding chapter addressed the issue of whom to ask; now we shall take up the issue of what to ask. What forms should questions take? How should questions be worded? What response choices should be offered? In what sequence should the questions be asked? In order to conduct a survey, these practical matters must be settled.

Survey questions should be directly related to the theory and concepts that you are investigating. Great care must be exercised in writing questions in order to get the information you are seeking. Naturally, the first step in writing questions is to spell out precisely what it is you would like to learn from each question or set of questions. Once this is done, a researcher constructs the questionnaire.

QUESTION FORM

When constructing a questionnaire, the first decision to make is what form of question will be used to measure each variable. There are two basic forms, closed-ended and open-ended. *Closed-ended questions* offer a series of alternative answers among which the respondent must choose, like a multiple-choice examination question. *Open-ended questions* allow people to answer in their own words—like an essay examination question.

Open-Ended Questions

Some examples of open-ended questions:

- What do you like about the Republican party? What do you dislike about it? What do you like about the Democratic party? What do you dislike about it?
- What do you think is the cause of the crime and lawlessness in this country?
- What do you consider the most important problem facing the nation today?

In these questions, respondents can reply using any framework they choose.

Open-ended questions have the advantage of allowing respondents to express their thoughts and feelings in their own words instead of in words chosen by the researcher. Thus these questions permit the analyst to study how the public thinks rather than just what their opinions are. For example, the question series asking what the person likes and dislikes about the political parties can be used to assess how positively or negatively a person feels about each political party. That series can also be used to reveal the terms in which people think about politics—do they mention ideological concepts? Specific issues? Do they justify their opinions with lots of information?

Thus, one advantage of open-ended questions is that researchers can see how respondents actually think about the topic. Another advantage is that different analysts with different research interests can find information of value to them from the answers to these same questions. However, the accompanying disadvantage is that different respondents may approach the same question from different perspectives, so that their answers are not fully comparable.

Open-ended questions are more difficult to analyze than closed-ended questions. This is so because researchers must code respondents' answers to open-ended questions into categories before analysis can begin. This involves grouping together respondents who provided similar answers. Because no two respondents ever give exactly the same answer, researchers must often fill in missing details of an answer by making guesses about what a respondent meant to say. Closed-ended questions are easier to analyze because the respondents code themselves into categories.

Closed-Ended Questions

Here are some examples of closed-ended questions:

- Do you think the penalties for selling marijuana should be made stricter, should be made less strict, or should remain as they are now?
- Which do you think is more responsible for crime and lawlessness in this country, individuals or social conditions?
- Which of the following is the most important problem facing the country today: inflation, unemployment, the federal budget deficit, or the threat of nuclear war?

In each of these questions, respondents are asked to choose one from among a set of response alternatives.

A common format for closed-ended questions is to read a statement and ask the respondent to agree or disagree. However, simple agreement or disagreement with a statement gives no clue to the intensity of the person's views. Intensity can be measured by asking if the respondent

- Agrees strongly
- Agrees
- Neither agrees nor disagrees
- Disagrees
- Disagrees strongly.

This is a *rating scale*.

Rating Scales.   Rating scales are, of course, ubiquitous in daily life. Restaurant reviewers, for example, give an establishment a certain number of stars to indicate its quality. More stars indicate higher quality. In surveys, many variables can be measured using rating scales. For instance, people can be asked to indicate how much they like a person (such as a political candidate) or a group of people (such as blacks, Catholics, or police) on a six-point scale with end points labeled "like a great deal" and "dislike a great deal" (Table 4.1). Alternatively,

Table 4.1   Rating Scale

How much do you like Ronald Reagan?					
1 Dislike a great deal	2	3	4	5	6 Like a great deal

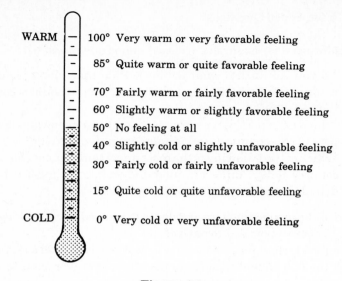

Figure 4.1
Feeling Thermometer

respondents could be asked to indicate their feelings toward a person or group using a *feeling thermometer* (Figure 4.1), where a rating of 0° means the respondent feels very cold, 50° represents the neutral point, and 100° is a very warm rating.

Tables 4.2, 4.3, and 4.4 show three other popular rating scales. For the *card sort* (Table 4.2) the person is handed a set of cards, each with a statement such as "I like the Republican party," and is asked to sort these cards into seven boxes. The *semantic-differential* approach (Table 4.3) has the person rate entities such as the Republican party along several seven-point bipolar scales such as good-bad, strong-weak, and fast-slow by checking the appropriate boxes. A common *seven-point scale* (Table 4.4) calls for stating two opposite extremes — "Some people feel that women should have an equal role with men in running business, industry, and government. Others feel that women's place is in the home" — and then asking the respondent to indicate his or her

Table 4.2   Card Sort

How strongly do you agree or disagree with the following statement: Marijuana should be legalized.

Strongly Agree						Strongly Disagree
+ + +	+ +	+		−	− −	− − −

Table 4.3   Semantic Differential

Here is a list of pairs of words you might use to describe political leaders, and between each pair is a measuring stick of seven lines. Taking the first pair of words—"Good/Bad"—as an example, the line on the extreme left would mean that the leader concerned is very good, the next line would mean he was fairly good, and so on. The words at the top of your card will help you to choose the line you think is appropriate.

Now will you tell me which line you would use to describe Ronald Reagan?

	Very	Fairly	Slightly	Neither	Slightly	Fairly	Very	
Good:	___	: ___	: ___	: ___	: ___	: ___	: ___	:Bad
Weak:	___	: ___	: ___	: ___	: ___	: ___	: ___	:Strong
Fast:	___	: ___	: ___	: ___	: ___	: ___	: ___	:Slow

position along a numbered seven-position scale with the two end points labeled to represent those two extremes.

If a rating scale is to be used, three decisions must be made. First, one must decide how many points to include in the scale. Since psychological research has shown that people have difficulty reliably making more than seven distinctions,[1] it is usually not a good idea to construct scales with more than seven points. Indeed, if respondents are expected to remember the answer categories in a phone survey, it is safer to use only five response categories. When people are given a 101-point scale like the thermometer (Figure 4.1), they typically simplify their task by using only the few points that are labeled and ignoring the rest.

Table 4.4   Seven Point Scale

(HAND R CARD G10) Recently there has been a lot of talk about women's rights. Some people feel that women should have an equal role with men in running business, industry, and government. Others feel that women's place is in the home.

Women and Men
   Should Have
   an Equal Role

Women's Place Is
in the Home

1	2	3	4	5	6	7

_____   Where would you place yourself on this scale, or haven't you thought much about this?

[1] George A. Miller, "The Magical Number Seven, Plus or Minus Two," *Psychological Review* 63(1956):81–97.

The second decision one must make is whether or not to provide a middle alternative. The feeling thermometer in Figure 4.1 includes one (50 = no feeling at all), whereas the six-point scale in Table 4.1 does not. It is generally good to include a middle alternative, since it represents the best description of some respondents' feelings. However, in some situations, researchers prefer to force respondents to take a stand one way or the other.

The third decision to be made when using a rating scale is how many points to label with words. One could label only the end points with words and label the other points with numbers (Table 4.1). One could put verbal labels on the end points and on some of the points in between (Figure 4.1). Or one could label all of the scale points with words (Table 4.3). In general, verbal labels clarify the meanings of scale points for respondents, but they may be distracting for respondents in some cases. It is best to include them only when necessary.

If verbal labels are used, they must be chosen carefully, a process that is sometimes difficult. For example, should people be given the chance to evaluate the president's performance in office as "very good, good, bad, or very bad," or do a different set of descriptors work better? Research on this topic has found that people see little difference between very good and good. A better set of labels is *excellent, good, so-so, bad*, and *terrible*. These terms capture the gradations from one end to the other better than the very good through very bad scale. If one wanted even more extreme terms for the two ends of the scale, *perfect* and *disgusting* could be used as anchors.[2]

Remembering Response Alternatives.   During a face-to-face interview, the respondent can be handed a show card, on which are printed the response alternatives for a particular question. This is a useful technique when the choices are difficult to remember after just hearing them read aloud. Before telephone interviews are conducted, respondents are sometimes mailed sets of show cards in advance of the interview so they are on hand when the interviewer calls. Most often, though, telephone interviews are conducted without show cards. Therefore, response categories used in telephone interviews must be easy to remember.

One way to help telephone interview respondents to answer closed-ended questions is to use a branching format. For example, asking

---

[2]Milton Lodge, et al., "The Psychophysical Scaling and Validation of a Political Support Scale," *American Journal of Political Science* 19(1975):611–49.

whether a person "strongly agrees, moderately agrees, slightly agrees, neither agrees nor disagrees, slightly disagrees, moderately disagrees, or strongly disagrees" with a statement can lead to unnecessary confusion. It is better to ask first whether the respondent agrees or disagrees. Then, respondents who say they agree can be asked if they agree strongly, moderately, or only slightly, and similarly for respondents who disagree. This is called a branching format because which questions are asked depends upon the respondent's answers to earlier questions.[3] If several questions using the same branching format are asked, many respondents will eventually become familiar enough with the categories to give the complete response at once.

Response Choice Order.   Unfortunately, the order in which answer choices are presented to respondents can affect their answers to closed-ended questions. The effect of order seems to depend upon whether answer choices are read aloud to respondents (as occurs in face-to-face and telephone interviews) or are presented in written form (as occurs in self-administered questionnaires and in face-to-face interviews using show cards). When answer choices are read aloud to respondents, they are more likely to choose alternatives at the end of a list. When answer choices are printed on a questionnaire or on a show card, people are more likely to choose the alternatives at the beginning of the list. These order effects seem most likely to occur when many answer categories are offered to the respondent, so it seems better to offer only a few alternatives that are easy to remember.[4]

Choosing a Question Format

The main advantage of the closed-ended question format is that it provides the same frame of reference for all respondents to use in determining their answers. It is also easy and inexpensive to work with the resulting data. If the closed-ended format is chosen, however, care must be taken in writing the choices so that all possible opinions are included and none of the categories overlap.

---

[3]See John H. Aldrich, et al., "The Measurement of Public Opinion about Public Policy: A Report on Some New Question Formats," *American Journal of Political Science* 26(May 1982):391–414.

[4]Howard Schuman and Stanley Presser, *Questions and Answers in Attitude Surveys* (New York: Academic Press, 1981); Jon A. Krosnick and Duane F. Alwin, "An Evaluation of a Cognitive Theory of Response Order Effects in Survey Measurement," *Public Opinion Quarterly* 51(Summer 1987):201–19.

Open-ended questions take more time to analyze, so if instant analysis is required, closed-ended questions are better. Commercial pollsters who have to meet newspapers' deadlines for stories use closed-ended questions almost exclusively. Academic researchers, who can take years to analyze interview data, use open-ended questions more often.

THE WORDING OF QUESTIONS

Once the investigator has decided which question forms to use in measuring each variable, the specific wording of each question must be worked out. When wording a survey question, there are a number of general rules to keep in mind.

Ambiguous Wording

The meanings of words in survey questions must be clear to all respondents. Consider, for example, a question asking whether respondents favor or oppose racial integration. This question is likely to be confusing to some respondents because it isn't completely clear what is meant by racial integration. Does it mean blacks and whites eating in the same restaurant? Or does it mean blacks and whites living in the same house? If different respondents interpret a question differently, their answers will be difficult to interpret.

In order to avoid ambiguity, survey questions should be short and direct. Also, one must keep respondents' cognitive abilities in mind. When interviewing a sample of physicists about their work, it may be perfectly appropriate to use jargon to save time. But when interviewing a representative sample of Americans, one should use ordinary everyday language and should avoid social science jargon or technical terms. Misunderstandings and confusion produce useless data.

A notable ambiguous question is one that was used by the University of Michigan's Center for Political Studies: "How many public officials do you think are a little bit dishonest—most, some, a few, or none?" Researchers included this question in surveys for years to measure how cynical Americans were about politicians. Needless to say, they were surprised to learn from a test of the questionnaire that some very cynical people were answering "none" because they believed that most public officials are very dishonest and that none are only a little bit dishonest! As a result, this question was changed to "Do you think that quite a few of the people running the government are crooked, not very many are, or do you think hardly any of them are crooked?" As this case clearly illustrates, questions should be examined carefully to see if unintended double meanings exist.

In addition to agreeing with question writers about the meanings of words, respondents must share assumptions of those who write the questions. Unfortunately, this is not always the case. For example, political scientists generally agree on the meanings of the words *liberal* and *conservative* and often speak about how liberal or conservative political candidates are. However, members of the public may not see candidates in this way, so asking them to report their perceptions of how liberal or conservative a candidate is might not yield useful results.

Bias in Questions

People designing surveys must be careful to avoid writing biased questions. Biased questions are those that make one response more likely than another, regardless of the respondent's opinion. Examples of biased questions (taken from actual questionnaires) are "Do you favor murdering babies in the womb?" and "Should we continue disarmament so as to give this country to the Communists?" The bias in these questions is obvious, but unfortunately, subtle forms of bias can creep into survey questions in spite of researchers' best efforts to be objective.

One subtle form of bias results from citing authority figures such as the president. The question "Do you support the president's position on aid to India?" is likely to attract more support than stating the president's position without mentioning him and then asking respondents whether they support it. Generally, questions that identify the president with a program exaggerate support for that program in comparison with questions asking about the program without mentioning him.

How a question is worded sets a frame of reference for the respondent. Thus, asking about forced busing frames the problem differently than does asking about school integration. People may think about those two topics differently, so which frame is used in a question may determine the answer. Close inspection of poll results reported in newspapers often reveals that wording of the question may evoke one answer more than another.

An important rule in question wording is that it should be as easy for a person to say no to a question as to say yes to it. Rather than just asking whether the person agrees with the proposed policy, the question can indicate that there is a legitimate disagreement on the proposal so the person will not feel that automatic approval is required. So instead of asking, "Should penalties for selling marijuana be made stricter?" it is preferable to say: "Some people think the penalties for selling marijuana should be made stricter, and other people think they should be made less strict. Do you favor stricter penalties, less strict penalties, or do you think the penalties for selling marijuana should remain as they are today?"

Some survey questions produce useless data because of *social desirability bias*. This occurs when respondents are unwilling to admit certain behavior or attitudes because they are not considered socially acceptable. As a result, when polling about sensitive topics, it is important to make it easy for the respondent to give a truthful answer. For example, simply asking people whether or not they voted in the last election makes it difficult for some people to admit that they did not vote. Instead, it is common to assure people that such behavior is reasonable, as in the question: "In talking to people about elections, we often find that a lot of people were not able to vote because they weren't registered, they were sick, or they just didn't have time. What about you—did you vote in the elections?"

Over the years, survey researchers have found that some wordings yield more biased results than others. For example, people may round or understate their ages but generally will report their birthdates accurately. Similarly, people often refuse to tell strangers their income, but they are more willing to state the range in which their income falls (a. less than $3,000, b. $3,001–$6,000, . . ., g. over $50,000, with people being asked to give the letter corresponding to their income bracket).

Double-Barreled Questions

It is important to avoid double-barreled questions—those that ask two questions at once. For example: "Do you favor reducing American use of gasoline by increasing our taxes on foreign oil?" There are two issues here—one is whether or not to reduce gasoline consumption, and the other is whether or not to use taxes on foreign oil as a means of accomplishing that end. Some respondents might say no to the question because they do not feel that consumption should be reduced; others might say no because they feel some other means of reducing consumption should be used. Asking two questions would be better: (1) "Do you think that American use of gasoline should be reduced?" If the person answers yes, ask, (2) "Do you favor or oppose a tax on foreign oil as a way to cut gasoline use?"

Another version of this problem sometimes occurs with seven-point scales. When respondents are given two opposite sides to an issue and are asked to locate their own position along a scale (Table 4.4), it is important that the two extremes really be opposites in the minds of the respondents. If respondents do not see them as mutually exclusive, then answers will be meaningless. For example, during the Vietnam war days, the National Election Studies included a seven-point scale asking people whether they favored immediate American withdrawal from the war on the one hand, or the pursuit of military victory on the other hand. It has become apparent that many respondents actually favored both these supposedly polar extremes over what they considered to be the unacceptable status quo: fighting on in an indecisive war.

Nonattitudes

Survey designers must always keep in mind that some people who lack a real opinion on an issue may nonetheless offer one when asked about the issue in a survey. Consider people asked for an opinion on some new proposed public policy that they have never heard of or know only very little about. In this situation, some respondents develop instant opinions in order to avoid appearing uninformed to the interviewer. The answers they give, though, do not reflect well-informed opinions and sometimes reflect incorrect guesses about what the policy is.

Two techniques can be used to avoid measuring instant opinions. The first is to explain the policy in neutral terms (if there are any) before asking the question. Better yet, the interviewer could first ask whether the person has read or heard much about the proposed policy. If the respondent answers no, the interviewer can skip the policy question and go on to the next topic. Only if the person claims to know something about the policy is he or she asked about approval of it. Filtering in this fashion typically increases the proportion of don't-know responses by about 22 percent.[5] The argument in favor of filtering is that only real attitudes should be measured, rather than making respon-

---

[5]Howard Schuman and Stanley Presser, *Questions and Answers in Attitude Surveys* (New York: Academic Press, 1981), Chapter 4.

dents think they must take sides on topics on which they have no opinions. However, some pollsters feel that this discourages expression of opinions by respondents who actually have some feelings on the topic but who are not absolutely certain of their attitude.

Academic surveys generally prefer filtering in order to avoid measuring nonattitudes. Commercial pollsters are less likely to filter so they can report simpler results—the proportions of the public favoring and opposing a policy reform. This often means that the public is less decided on an issue than newspaper reports of poll results suggest. Surveys should be interpreted cautiously if it is not clear whether respondents were given a chance to indicate no opinions.

A related problem involves asking how the respondent would behave in a hypothetical situation. Respondents may answer the question, but the answers may tell little about how they actually behave. For example, asking legislators if they vote their own minds or follow constituents' wishes produces meaningless results. At best the legislators give answers that will put them in a good light. A better tactic is to ask them what they considered in deciding how to vote in a recent specific vote in the legislature. Dealing with a specific case is more likely to get meaningful answers than asking hypothetical questions.

The Importance of Question Wording

Even after taking account of all the question-wording problems described so far, there is no way to word a question perfectly. The same question can be asked in different ways, all of which seem good, and the different wordings may yield different results.

For example, pollsters Gallup and Harris ask monthly questions measuring the president's popularity, but they ask different versions. The Gallup Poll asks, do you approve or disapprove of the way the president is handling his job as president? The Harris Poll asks, how would you rate the job the president is doing—excellent, pretty good, only fair, or poor? Harris then combines *excellent* with *pretty good* to yield *positive*, and *fair* and *poor* for *negative*. These questions generate different results. For example, one year after Gerald Ford became president, Gallup reported 45 percent approval of the president, while Harris found only a 38 percent positive rating.

Consider another example. On the face of it, answering yes to "Do you think the United States should forbid public speeches against democracy?" seems equivalent to answering no to "Do you think the

United States should allow public speeches against democracy?" However, only 20 percent of respondents in a 1976 survey said yes to "forbidding" such speeches, compared with 45 percent who said no to "allowing" such speeches. It is difficult to know why people answered these two questions differently, but this example illustrates how even trivial changes in question wording can substantially alter answers.[6]

As a final example, a 1980 *New York Times*/CBS News Poll found that half of a national sample favored a constitutional amendment "protecting the life of an unborn child" versus only 29 percent favoring a constitutional amendment "prohibiting abortion." In this instance people on both sides of the issue can find poll evidence showing public support for their point of view because question wording can be manipulated to yield results that favor either.

In these examples, question wordings are logically equivalent, but different versions produce different results. It is certainly natural to wonder which wording of each question is the "correct" one, but it is impossible to decide which result is right. It therefore seems best to recognize that there is no such thing as a correctly worded question. Instead of looking for perfect questions, researchers have learned to measure attitudes using a variety of question wordings and to interpret the results of polls cautiously, since they can be sensitive to rewording of questions.

Therefore, researchers tend not to try to determine how many people favor or oppose legalized abortion, for example. Instead, they study which types of people are more favorable and which types are less favorable, how opinions change over time, and what causes them. Researchers generally believe that the same results regarding subgroup differences, change, and cause will be obtained regardless of the exact question wording used. For example, if Protestants and Catholics differ in terms of favorability toward abortion, any wording of an abortion question probably will reveal that difference. Similarly, changes in attitudes over time and the causes of attitudes should be apparent regardless of the attitude measure used.

Using Standard Questions

A useful short-cut to wording your own questions is using standard questions that have been developed and employed by major sur-

---

[6]This experiment is reported in Schuman and Presser, 276–80.

vey organizations. Through extensive experience, these organizations have refined measures of political and psychological concepts as well as standard background questions about income, age, occupation, education, and so on.[7] A survey researcher can benefit from the experiences of others by using their questions and by modifying them only when necessary to suit particular objectives. Using questions that have been employed in previous surveys allows one to compare new results with older ones in order to study changes in attitudes over time. This also permits one to replicate findings of previous research, a task that is important in science but that is rarely done.

When designing a survey, there is a constant tension between the desire to use standard questions in order to compare results with those of previous surveys and the desire to improve the wording of questions. After some experience using a standard question, researchers sometimes realize that it could be improved through rewording. However, changing wording makes it more difficult to examine attitude change, since the stimuli given to respondents are different. This means that minor tinkering with the wording of standard questions is not worthwhile; standard questions should be reworded only if serious problems are found with them.

Sometimes rewording questions is necessary because of changes in the meanings of words or in the acceptability of certain terms. For example, it was common to refer to blacks as Negroes in the 1950s. Asking a question about Negroes today would seem odd to many respondents. Therefore, if one were tracking changes in racial attitudes over time, it would have been necessary to replace the word *Negroes* with the word *blacks* at some point since the 1950s.

Another reason for rewording questions has to do with changing meanings. Consider a question that asks respondents whether they favor or oppose racial integration. In the 1950s, most Americans probably interpreted this term as referring to whites and blacks eating in the same restaurants, sleeping in the same hotels, and so on. Today, most respondents would be unlikely to think of racial integration as referring to these circumstances because most of us take them for granted. Instead, it is more likely that people will think of controversial aspects of racial integration, such as busing children in order to integrate

---

[7]A useful source of standard social science batteries of questions is Delbert C. Miller, *Handbook of Research Design and Social Measurement*, 4th ed. (New York: Longman, 1983).

schools. In order to track changes in attitudes toward the same concept, it is necessary in cases like this to reword the survey question.

It is useful to think of a survey question as a *stimulus* to which respondents respond. In order to track variations in attitudes across subgroups or changes in attitudes over time, the same stimulus must be presented to respondents in all subgroups and at all times. It is tempting to think of the stimulus as the *wording* of a question, but it seems more appropriate to think of the stimulus as the *meaning* of the questions. Wording should therefore be changed when necessary in order to keep meaning constant.

Batteries of Questions

It is often impossible to measure a complex concept with only a single question, so several questions may be needed to measure the various aspects of the concept. For example, to measure how cynical people are about government, one might ask: "How much of the time do you feel you can trust the government in Washington to do what is right? Do you think that people in the government waste a lot of the money we pay in taxes, waste some of it, or do not waste very much of it? Do you think quite a few of the people running the government are a little crooked, not very many are, or do you think hardly any of them are crooked?" No one of these questions provides a perfect measure of political cynicism, but the set of questions can be combined into an overall index of cynicism. The results produced by this index are not as much influenced by the wording of particular questions as would be the case if only one question were used.

Tailoring Questions to Respondents

Questions should be written specifically for the group being interviewed. For a sophisticated political elite the questions could be phrased differently than for the general public. Legislators, for example, could be asked their opinions on specific policies that would be meaningless to most people.

When dealing with the mass public, it is important to keep questions at a level the respondents understand. Minimally, this means avoiding social science jargon and terms that the public would not recognize. It also argues for phrasing questions and alternative responses in the way that the public thinks about the topic, rather than as researchers think about it.

EVALUATING QUESTIONS

Once a survey question has been written, the investigator must evaluate how well it does what it is intended to do. That requires assessing the reliability and the validity of each question.

Reliability

For a survey question to be useful, it must be reliable, meaning that people should answer it the same way each time they are asked. Imagine measuring the length of a pencil with an elastic ruler. One person may measure its length to be four inches, while another person may find its length to be three inches because he or she stretched the ruler. This is an example of an unreliable measure. Using a reliable measure, repeated measurements of the same object produce similar results, as is the case when measuring the length of a pencil using a wooden ruler.

The best way to assess the reliability of a question is by comparing answers people give to it on one occasion with the answers those same people give to it a short time later. Of course, if the time interval is too short, the apparent reliability of a question may be exaggerated because people simply repeat what they remember saying the first time they were asked. If the time interval is too long, people's answers may change because their attitudes changed, thus causing the question's apparent reliability to be artificially low. If answers to a question are pretty consistent over a period of a few weeks, the question is probably adequately reliable, but if people's answers are very different on the two occasions, the question must be rewritten.

A battery of questions measuring the same concept is considered reliable if a person's answers to them are consistent with each other. For example, on the cynicism battery described above, if the people who give cynical answers to one question are trusting on a second question, while those who give trusting answers to the first question are cynical on that second question, then the two questions are not consistent. The researcher should try to determine which question is the least consistent with the remaining questions and drop that question in order to improve the overall reliability of the battery.

Validity

Good survey questions must also be valid, meaning that they should measure the concepts they are intended to measure. Sometimes a question may actually measure a related concept rather than the one the researcher wants to measure. There are a number of ways to evaluate the validity of a survey question, the simplest of which is to assess its *face validity*, the degree to which it seems to measure the appropriate concept on its face. For example, to measure how cynical people are about politics, asking whether all politicians should be trusted has more face validity than asking whether all politicians should be jailed. Yet face validity is a subjective matter, so it should not be the only test of the validity of a question.

Two other sorts of validity are *convergent validity* and *divergent validity*. The principle underlying these forms of validity is that measures of the same concept should receive similar answers, while measures of different concepts should receive different answers. Convergent validity is assessed by comparing people's answers to one question with their answers to another question intended to measure the same concept. For example, if answers to two questions measuring political cynicism are quite similar, they have high convergent validity. Divergent validity is assessed by comparing people's answers to a question measuring one concept to their answers to a question intended to measure a different concept. For example, a question on political cynicism should not yield identical answers when compared with a question on political efficacy (whether people feel they can influence government actions); if answers are not highly similar, they are said to have high divergent validity. A question with low convergent or divergent validity must be rewritten.

Another form of validation is *criterion validity*, which can be assessed by comparing people's answers to a survey question with a direct measure of the concept of interest. For example, a question asking people whether or not they voted in an election can be validated by checking official records in voting registration offices. Unfortunately, it is impossible to obtain official criteria for most survey questions, particularly those measuring attitudes. When it is possible to assess criterion validity, though, it often turns out to be surprisingly low. It is therefore important to assess criterion validity whenever possible in order to identify inadequate questions.

Sometimes a survey includes a battery of questions intended to measure different aspects of the same concept. Investigators speak of the *content validity* of such sets of questions, the degree to which they measure all the important aspects of the concept. For example, if a researcher wishes to measure how knowledgeable respondents are about politics, a single question asking how many justices are on the United States Supreme Court would be insufficient. Other questions should be added, perhaps asking how many years a senator's term in office is, how many times a person can be reelected president, and so on. If a battery of questions lacks content validity, one can solve the problem by adding new questions to measure additional aspects of the concept.

A final form of validity is *construct validity*. A theory may indicate how the concept being measured should be related to other concepts. If the measure of the concept is not related to other concepts as the theory suggests, then either the theory is disproved or the measurement is invalid. If the theory is widely accepted, the construct validity of the measure is considered low. As an example, say much previous research shows that people who are more cynical about politics are less likely to vote, but we find the opposite in our survey. This could be a disproof of the theory, but it is more likely that the construct validity of our cynicism and/or voting turnout measures is low.

Always be cautious in interpreting survey results, since those results may be the product of poor question wording. Before taking the results literally, make some appropriate checks. Does the question wording seem reasonable (have good face validity)? Does it give results similar to other measures of the same concept (have good convergent validity)? Does it give different results from questions that are supposed to be measuring different concepts (have good divergent validity)? Can it be compared against a direct measure of the concept (have good criterion validity)? Does it measure the full breadth of the concept (have good content validity)? Does it relate to other variables as theory and previous research suggest it should (have good construct validity)?

CONSTRUCTING THE QUESTIONNAIRE

After deciding upon the wording of each question, the questionnaire must be assembled. This involves deciding upon the order of topics to be discussed and the order of questions on each topic.

Topic Order

The organization of questions in the questionnaire is extremely important, partly because the interview may be terminated at the beginning if it starts with questions that anger or embarrass the respondent. Also, people may not give candid answers to personal questions unless they have developed some rapport with the interviewer. Therefore, interviews should begin with general warm-up questions that put respondents at ease and show that the interviewer and researchers are interested in learning their views rather than in testing their knowledge. Open-ended questions encourage people to speak freely and help them to become comfortable, so they make good early questions.

It is especially important that the early questions in an interview correspond closely to the purpose of the survey as it was originally described to the respondent. So many salespeople call or visit houses claiming to be conducting a survey and later switch to a sales pitch that people may distrust surveys until the interviewer has proved that the study is legitimate by asking many questions on the stated topic. Trust between interviewers and respondents is more difficult to establish on the phone than in person, so early questions in telephone interviews must be especially good at building rapport.

Routine demographic background questions (about the person's education, occupation, religion, and so on) are usually placed toward the end of a questionnaire. Questions that might anger or embarrass some respondents or that they might be reluctant to answer (such as questions about their family income) are customarily put at the end of the interview as well.

Question Order

Each question in a questionnaire should flow naturally from the previous one. It is very confusing to people if the questionnaire skips around from topic to topic, so questions on the same topic should be grouped together. Each section should begin with an introductory sentence telling the respondent the topic of the next series of questions ("Now we will turn to some questions about politics"), particularly when there is a sharp change in subject matter.

The order in which questions on the same topic are asked sometimes makes important differences. Asking one question before a second can yield different results from asking the second question first. This is especially important in the presence of *consistency bias*—the desire of respondents to appear consistent to the interviewer by answering related questions in a consistent manner. For example, studies find that people are more likely to agree that Japan should have the right to limit its imports if they are first asked if the United States should have the right to limit its imports. Consistency bias is reduced if people do not notice that separate questions are interrelated. Still, it is worth avoiding this problem by not asking a series of questions that might make respondents feel that they are being tested for the consistency of their answers.

Earlier questions can affect what comes to mind for the respondent when asked a later question. Say that you wanted to measure what people consider the most important problem facing the country (measured via an open-ended question) and how they feel on specific policy questions such as foreign aid, our relations with Russia, the state of the economy, and so on (measured with closed-ended questions). If the most important problem is asked for later, people will naturally think back to their answers to the specific policy questions and will often choose among the issues mentioned in those earlier questions. In order to avoid inadvertently limiting responses in this way, open-ended questions should be asked before closed-ended questions on similar topics.

Avoiding Response Set

A final question-wording problem is related to the sequence of questions that all use response options such as yes/no or agree/disagree. Sometimes people do not seriously consider each question but are just in an acquiescent mood and simply say yes or agree to all the questions. This problem, called response set, can seriously distort results. Say that you have a series of yes/no questions designed to measure how conservative a person is, with a yes on each question being the conservative response. An acquiescent person would be scored as extremely conservative. The impact of response sets can be reduced by introducing some variety into the questions, so that for example yes is the conservative response to some questions and no is the conservative response to others. An acquiescent person would then be scored as conservative on some questions, liberal on others, and therefore be viewed as neither conservative nor liberal. Overall, the result would be a more accurate measure of conservatism.

Questionnaire Layout

When the questions and their order are determined, it is necessary to lay out the questionnaire so it can be read easily. If the physical

Table 4.5   A Page from an Interview Schedule

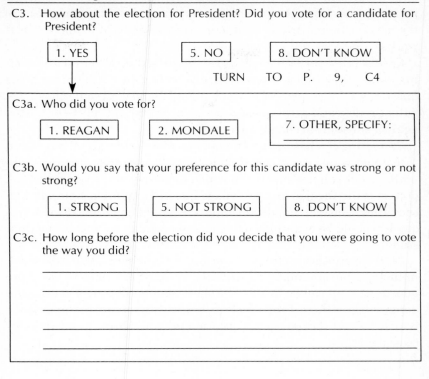

C3.   How about the election for President? Did you vote for a candidate for President?

| 1. YES | | 5. NO | | 8. DON'T KNOW |

TURN   TO   P.   9,   C4

C3a. Who did you vote for?

| 1. REAGAN | | 2. MONDALE | | 7. OTHER, SPECIFY: |

C3b. Would you say that your preference for this candidate was strong or not strong?

| 1. STRONG | | 5. NOT STRONG | | 8. DON'T KNOW |

C3c. How long before the election did you decide that you were going to vote the way you did?

_____

_____

_____

_____

_____

layout of the questionnaire is too confusing, even a good interviewer will skip questions by accident. This is especially a problem with self-administered questionnaires, since there is no way of calling to the respondent's attention a question that was missed.

A good questionnaire is laid out so that the pages are not cluttered. Arrows may help the interviewer follow the intended sequence. Important questions should not be hidden at the bottom of the page. Table 4.5 reproduces a page of a questionnaire showing a type of layout that is very readable.

Pretesting the Questionnaire

Questionnaire construction is really an art, much of which is learned through practice. In fact, it is so difficult that researchers rarely use a questionnaire in a survey without first pretesting it. They interview some people who will not be in the final sample in order to try out the questions. Taking twenty-five to seventy-five pretests for a major survey has been recommended,[8] but minimally it is important to try the questionnaire out on at least a few people just to make sure it works.

Pretest interviewers generally report to the researchers at a debriefing, when they indicate any difficulties they encountered with the questions. Often unexpected problems are found with some questions. After the debriefing, the questionnaire is revised and may be pretested again if substantial changes are made.

Pretesting can be used as a tool in question formulation. Say that a researcher wants to use closed-ended questions so answers can be tabulated quickly but is unsure on which issues people have opinions. A pretest could include an open-ended question asking people what issues they consider important, and the issues mentioned most frequently could be examined using closed-ended questions in the final study.

Pretests are also useful for determining how long it will take to administer a questionnaire. Inevitably, researchers want to ask more questions than can be fit into the short amount of time most respondents will give them. Pretests often force questionnaire designers to be realistic about the length of a questionnaire and to drop questions for reasons of time.

SUMMARY

To sum up the general rules of questionnaire design:

- Use open-ended questions to let respondents define their own frame of reference for the answer, but use closed-ended questions when a quick tabulation of results is required.
- Word the questions simply and avoid bias.
- Avoid questions that are too sophisticated or complex for respondents.
- Organize the questions so that they flow smoothly, so that early questions are not threatening, and so that early questions do not direct later answers.

Remember, what you ask is what you get. Ask a good question, and you get useful information. Ask a bad question, and you get useless in-

---

[8]Jean Converse and Stanley Presser, *Survey Questions* (Beverly Hills: Sage Publications, 1986).

formation. Questions must be structured with the purposes of the survey clearly in mind, so be tenacious in asking "What is it that I really want to know? How will I use this information when I get it? What is the purpose of this question? Does it accomplish that purpose?"

Finally, do not take survey results as absolute, because they are dependent upon the wording of questions. Slightly different wordings can yield results that differ by 5 percent or 10 percent and sometimes more. But if the wording is reported, readers can form their own ideas as to how valid the questions are. All surveys have flaws, but high-quality surveys make an honest attempt to accomplish their purposes with accurate, unbiased questions.

Questions

1. You are designing a survey on attitudes toward various life-styles and you expect educational differences to be a major factor in determining people's attitudes. To test this hypothesis, you want to measure each person's education. First list the different things that might be meant by amount of education; there are at least three major meanings of the term. Write a question or series of questions to use in asking about the person's educational background that would permit analysis of the effects of all of these types of education.
2. It is very difficult to phrase unbiased questions on emotionally charged issues. Assume that you want to study people's opinions on abortion—more precisely, that you are interested in the circumstances in which people would permit abortion. What are the most basic types of circumstances that should be included in a question? (There are a large number of distinct alternatives, so concentrate on a few major types.) How would you phrase a closed-ended question on this topic?

5

The Data Collection Stage

Once the questionnaire has been prepared, the next stage in a survey is to collect the data. The three primary methods for data collection are face-to-face interviewing, telephone interviewing, and self-administered questionnaires. In this chapter, we describe the mechanics involved in each method and compare their strengths and weaknesses.

FACE-TO-FACE INTERVIEWING

Historically, face-to-face interviewing has been the most common method of survey data collection, and most commercial survey organizations make frequent use of this technique. To use this method, an organization begins by hiring a staff of interviewers and teaching them how to conduct interviews. Letters describing the purpose of the survey and telling residents to expect a visit from an interviewer are then mailed to all the residences (houses, apartments, trailers, and so forth) where interviews are to take place. Each interviewer is given a set of blank questionnaires and is assigned a set of residences to visit, and after the interviews are completed, the questionnaires are returned to the survey office for data processing.

Selection of Interviewers

Regardless of how much care is taken in drawing the sample and writing the questions, the success of a survey is in the hands of the interviewers. They ask the questions and record the responses by writing them on the questionnaire. If they do a good job, the study is in good shape; if they do a poor job, the results are meaningless.

One of interviewers' most important tasks is to get respondents to agree to participate in the survey, since getting in the door for an interview can be difficult. Even when the interviewer identifies herself, shows credentials, and reminds the resident about the letter that he or she presumably received a few days earlier, it is natural for the person to wonder whether the interviewer is being truthful. Encyclopedia salespeople often claim to be taking a survey until they are well into their sales pitch, so it is not surprising that many people are suspicious of interviewers.

Questioners who seem credible and do not make respondents feel threatened are most likely to obtain entry into their homes. Because initial perceptions of an interviewer's credibility and threat are based largely on appearance, survey organizations prefer to hire middle-class, middle-aged women. (As a result, we refer to interviewers as female.) Young people and men have a harder time gaining access to people's homes, and men with long hair or a beard are especially likely to have trouble obtaining interviews. Black interviewers are typically employed in predominately black neighborhoods, since these individuals are more likely to gain entry there.

A second primary task of the interviewer is to measure respondents' attitudes as accurately as possible. To do so, the interviewer must gain the trust of the respondent and must induce him or her to speak freely. Understandably, most people are reluctant to express their opinions to a person they do not know at all, but candid responses are essential for survey data to be useful. Respondents speak most freely with interviewers who they believe have opinions similar to their own, a judgment that is made in part on the basis of the interviewer's appearance. This is another reason why white interviewers are usually assigned to interview white respondents, black interviewers are usually assigned to interview black respondents, Hispanic interviewers are usually assigned to interview Hispanics, and so on.

Interviewer Training

Once interviewers are chosen, they must be taught how to initiate interaction with a potential respondent and how to administer the questionnaire. The training usually begins with showing the interviewers some play-acted interviews so that they can see which interview practices are useful. Interviewers must also become familiar with the questionnaire and must be briefed on the purposes of the study and on the objectives of each question. This knowledge helps them to handle problems they may encounter during interviews. Finally, they conduct practice interviews to familiarize themselves with the questions before they take the real interviews. During the training, interviewers are taught a number of basic rules for obtaining the interviews.

Organizations that regularly conduct surveys hire a permanent staff of interviewers in their primary sampling units. The same interviewers are used for several different surveys. This leads to better-trained interviewers than would be obtained by hiring new interviewers for each study.

Obtaining the Interview

It may sound as if face-to-face interviewing is easy — that the interviewer just goes to the person's house and conducts the interview. However, survey research is never that simple. Instead, the interviewer must handle a number of preliminary problems before starting the interview.

Initiating Contact.   When an interviewer rings a doorbell and someone comes to the door, the interviewer must make sure that the person does not slam the door in her face. Usually, she begins by introducing herself and showing some credentials from the survey organization. She explains the nature of the study in general terms ("We are getting information on how people feel about important problems facing the country today") and assures the person that the opinions collected will be kept confidential. Finally, the interviewer tells the person how his or her home was chosen. ("We talk to people of different ages and walks of life in all parts of the country and put their answers together to get a cross-section of the people.")

Sometimes, an interview gets no further than this stage. The person may not trust the interviewer's explanation or may be fearful of being interviewed. Further explanations or assurances may help, but sometimes the refusal is adamant and the interview terminates. If the interviewer came at an inconvenient time, perhaps a later appointment can be made for the interview. Occasionally, interviewers encounter situations that do not permit interviews — the respondent may be mentally or physically ill, drunk or stoned, or so busy that the interview is constantly interrupted. Every survey loses a few interviews for such reasons.

The problems inherent in interrupting someone's life should not be minimized. People are always doing something when interviewers knock on their doors. Most people stop what they are doing to answer the door, and most agree to be interviewed, but sometimes a respondent is caught in an embarrassing moment. Every survey organization has a story about the interviewer who rings a doorbell and is greeted by a naked person. The story often continues that the interviewer explains that she is not permitted by her organization to take interviews unless the person is clothed. Usually, the individual agrees to get dressed. If an interview is truly impossible at a given time, the interviewer is instructed to excuse herself politely and return later to try again.

Selecting a Respondent.   Once the person answering the door agrees to speak with the interviewer, she asks who is living in the house and what their sexes and ages are. Using the household listing, she follows instructions and selects the person to be interviewed—perhaps the oldest male (if there is one) in the first household, the youngest female over age 18 (if there is one) in the next, and so on. It is important to the sampling that the interviewer carry out this respondent selection procedure carefully.

After the respondent has been selected, a time for the interview must be settled upon. If the person answering the door is the person to be interviewed, the interview is usually conducted at that time. If the person to be interviewed is not at home, an appointment can be made for the interviewer to return to the house.

Interview Conditions.   Whenever possible, interviews should be conducted without an audience. If friends or family members are present, the respondent may give the answers that these people would approve of instead of reporting his or her own attitudes. Furthermore, children playing in the same room can be distracting and therefore decrease the quality of answers. Unfortunately, it can be difficult to get the respondent alone, so in some national studies as many as half of the interviews are taken with family or friends present.

Informed Consent.   The participation of respondents in surveys should be voluntary and based on an understanding of the nature of the research project and of any risks involved. However, the more one reminds people that they need not participate, the less likely they are to do so. The lower response rates that result from stressing voluntary participation make the research findings less generalizable to the population of interest. As a result, interviewers typically mention the voluntary character of participation only briefly while attemping to secure the person's cooperation.

At the beginning of interviews, respondents are usually told what topics will be covered and are given a rough idea of the length of the interview. They should also be apprised of what rights they have in the interview. This is done by saying something like "Feel free to ask any questions at any time. If you do not wish to answer a particular question for any reason, just let me know, and we'll go on to the next question."

Guidelines for Interviewing

There are a variety of guidelines for interviewing, designed to help get candid answers from respondents.

Asking the Questions.   Generally, the interviewer is expected to read the questions using exactly the same wording and in exactly the same order as they appear in the questionnaire. Because even small changes in wording or order of the questions can sometimes change respondents' answers dramatically, it is essential that all interviewers administer the questionnaire in an *identical* manner. Chaos would result if every interviewer asked a different variant of the same question, or changed the order of questions to suit the interviewer's tastes.

Recording the Answers.   Interviewers usually record respondents' answers exactly, including a verbatim record of open-ended answers. This allows researchers to analyze the respondent's answers in whatever manner they desire, without being dependent on the interviewer's interpretations of those answers. Imagine a respondent giving a lengthy answer explaining why America should not trust Communist countries only to have the interviewer write down, "Russia is our enemy." The richness of an answer can be preserved only by recording it in full, which permits researchers to study how people think by evaluating their choice of words. Though it may seem sensible, tape-recording interviews is extremely rare in surveys of the general public because many people are uncomfortable being recorded, some are unwilling to be recorded, and transcription of the recordings is costly and time-consuming.

Not Giving Opinions.   The primary purpose of an interview is to measure the respondent's attitudes. This means that interviewers should simply ask the questions and should not express their own opinions to the respondent. If the interviewer expresses her own attitudes, the respondent might feel pressure to give answers that the interviewer will like. If this pressure actually influences some respondents' answers, their validity is compromised. On occasion respondents pressure interviewers for their opinions. In those cases, interviewers are trained to say they are not permitted to state their own opinions during the interview but that they would be happy to discuss the issue at the end of the interview. Interviews sometimes conclude with an informal conversation, during which the interviewers express some of their own attitudes.

Building Rapport With the Respondent.   Obviously, the interview situation is unusual for respondents. Rarely do strangers come to a person's door inquiring about his or her opinions. Indeed, the respondent may not be used to stating his or her opinions on political or other controversial matters, so he or she must be made to feel comfortable in this unsual situation. Furthermore, respondents sometimes feel inadequate; they may be afraid that they do not know enough to give an answer or that they will give the "wrong" answer.

Ideally, the respondent should find the experience pleasurable and should feel happy that someone is interested in his or her opinions. In order for this to occur, the interviewer must build rapport with the respondent. That is, both people should develop feelings of confidence, understanding, and trust. Two ways an interviewer can build rapport are by expressing appreciation for each answer (such as by saying thank you or nodding affirmatively) and by permitting the respondent to talk as much as he or she wishes to. It is also important to assure respondents that there are no right or wrong answers to most survey questions and that the reseachers are interested in their opinions. One of the common ways interviewers reassure respondents is borrowed from psychotherapy: a nondirective "uh-huh." Using this and other techniques, interviewers should be good listeners; they should inspire trust and encourage expression of frank opinions.

Probing.   Researchers need clear, complete, and relevant answers to their questions. Often, a respondent's initial reply to an open-ended question is unclear, is just a fraction of his or her views, or is off the track. When this occurs, the interviewer must probe, getting the person to clarify his or her answer. Questionnaires sometimes list additional questions that the interviewer can ask to clarify answers. Also, interviewers are taught a set of general techniques to be used whenever necessary: saying yes, pausing, repeating the question, repeating the respondent's answer, asking "How do you mean that?" or "Anything else?" or "Could you tell me more about what you mean?"

The most common answer that requires probing is "I don't know," since it has so many possible meanings. It may mean that the person has never thought about the question and has absolutely no opinion. At the opposite extreme it may just be a phrase the respondent uses while thinking for a second before giving an answer. In response to a closed-ended question, "I don't know" may mean that a respondent knows exactly how he or she feels on the issue but isn't sure which choice fits that opinion best. Respondents should not be badgered to determine the meaning of "I don't know," but the interviewer should not accept don't-know responses too easily.

Refusal.   Another problem that sometimes occurs is the respondent's refusal to answer a particular question. This rarely occurs, but when it does, the interviewer should try to get the answer. However, she should not try so hard as to jeopardize the rapport for the rest of the interview.

Interviewing Elites.   When surveying members of elite groups such as politicians and civic leaders, some exceptions are made to the usual interviewing rules. For example, in these situations it is common for interviewers to memorize the questions and ask them in whatever order the conversation follows. The argument behind this practice is that members of an elite group are not likely to accept interviews that are not tailored directly to them. Also, writing the respondent's answers down during such an interview is uncommon, because it is felt that doing so would be viewed as a discourtesy and a distraction, taking away from the flow of the interview. Instead, interviewers usually record a few key phrases during the interview to aid their memories and then transcribe the interview immediately afterward, while the experience is still fresh in their memories. Political elites are used to being interviewed by reporters using tape recorders, so they are often willing to have the interviews taped once they are sure of the purposes and confidentiality of the interview.

Benefits to the Respondent. Perhaps most important of all, interviewers must bear in mind that respondents should benefit from the experience. We usually think that an interview is valuable and useful mainly to the researcher who is gathering the information. But surveys would not be possible if the benefits were only one-sided. Surveys offer respondents opportunities to speak to a good listener, to reflect on things, to reminisce about past experiences, to be stimulated intellectually by thinking about issues they don't often consider, and to express attitudes candidly without fear of the consequences. When the interviewers do their jobs well, the experience is a pleasant break in the respondent's daily routine.

Supervising Interviewers

Most survey organizations sooner or later discover that a few of their interviewers fake interviews. Often this is apparent from the completed questionnaires — real people tend to have somewhat inconsistent attitudes; fake interviews tend to be too consistent. Also, interviews often include a question designed to check some known information about the respondent; a wrong answer recorded here can be a clue that the interview is a fake. Survey organizations increasingly employ some technique to validate each interview, usually either sending a letter or making a telephone call to the respondent to verify that the interview took place. In general, though, interviewers who are paid good wages almost never fake interviews.

Confidentiality

When surveys address sensitive topics, respondents run the risk of being injured if their responses become public. Imagine, for example, that a newspaper publishes a survey detailing the extent of drug use on a college campus, and the local police subpoena the questionnaires to identify respondents who admitted illegal drug use. Or imagine a survey in which respondents reported their family incomes, the results of which the Internal Revenue Service subpoenas in order to identify tax evaders. Or imagine a survey of political attitudes, the results of which are subpoenaed by the Federal Bureau of Investigation to identify Communist sympathizers. Respondents are well aware of this danger and are usually reluctant to discuss such topics with interviewers.

The best way to handle this problem is to explain to respondents that their responses will be kept confidential and that only statistical analysis of the results will be published. Names and other identifying materials (addresses, phone numbers) are generally removed from interview schedules after the interview has been conducted and validated. From that point on, each questionnaire can be identified with a unique number, with the respondent's identity being kept confidential.

TELEPHONE SURVEYS

At a superficial level, telephone interviews are very similar to face-to-face interviews. In both cases interviewers read questions to respondents and record their answers. However, many aspects of these two data collection methods are quite different. Below, we describe the most notable procedural differences between face-to-face and telephone interviewing.

Survey Administration

Telephone interviews are generally conducted from a single site. Most major survey organizations have a large number of telephones in the same room from which all interviewers make their calls. Even a national sample can be interviewed from a single location using relatively inexpensive WATS (wide-area telephone service) lines. For example, the CBS/New York Times Poll does its interviews from a New York City location that is convenient for the unemployed Broadway actors and actresses that it sometimes hires as interviewers.

Conducting all of the interviews from a single site also serves to increase the amount of supervision that is possible. Supervisors often listen in on another phone to check how the interview is being conducted. Thus, they can notice problems when they occur. Unanticipated problems can be dealt with immediately. In some cases this means further training for a particular interviewer; in other cases it means adding new instructions for all of the interviewers.

Data collection through telephone interviews is often done by using computer assisted telephone interviewing (CATI). Instead of reading questions out of a booklet and writing answers down with a pencil, interviewers read questions displayed by computers on video screens and type responses on a computer keyboard. CATI has numerous advantages. First, the data are recorded directly on a computer, which eliminates the time usually spent transferring written responses onto computers for analysis, and eliminates errors made in this transferring process. Second, the computer can immediately inform the interviewer if an invalid response has been recorded. Third, the computer can be programmed to implement skip patterns or branching, changing the questions to be asked on the basis of answers a respondent has already given. Computers can make these decisions more quickly and accurately than a person can, which saves time and eliminates error. The disadvantage of CATI is that it is costly and time-consuming to set up a CATI system. As a result CATI would not be reasonable for doing a small survey; its use makes most sense for ongoing survey organizations that can capitalize on their investment. CATI is becoming the state of the art for telephone interviews.

Conducting the Interview

The guidelines described above about good face-to-face interviewing technique are generally applicable to telephone interviewing, though there are some necessary differences. Of course, because the respondent cannot see the telephone interviewer, nonverbal gestures are not possible. Furthermore, the telephone requires a somewhat different start to the conversation between interviewer and resident.

A telephone interview begins with an introduction and explanation to convince the answerer that the call is legitimate. Generally, interviewers begin by asking if they have reached the number they intended to call; needless to say, the call is terminated if a wrong number has been reached. Next, the interviewer must determine whether the number reached is a business or a residence. Most surveys involve residences only. Questions might also be asked at this point to make sure that the residence reached is located in the area targeted for the survey. For example, for a study of Tucson, Arizona, interviewers might need to confirm that the phone they have reached is in Tucson or one of its suburbs. The interviewer politely terminates the call if the person lives in a suburb not to be included in the survey.

If the correct number has been reached and the residence is within the region to be sampled, the interviewer identifies herself, identifies the organization for which she is calling, and explains that they are conducting a survey on a specified topic. At this point, the interviewer checks whether the person who answered the phone is the proper respondent (see Chapter 3). If the proper respondent is someone else, the interviewer asks to speak to that person; if the person is not home, the interviewer makes an appointment to call back at another time. From this point on, telephone interviews closely resemble face-to-face interviews.

SELF-ADMINISTERED QUESTIONNAIRES

The third method through which survey data can be collected involves giving questionnaires to respondents and asking them to fill them out. Typically, questionnaires are distributed to respondents by one of three methods. First, questionnaires can be mailed to individuals or delivered to their homes. People are asked to fill the questionnaire out and either to mail it back to the researcher or to give it to a messenger who returns a few days later. Second, people may be stopped on the street or in public places like shopping malls and asked to complete the questionnaire on the spot. Finally, individuals can be assembled in groups in large rooms and can be asked to complete questionnaires at that time. This can be arranged most easily in institutional settings, so this approach is commonly used to survey school children, members of the armed forces, employees of a company, and so on. Using this method, only a few staff people are required to distribute questionnaires to respondents, answer any questions, and collect the completed questionnaires.

When questionnaires are distributed in institutional settings or in places like shopping malls, the person distributing them usually explains the purpose of the study to respondents and asks them to participate. If necessary, the distributor can give the questionnaire to only certain types of people. In contrast, when questionnaires are mailed to respondents, the purpose of the study is typically explained in a cover letter, and respondent selection is much more difficult. Usually, researchers using mail questionnaires don't ask a particular person to complete the questionnaire but instead simply ask anyone who lives at the address to fill it out.

In institutional settings and when respondents are recruited on the street, response rates tend to be reasonably high. Unfortunately, though, many people throw questionnaires they receive in the mail into their wastebaskets; response rates for mail questionnaires tend to be between 10 percent and 50 percent. Survey researchers compensate for this problem in two ways. First, they send questionnaires a second, third, or even fourth time to households that do not return them. Included in the follow-up mailings are letters asking respondents to reconsider participating in the survey. Alternatively, some survey organizations include small amounts of money (such as $1) or material incentives with the questionnaire as a way of thanking respondents for their time in advance. Over the years, material incentives have included golf balls, letter openers, tobacco pouches, photograph holders, pens, lottery tickets, pencils, instant coffee packages, stamps, tie clasps, books, and key rings. Such incentives have been shown to increase response rates when few follow-up mailings are conducted, but the effect of incentives is eliminated if multiple follow-ups are implemented.[1] Through the use of follow-up mailings and incentives, response rates as high as 70 percent can be achieved for mail questionnaires.

CHOOSING AN ADMINISTRATION METHOD

Having reviewed procedures for face-to-face interviews, phone surveys, and self-administered questionnaires, a natural question is which is the best procedure to use. The answer is that it depends. In designing any study, the researcher must balance considerations of cost, speed, length of interview, and quality of data. The best choice in one setting will not necessarily be the best choice in another setting. Table 5.1 summarizes some of the considerations that have been discussed in this chapter and introduces some further points discussed below.

Practical Differences

Expense. First, the procedures differ in cost; mail questionnaires are the cheapest, even after taking into account the expense of wasted questionnaires and of postage. Face-to-face interviews are the most expensive because interviewers and supervisors must be paid, and because of transportation costs.

Telephone interviews are about half as expensive as face-to-face interviews. For one thing, the smaller required number of interviewers sharply cuts the costs of hiring, training, and supervising interviewers. Transportation costs, often one of the most expensive aspects of face-to-face interviewing, are eliminated when telephone interviews are conducted. Indeed, most other components of the data collection

---

[1]A. J. Nederhof, "The Effects of Material Incentives in Mail Surveys: Two Studies," *Public Opinion Quarterly* 47(1983):103-111.

Table 5.1   Comparison of Interviewing Situations

Feature	Administration Method		
	Mail	Phone	Face-to-Face
Cost of interviewing	Cheap—no interviewers	Cheap—no transportation	Expensive
Response rate	Very low without reminders and/ or incentives	Good: 60%	Highest: 70%
Length of interview	Short	Medium: 20 to 30 minutes	Long: up to an hour
Candor of interview	Limited	Good on sensitive items	Good
Data collection time	Several weeks	Less than a week	Intermediate
Interviewer supervision	—	Good	Minimal
Respondent selection	Low SES* bias; hard to control who fills out questionnaire	High SES* bias	Good
Quality of interview	Good candor; cannot probe	Terse answers	Good rapport

*Socio-economic status.

process are cheaper with phone surveys, including the pretest, debriefing of interviewers, verifying that interviews were not forged, printing, field office expenses, record keeping, salaries, and sample selection. Communication costs are, of course, higher for phone interviews, but that greater expense is more than balanced by the decreased travel costs.

Response Rates.   Response rates are best for face-to-face interviews. Telephone interviews do reasonably well, but it is so easy for people to terminate a call by hanging up that response rates are lowered by break-offs. If something important comes up, it is apparently easier to hang up on an interviewer than to ask one sitting in your living room to leave. As result, completion rates in the late 1980s were about 60 percent for national telephone interviews, still respectable but less than the 70 percent obtained for face-to-face interviews. Mail questionnaires typically have the lowest response rates, though as we have seen, the response rates can be increased by persistent mailings to uncooperative respondents and by including incentives with the questionnaires.

Interview Length.   Face-to-face interviews allow for longer interviews. The main expense in face-to-face interviews is getting the interviewer to the person's house. It is not worth going to the trouble of sending out interviewers and persuading people to be interviewed for only a five-minute interview. Consequently, face-to-face surveys tend to average an hour in length. Researchers initially assumed that telephone interviews had to be kept short, just five to ten minutes. As researchers gained more experience writing questionnaires that are effective on the phone and as interviewers gained more experience in building rapport in phone interviews, interview length has increased. Now twenty-to-thirty minute telephone interviews are common. Self-administered questionnaires pose the greatest length difficulty. The researcher always wants to add more and more pages of questions, but the longer the questionnaire, the less likely it is that the respondent will bother to fill it out. Consequently, they tend to be short.

To give an idea of how some of these considerations combine, in 1987 the University of Michigan's Survey Research Center estimated its interviewing costs at $150 to $170 for a one-hour face-to-face interview, compared to $65 for a half-hour phone interview. These figures certainly will go up over the years, but their relative sizes are informative. The longer face-to-face interview produces more information, but many more people can be interviewed within a fixed budget with telephone interviews.

Data Collection Time.   Using self-administered questionnaires distributed in institutional settings can save a great deal of time, since hundreds of people can fill them out simultaneously. Self-administered questionnaires distributed by mail take much longer to implement, especially if researchers try to improve response rates through follow-up mailings to those who have not sent back the questionnaire.

When face-to-face interviewing is used, the geographical dispersion of the sampled residences limits the number of interviews that any one interviewer can take. The interviewer must spend time driving from one area to another, and interviewers sometimes visit a residence many times before they finally find someone home. As a result, these studies are generally in the field for one week to two months. With phone surveys an interviewer can conduct many more interviews in a short time. Calling a residence where no one is at home wastes less than a minute. Consequently, telephone interviewing requires much less time for data collection and requires fewer interviewers. In a national study four times as many interviewers are needed for face-to-face interviews as are needed for telephone interviews.

Since telephone surveys require less time than face-to-face surveys, the former are especially attractive to news organizations that wish to publish up-to-the-minute polling results and to researchers who wish to study the impact of an event immediately after it happens. For example, telephone surveys are frequently used by politicians to measure public reactions immediately. A president may give a speech and have a pollster measure the public's reaction that same night, expecting to get a report on public attitudes the next morning. Television and newspaper polls are often conducted to assess immediate reactions to dramatic political events, something that was not possible before the advent of telephone polling.

Interviewer Supervision. One advantage of telephone interviewing over face-to-face interviewing is that supervisors can easily monitor each interviewer's telephone conversations. This permits quality control that is not feasible when face-to-face interviews are conducted. If the supervisor notes some problem in the way an interviewer conducts herself, it can be corrected immediately, either by telling the interviewer what she is doing wrong or by changing the instructions that all of the interviewers receive. On-line interviewer supervision is impossible when face-to-face interviews are conducted in respondents' homes.

Interviewer Effects. Interviewer bias is another important form of bias in a survey. The interviewer-respondent interaction is an unusual interaction in the life of the respondent, and the respondent often does not know just how to act. Some respondents try to please the interviewer in their answers, and avoid giving answers that the interviewer might not approve. The interviewer may also inadvertently ask a question differently than it is written, or ask the question in such a tone that one answer seems preferred. These are all sources of interviewer bias. Such bias can never be eliminated, but it is minimized by care in selection and training of interviewers.

One advantage of self-administered questionnaires is that responses are not influenced by interviewer effects, since there are no interviewers. Interviewers read questions slightly differently from each other, whereas self-administered questionnaires appear identical to all respondents. However, when filling out questionnaires respondents can make mistakes that could be avoided if a face-to-face or telephone interview were conducted.

Interviewers hired for face-to-face interviews require the most training, since personal interviews are so sensitive to how the interviewer handles the interpersonal relations involved. Phone interviews tend to require less interviewer training. Unfortunately, the fact that telephone surveys typically use fewer interviewers than do face-to-face interviews increases the risk that a single interviewer's style of asking questions will distort the results of a telephone survey. If a particular interviewer happens to ask questions in a way that biases answers, the effect on results will be relatively small when there are fifty other interviewers collecting data for the study. However, when this interviewer is one of only fifteen, a greater proportion of interviews will be biased. The closer supervision possible in telephone interviewing probably allows researchers to identify and eliminate many of these biases, but some are so subtle that they cannot be detected by supervisors.

Respondent Selection.   Some of the sampling issues involved in a choice between face-to-face interviews, phone samples, and self-administered questionnaires were discussed in Chapter 3. To summarize briefly, phone respondents tend to have somewhat higher income and education levels than face-to-face interviewees,[2] and mail questionnaires result in respondents with even lower income and education levels. Still, with more than 90 percent of the households in the United States having telephones, the choice of procedure today has less effect on the demographic composition of the sample than it once did.

A disadvantage of mailed self-administered questionnaires is that it is impossible to coordinate respondent selection the way an interviewer can. In most telephone and face-to-face interviews, the interviewer obtains a household listing and selects one adult to be interviewed using a selection table. Obviously, this cannot be done with mail questionnaires. In houses where more than one adult lives, the decision as to who will fill the questionnaire out is made by the residents. Therefore, respondent sampling is less controllable using this data collection method, and sampling is likely to be biased as a result.

Differences in Respondent Satisfaction

Respondents say that they prefer face-to-face interviews over telephone interviews. The rapport with the interviewer is greater in the former case, and people are more comfortable giving open-ended

---

[2]Robert M. Groves and Robert L. Kahn, *Surveys by Telephone* (New York: Academic Press, 1979), 94-97.

comments in the face-to-face interview. However, differences between the two types of interview are not substantial, so telephone interviewing is done widely. When asked to compare self-administered questionnaires with interviews, respondents generate some reasons in favor of each. On one hand, they say, a self-administered questionnaire gives more time to think about each question and allows the respondent to complete the questionnaire at his or her convenience. On the other hand, self-administered questionnaires are said to require more effort than interviews and to feel less personal.[3]

Differences in Results

When telephone interviewing was first being tried, some researchers raised questions about the validity of data gathered over the telephone. A few studies have compared the results of surveys done using face-to-face and telephone interviewing and found that the two methods produce similar results for the most part. However, there are a few important differences.

People typically provide more information in face-to-face interviews than in telephone interviews. For example, more people refuse to reveal their incomes during telephone interviews, though this reluctance to reveal sensitive information does not seem to extend to other items. Some research suggests that people are more likely to answer sensitive questions and less likely to give socially acceptable answers on mail questionnaires. Apparently respondents give more candid answers when they can fill out the questionnaire in complete privacy, both from other people in the household and from the interviewer as well.

Similarly, telephone interviews obtain fewer comments in response to open-ended questions. This is especially true among people who have difficulty expressing their thoughts verbally. Because respondents are terser in answering questions on the phone, face-to-face interviews are preferable if open-ended material is critical. Self-administered questionnaires obviously are not useful when the researcher feels that probes of respondent answers are important.

Another interesting difference between results obtained by face-to-face and by telephone interviews has to do with the use of rating scales. When respondents are presented with scales on which some but not all

---

[3]Peter H. Rossi, James D. Wright, and Andy B. Anderson (eds.), *Handbook of Survey Research* (New York: Academic Press, 1983), p. 724.

of the points are accompanied by verbal labels, face-to-face interview respondents tend to use the points with verbal labels more often than telephone interview respondents do. As a result, responses from the latter group are spread more evenly across the points of the rating scale.

Otherwise, telephone interviews seem to obtain responses that are just as valid as and sometimes more valid than responses from face-to-face interviews. For example, a study of crime victimization found that people reported more incidents of crime directed against them when interviewed on the phone than in person. People seem unwilling to mention to an interviewer in their homes some crimes that they were willing to mention on the telephone. This may be due in part to the greater secrecy associated with phone interviews: It is sometimes impossible to conduct a face-to-face interview without other members of the family present, whereas in phone interviews, the respondent can say yes or no without other members of the family knowing what the question was. This increased privacy during telephone interviews may yield more candid data in response to some questions.

SUMMARY

Over the years researchers have learned many valuable lessons about how to conduct surveys. The procedures used by survey organizations across the country for obtaining interviews and for administering questionnaires are remarkably similar and successful. Good interviewing requires careful selection, training, and supervision of interviewers. Interviewers must ask questions as written, record the answers exactly, not give their own opinions, build rapport with the respondent, probe answers where they are unclear, and not accept refusals too easily.

Choosing a method for collecting survey data is a complex decision, involving considerations of expense, response rates, the sorts of questions being asked, the amount of information needed, and so on. Face-to-face interviews were once seen as the only way to obtain high-quality data, but phone surveys are now used extensively, since they are less expensive, faster, and can be carefully supervised. Self-administered questionnaires are also useful, though extra efforts are necessary to get an acceptable response rate from mail questionnaires. Different types of people may respond in face-to-face, telephone, and mail studies, so researchers should compare the demographics of their samples with census statistics in order to detect any biases that result.

Questions

What should the Interviewer (I) do next in each of the following three exchange with the Respondent (R)?

    I: What do you think are the most important problems facing this country?
    R: Our relations with Russia.

*   *   *   *

    I: Now looking ahead—do you think that a year from now you (and your
        family) will be better off financially, or worse off, or just about the same
        as now?
    R: Hmmm. Let me see about that. I don't know.

*   *   *   *

    I: What is your main occupation?
    R: Engineer.

6

Coding Practices

Unfortunately, it is impossible to analyze a set of interviews simply by leafing through them. Computers are required to analyze the large amount of data in large-scale surveys. In order to use a computer to analyze survey data, the verbal answers to survey questions must be translated (coded) into numbers in the computer's memory.

In this chapter we will describe the coding process, which has three parts. First, one must develop the coding scheme for each question, deciding which numbers correspond to which answers. Then a codebook must specify where each question's answer will be recorded on coding sheets. Finally, numbers representing each questionnaire's answers, must be written on the coding sheets and entered into the computer.

DEVELOPING CODING SCHEMES

Procedures for developing codes differ for closed-ended and open-ended questions.

Closed-Ended Questions

It is much easier to develop coding schemes for closed-ended questions than for open-ended ones because all the possible answers to a closed-ended question are known before the interviews take place. Each possible answer is printed in a box on the questionnaire with a

Table 6.1   1984 Presidential Vote Question

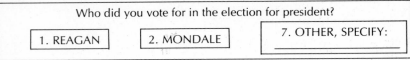

Who did you vote for in the election for president?		
1. REAGAN	2. MONDALE	7. OTHER, SPECIFY:

number corresponding to that particular answer. When a respondent answers a question, the interviewer checks the box corresponding to the respondent's answer. As an example, Table 6.1 displays the coding format of the 1984 National Election Study question asking how respondents voted in the presidential election. If a respondent said that he or she voted for Reagan, the interviewer should check box 1; box 2 should be checked for Mondale voters; and so on.

The numbers in the questionnaire boxes are used to code answers to closed-ended questions. These response categories for each question must be *mutually exclusive*, so no answer can fit more than one category, and the categories must be *exhaustive*, so that every answer fits some category. Sometimes additional coding categories must be assigned after the interviews have been conducted to handle unanticipated responses to closed-ended questions. Also, if an interviewer does not record a respondent's answer to a particular question for some reason, the respondent must be assigned a code for that question describing why no answer was recorded.

Table 6.2 shows the coding scheme that was used for the 1984 presidential-vote question. It corresponds closely to the original questionnaire but also includes some additional coding categories. In order for the coding categories to be exhaustive, allowance was made for respondents who refused to say for whom they voted, who voted for other candidates, who did not remember how they voted, who did not vote for a presidential candidate, and who—accidentally or not—were not asked the question. Categories 6, 7, 8, 9, and 0 handle these special situations. When there are five or fewer alternative answers to the ques-

Table 6.2   Closed-Ended Question Code

(If reports voting in 1984)
Who did you vote for in the election for president?

1. Reagan
2. Mondale
6. Refused to say who voted for
7. Other
8. Don't know
9. Not ascertained
0. Inappropriate—did not vote for president (or no postelection interview)

tion, it is conventional to use 6 for *refused to say*, 7 for *other*, 8 for *don't know*, 9 for *not ascertained*, and 0 for *inappropriate*. When there are more than five answers to a closed-ended question, these situations are usually assigned codes of 96, 97, 98, 99, and 00, respectively.

Categories 9 (for questions with five or fewer valid answers) and 99 (for questions with six to ninety-five valid answers) are used to code lack of response for a question. This could occur if a respondent terminated the interview prior to being asked the question or if a coffee stain made it impossible to read what the person's response was. In any case, the number of responses coded *not ascertained* is usually quite small.

The 0 category is required when a question is asked of some but not all respondents. This code is most often used when an answer to a preceding question causes the interviewer to skip a later question because it is inappropriate for a particular respondent. For example, people who say they did not vote in the election are not asked for whom they voted. We use the 0 code for these cases. The 0 code can also be used in panel studies if a respondent has not been reinterviewed. For example, the 1984 American National Election Study interviewed the same people both before and after the election. However, some people who were interviewed before the election could not be contacted for a reinterview, so they are given the 0 code for all the reinterview questions.

Open-Ended Questions

Open-ended questions are usually the most interesting (and possibly the most valuable) questions in a survey. Respondents say whatever they wish in response to these questions, and interviewers record their answers verbatim. These questions allow respondents to express themselves; if respondents give inconsistent, bigoted, witty, dumb, sophisticated, or knowledgeable answers, all that is preserved on the questionnaire. Because people give a variety of answers to these questions, most of which couldn't be anticipated, researchers develop coding categories for them only after the interviews are completed.

There are several considerations when developing code categories for open-ended questions. First, the code categories should satisfy the objectives of the question. If a question has more than one objective, the same answers might be coded in more than one way. For example, answers can be coded in terms of either manifest or latent content. *Manifest* coding focuses on the meaning of the respondent's answer to a question; *latent* coding focuses on the style of the person's answer. Consider a survey that asked respondents how they decided which presidential candidate to vote for. Obviously, the manifest reasons respondents give would be coded, and it might also be useful to code evidence about *how* each respondent thinks about politics. If a respondent used the words *liberal* or *conservative*, his or her answer might be coded as having ideological content. Often the same open-ended question is coded at the manifest level and at one or more latent levels.

Manifest codes for open-ended questions can be developed in two ways. The first is the theoretical or a priori method: the researchers develop the codes in advance based upon the answers they expect, just as they do with closed-ended questions. For example, suppose respondents in a survey were asked, "What do you think this country will be like in ten years?" If the researchers wanted to know simply whether people are optimistic or pessimistic, they could develop code categories (optimistic and pessimistic) before seeing the respondents' answers. A second strategy for developing codes is the contextual approach: researchers read a large number of answers and develop codes by grouping similar answers together. If they were working on the above question, they might find overcrowding and increasing land values mentioned by a number of respondents, so a category would be created for each.

Researchers usually combine these methods to develop code categories for open-ended questions. Researchers almost never let data speak for themselves (by using only the contextual method) and almost always impose their own theoretical or a priori view to some extent. In other words, they usually look in the data for things they are interested in. An economist might code the question about the future in economic terms; a sociologist might look for references to changes in the racial and ethnic character of the country; a psychologist might mine the data for information about whether the respondent feels threatened by the changes. In the end, coding schemes depend upon the researchers' objectives.

Consider the question, "What is the most important problem facing the country today?" The manifest coding scheme for answers to this question is complicated because so many different problems are mentioned by respondents. Furthermore, various coding schemes for the latent content of answers are conceivable. For example, answers could be categorized according to whether the respondents believe the problem can be solved by government, business, or not at all. Or answers could be categorized as social, political, economic, or structural problems.

Table 6.3 shows the outline of the code categories used by the Na-

Table 6.3   Part of an Open-Ended Code

What is the most important problem facing the country today?

General Category Codes

001–099 Social welfare problems
100–199 Agricultural and national resource problems
200–299 Labor problems, union-management problems
300–399 Racial and public order problems
400–499 Economic and business problems; consumer protection
500–699 Foreign affairs problems
700–799 National defense problems
800–899 Problems relating to the functioning of government
900–999 Miscellaneous and missing data

Some Detailed 800–999 Codes

800 Power of government; general reference
805 Government control of information; secrecy
810 Honesty in government; ethics in government
811 Lack of personal ethics of people in government
815 Media bias
819 Other specific references to honesty in government
820 Campaign donations
830 Confidence/trust in political leaders
831 Increased trust in political leaders
832 Decreased trust in political leaders
833 Quality, efficiency, cost of government
834 Increased quality/cost of government
835 Decreased quality/cost of government
836 Compensation of government employees
837 Waste in government
840 Size of federal government
841 For a more powerful federal government
842 Against power of federal government
850–859 Power of president, Congress, Supreme Court
860–869 Apportionment and election procedures
870 Other qualities of political leaders
871 Lack of devotion to general welfare
872–882 Comments on current president
885 Public apathy
886 Getting people together; unity of people
890 Other specific references to functioning of government
995 "There were no issues"
996 "There was no campaign in my district"
997 Other
998 Don't know
999 Not ascertained
000 Inappropriate; no problems mentioned; no further mention

SOURCE: Codebook for 1984 American National Election Study.

tional Election Studies in coding this question. The responses are sorted into basic types. One range of code numbers represents social welfare problems (aid to education, helping the poor, and so on), another set of numbers represents various agricultural and natural-resource problems, and so on. To illustrate the detailed codes more directly, Table 6.3 also lists some of the 1984 NES codes relating to problems involving the functioning of government. There are several specific codes for particular problems plus a general code (800) for a respondent who makes a nonspecific reference about governmental power and a catchall code (890) for references to governmental problems other than those being coded specifically. Note the variety of missing-data codes that are available if a person (a) gives an answer beyond the basic types being coded, (b) says "I don't know," (c) is not asked the question by accident, or (d) is not asked the question for some other reason.

Developing coding schemes for open-ended questions is often difficult. People sometimes give answers that cannot easily be put into simple categories, and their answers sometimes span several categories. The coding scheme in Table 6.3 seems relatively simple to use, yet what if someone answers that the major problem facing the country today is "all the crooked politicians in the control of those big fancy corpo-,rations." Is that an 810 answer (honesty) or an 871 (lack of devotion to general welfare)? The best coding schemes make it easy to categorize answers.

Researchers usually try to preserve as much detail as possible in their codes of open-ended questions. For example, the question about major problems could be coded into hundreds of detailed categories or a few general headings. If only general codes were created in the first place, a later decision to capture more detailed information would require repeating the coding process, a very expensive move. On the other hand, if detailed coding is done initially, a later decision to move to a higher level of abstraction requires simply combining detailed codes into general categories, a fairly inexpensive process.

An extreme solution to this problem is to record all the open-ended answers verbatim in a computer file so that researchers can develop their own coding schemes each time they analyze the data. The researchers make up specific instructions, indicating that an answer using some words (like *liberal* or *conservative*) go into one category, that those using other words go into another category, and so on. Computer content analysis lacks the discernment of human coding, but it has the advantage of permitting different researchers to use different coding schemes on the same answers without requiring a costly rereading of all the original questionnaires.

THE CODEBOOK

Once the coding schemes for a survey's questions are specified, the researcher constructs a codebook. The codebook lists the questions, shows what codes are used for each one, and shows the location of each question on the coding sheets onto which the numbers representing answers are written. In a small study, this information might fit on a single sheet of paper; in large studies, the information is put into books. The coders use an early version of the codebook when they do the coding.

As an example, Table 6.4 reproduces part of a page from the 1984 National Election Study codebook, which is several hundreds of pages long. The valid responses to the presidential-vote question are shown in this table. Presidential vote is listed as variable number 788, meaning it is the 788th variable coded in the data set. In analysis of the data, a researcher would direct the computer to analyze variable 788.

Note that the codebook has been annotated to show the number of people who gave each response. Needless to say, this is done after the data are all coded. Each missing-data category was employed. Incidentally, the reason for the large number of inappropriate responses is that 540 respondents did not vote, did not remember whether they had voted, or accidentally were not asked the question. Also, there was no

Table 6.4   Codebook Entry for Closed-Ended Question

Variable 788   Name: Respondent's 1984 vote for president

Question: (If reports voting for president in 1984) Who did you vote for in the election for President?

801	1.	Reagan
575	2.	Mondale
9	6.	Refused to say who voted for
13	7.	Other
4	8.	Don't know
47	9.	Not ascertained
808	0.	Inappropriate—did not vote for president (or no postelection interview)

SOURCE: Center for Political Studies, 1984 American National Election Study codebook. University of Michigan, Ann Arbor, 1985.

postelection interview with 268 people who were interviewed prior to the election.

CODING MECHANICS

Two different coding procedures will be described here: a mechanical procedure using coding sheets, and a computerized version. The computer approach is being used more and more nowadays, but coding sheets are still used frequently and give the novice a better idea as to what is involved in coding.

Using Coding Sheets

When completed questionnaires are turned in to the coding department after interviews, coders read through them and write the numbers for each person's responses onto coding sheets (Figure 6.1). Each row of a coding sheet has eighty columns; exactly one single-digit number is written in each cell. If all of a respondent's answers in a survey can be represented in eighty columns, the data for that respondent are written on one row on the coding sheet. If more than eighy numbers are required, as is typical in large surveys, more than one row is used for each respondent's data.[1]

Respondents are each given an identification number to preserve confidentiality while making it possible to compare the computer's record of what someone said during an interview with their questionnaire (on which the same interview number is written) if necessary. In order to keep track of which rows on the coding sheet correspond to which person's data, the respondent identification number is written near the beginning of each row of data. In order to keep each person's rows in order, a deck number is also written near the beginning of each row. The deck number ranges from one to the number of rows used for each person's data.

As an example, say that in the 1984 National Election Study each respondent's data occupied twenty-five rows on the coding sheets. Figure 6.1 shows a coding sheet. The respondent's identification number (0638) appears in columns seven through ten of every row of that per-

---

[1]The eighty columns correspond to the eighty columns of information that can be punched onto computer cards (Figure 6.2).

Figure 6.1
A Coding Sheet

son's data. The deck number, which ranges from one to twenty-five, appears in columns five and six. Also, a number identifying this particular survey (say 7010) appears in columns one through four of every row for every respondent. The numbers corresponding to people's answers to the survey questions appear in columns eleven through eighty of every row.

How exactly do the coders work? First, they write the identification numbers, deck numbers, and study numbers in the first few columns of each row. Then, they page through the questionnaire and write the numbers representing the answers in the appropriate columns. For example, here's what coders for the 1984 National Election Study would do to code the 638th respondent's report of her vote for president. The coding instructions indicate that the vote question is to be coded in column seventy of deck twelve. So for respondent 638 a 2 is put into that column of that row, since she claimed to have voted for Mondale. Since the coders go through the questionnaire sequentially, eleven full rows and sixty-nine columns of the twelfth row were filled up when he or she reached the vote question. Therefore, they don't have to check the coding instructions to check where the answer to each question goes— it goes in the next empty column.

It might seem that it would simplify the coding process if a blank on the coding sheet were used to indicate that a respondent did not answer a particular question for whatever reason. However, there are three reasons not to do so. First, leaving a column blank is a good way to indicate that the coder was not sure what code was appropriate, so a supervisor can scan the completed sheets and find the blanks to be filled in. Second, it makes it easier for the coder to keep his or her place, hence reducing coder error. Third, some computers do not read blanks accurately, so the data may not be easily analyzed. Therefore, it is better to code all responses and nonresponses with numbers.

The coding of some variables is complicated by the possibility of the respondent giving more than one valid answer. For example, the interview might ask people what the major problems facing the country are, and the interviewers might be instructed to prompt to obtain three answers per respondent, as by asking, "And what else do you consider an important problem facing the country today?" The coder would code up to three responses per respondent. Physically, that would mean setting aside three separate coding fields (for example, columns 15 through 17, columns 18 through 20, and columns 21 through 23) for the three responses. For the sake of completeness a special code would be created for no second or third response.

Data Entry

Once all respondents' answers have been translated into numbers on coding sheets, those numerical codes are entered into a computer's memory banks to be analyzed. The methods used to enter data into computers have changed in recent years. In the 1950s, the numbers on coding sheets were punched onto computer cards (Figure 6.2). Each computer card has eighty columns, and one digit can be typed into each column. One card would be used if a respondent's data could be represented with eighty or fewer numbers, and more cards would be used if not. The process of punching numbers onto these cards is called keypunching, and the machine used to do it is called a keypunch. A keypunch is similar to a typewriter, but instead of printing on a piece of paper, it punches holes into cards. These cards are read into a machine called a card reader, which enters the numbers into a computer's memory bank. By the 1970s, punching data on cards was the exception rather than the rule; instead, it became more common for a typist to sit at a computer terminal and type the numbers from coding sheets into the computer.

Improvements in computer technology now allow survey organizations to enter results into computers even more quickly through a process called *direct data entry* (DDE). Coding sheets are no longer used. The coder sits at a computer terminal and types each person's answers directly into the computer from the competed interview schedules. The questions are displayed on the screen in order along with the appropriate answer categories. The coder reads each person's answers directly from the questionnaire and types the appropriate numbers. An ex-

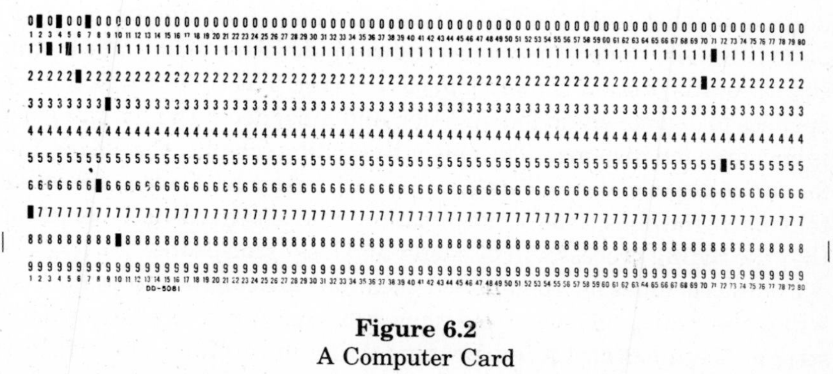

Figure 6.2
A Computer Card

treme form of direct data entry is CATI, computer assisted telephone interviewing. In CATI systems the interviewer types a respondent's answers into the computer during the interview. Telephone interviewers read the questions on the computer screen and type respondents' answers instead of writing them down on paper.

Direct data entry speeds up data processing a great deal. Also, as will be detailed in the next section, accuracy is increased, since the computer checks each number typed in to make sure that no obvious errors are made in coding the data. The major extra expense for DDE is programming a computer to display the questionnaire.

CODING ACCURACY

After carefully collecting a set of data, it is important to avoid errors during the coding and data entry stages.

Coding Reliability

Coding closed-ended questions is a very simple process. Nonetheless, a slight amount of human error always creeps into the computer data file. The interviewer may check the wrong box—a nonrecoverable error. The interviewer's check may be so unclear that the coder may misread which box is checked. The coder may enter the wrong number even if the interviewer's mark was clear. This error may be found by having a second coder check over the coding, but such clerical error is so rare (less than 1 percent on closed-ended questions) that check-coding is rarely done. Unlike other types of error, this type of error is unlikely to introduce any substantial bias into survey results, since the errors are likely to be infrequent and random.

Coding open-ended questions requires judgments to be made by the coder, so this process is more subject to error. The coder reads the responses to each open-ended question and must decide which category is best for each response. The better the coding scheme, the easier it is for the coder to choose a category for each response. Coders are often told about the objectives of the questions and of the coding schemes so that the coding process will be easier and less error-prone.

Coding schemes for open-ended questions are constantly evaluated while the coding goes on, and they are sometimes revised in midstream. Usually a preliminary coding of a few interviews is done to test the open-ended codes, just as a pretest is used to test the questionnaire before the actual interviewing. Then reseachers observe the coding process in order to spot coding schemes that do not work well. If coders frequently ask how to code answers to a particular question, the coding scheme for that question will probably be revised. Additionally, coders keep track of responses that do not fit the established categories so that the researchers can add new categories when an unanticipated response appears frequently.

Not only must an open-ended coding scheme be easy to use but it must also produce reliable results. That is, different coders ought to reach the same decisions about how to code particular answers. If this is not the case, the coding scheme is too ambiguous. One means of assessing the reliability of a coding scheme is to have several people code the same set of interviews. If they all code the questions the same way, then the researchers can be confident that the codes are good. However, if each coder puts an answer into a different category, then either the coders are not doing a good job, or as is more likely, the codes have not been adequately constructed. The researcher may compute a measure of the intercoder reliability of each open-ended question on the basis of the extent of agreement between two coders on that question. In some studies based on small numbers of interviews with elites, researchers actually have two or three coders code each question so the intercoder reliability of the open-ended questions can be fully measured.

Data Entry Errors

Once the numbers representing responses have been entered into a computer, the resulting data file must be cleaned. Many errors can be made during data entry, since typing thousands of numbers per hour can be very boring work. Therefore, it is essential to check the data file for errors. When numbers on coding sheets were punched onto cards, cleaning could be done partly be repunching each card on a machine that would signal the operator whenever a typed number differed from the number already on the card. When direct data entry is employed, the data can be entered into the computer a second time, and the computer signals the operator whenever the new numbers differ from the ones typed in first. Although this method is extremely effective at catching errors, it is expensive, since each data point must be typed twice.

Verifying at the data entry stage is a way to catch some errors, but errors that are made during coding and during data collection cannot be spotted this way. Therefore, once a set of survey responses are in a computer's memory, *wild code checking* must be performed. This is done by having the computer list all the numbers entered into the data set for each question in the survey. These are then compared to the codebook, which lists all the valid codes for each question. If some invalid codes are identified, the researcher must locate the original questionnaires and correct the values in the computer file. Direct data entry programs can prevent wild codes by storing in the computer a list of acceptable code values for each variable and then having the computer alert the typist to invalid entries.

Another form of error elimination is consistency checking. Some combinations of responses are logically impossible, so if they are observed, an error was made. For example, there would certainly be something wrong if a data file indicated that a respondent said no to the question, "Did you vote in the most recent presidential election?" and that he said Reagan in answer to the question, "For whom did you vote?" Computers can locate such logical inconsistencies in responses. The analyst must then fix each one by consulting the questionnaires. Again, direct data entry systems can be programmed to check for inconsistencies while the data are being entered, so the coder must correct such errors.

SUMMARY

In summary, coding is the conversion of verbal responses into a set of numbers representing mutually exclusive and exhaustive categories. The codes may represent manifest or latent information, and they must be reliable. Testing and revision of the code categories may be required along with careful training of coders, but the added expense is justified.

Open-ended questions are much more difficult and expensive to code than closed-ended questions. Also, coding a large study with many open-ended questions takes months. Although these questions permit great flexibility, including latent coding at various levels of abstraction, the most interesting abstract codes may well have the least reliability. Therefore, some researchers prefer to use closed-ended questions, which allow respondents to code their own answers into a preestablished set of categories. Clearly, each question form has its advantages, and the decision about whether to use open-ended or closed-ended questions must be made on the basis of considerations unique to each survey.

After the codes are constructed, they are assembled into a codebook. The coding can be done either manually on coding sheets or directly on the computer. It is important to check coding consistency, especially for open-ended questions. When intercoder reliability is low, it is necessary to train the coders better or improve the coding scheme. The computer can be programmed to check for some trivial data entry errors.

Question

Construct a code for the following question: "If you could vote for anyone, who would be your first choice for president?" You might try this question out on a few people to get an idea of the variety of possible responses before writing out the code. Make sure to provide an easy way to differentiate Republican from Democratic candidates. Also, you might choose to construct more than one code for this question.

7

Designing a Survey

We have traced the major steps in conducting a survey: sampling, questionnaire construction, interviewing, and coding. We can use that information to see how best to design a survey.

Unfortunately, there are no simple rules about good and bad survey designs. Instead, the best design for a survey is determined by its goals; different goals require different designs. In Chapter 1, we listed four main goals of surveys:

- To measure the prevalence of attitudes, beliefs, and behavior
- To determine the amount of change over time in those attitudes, beliefs, and behavior
- To examine differences between subgroups, as between men and women
- To analyze the causes of attitudes, beliefs, and behavior

The best design depends on which goal is predominant. For example, to predict the winner of an election, one would design the study differently than if one's goal is to examine the relationship between union membership and election turnout.

MEASURING THE PREVALENCE OF ATTITUDES, BELIEFS, AND FACTS

Measuring Facts

Surveys are frequently used to measure the frequency with which people have performed certain acts. For example, people can be asked how many times they visited a medical doctor during the last year, and it would seem likely that they can provide accurate information. This is true especially when the behavior in question was performed recently. Good examples of this are the exit polls taken by the news media on election days, in which interviewers approach people as they leave the polling area and ask them how they voted. Exit polls are typically highly accurate because people remember how they voted a minute earlier and are generally willing to disclose that information.

When people are asked to recall acts they performed long ago, though, their reporting typically becomes much less accurate. This is especially true when a particular time frame is involved. For example, if you ask people the number of times they went to the doctor in the past year, they would probably forget some visits that were several months earlier and would be unsure about exactly when other visits occurred. Because long-term recall is difficult, it is best to ask people only about recent behavior.

People somtimes misremember past events as having occurred more recently than they actually did (*forward telescoping*) or longer ago than they actually did (*backward telescoping*). A good strategy is to set the time frame for people, possibly by beginning with a throw-away question (such as how often they visited the doctor in the previous month), and then asking them the real question (say, how often they visited the doctor during the current month).

Sensitive Topics

Although people are usually able to report their behavior accurately, they are sometimes unwilling to do so. This is true especially when people feel that they will look more respectable to an interviewer if they say they behaved or will behave in a certain way. When asked whether or not they voted in the last presidential election, more respondents claim to have voted than official records show actually did.[1] Also, more people report having voted for the winner of an election than actually did, particularly when the winner's performance in office since the election has been good. Similarly, high-school students seem to overreport their use of alcohol and drugs rather than not sound "with it." Questions about sensitive behavior can be asked, but the re-

---

[1]See Aage Clausen,"Response Validity: Vote Report," *Public Opinion Quarterly* 32(1968–69):588–606.

sulting data may not be valid because of respondents' desire to present themselves favorably to the interviewer.

Fortunately, survey researchers have developed several techniques to improve the validity of reports of behavior on sensitive topics. One such technique is called the *bogus pipeline technique*. Here, interviewers ask respondents for permission to check an official record of their behavior (such as a voting record or medical records) in order to validate their report of it. When this is done, the accuracy of peoples' reports increases.

Another way to measure sensitive behavior involves giving respondents lists of acts and asking how many they have performed. The lists include several nonsensitive behaviors (such as having visited Europe). A random half of the sample is given a list that includes the sensitive behavior of interest (such as having used cocaine), while the other half of the sample is given the same list except for that sensitive behavior. This latter group is the control group. Because the two samples differ only by chance, one expects them to be similar in terms of having visited Europe and other nonsensitive acts. Therefore, any difference in numbers of acts performed between the two samples should be due to the sensitive behavior. If the average person in the control group performed 2.31 of the acts, and the average person in the other group also performed 2.31 of the acts, no one in the other group performed the sensitive act. If the average person in the control group performed 2.31 of the acts, and the average person in the other group performed 2.72 of the acts, then 41 percent (2.72 − 2.31) of the sample would be estimated to have performed the sensitive behavior. If the average person in the control group performed 2.31 of the acts, and the average person in the other group performed 3.31 of the acts, 100 percent (3.31 − 2.31) performed the sensitive act. Using this system, a researcher cannot determine *which* people in the sample performed the sensitive behavior, but he or she would be able to estimate how many did.

A particularly ingenious means of measuring sensitive attitudes or behavior is the randomized response technique. Say you want to know how many people cheated on their 1988 federal income tax returns. You could hand the respondent a coin and a card on which is printed:

- Did you cheat on your 1988 federal income tax return?
- Did you fill out your 1988 federal income tax return honestly?

The respondent is told to flip the coin and to conceal the result from the interviewer. The respondent is then told to answer question A if the coin turns up heads and to answer question B if the coin turns up tails.

Using this procedure, the interviewer and researcher never know which question the respondent answered. However, when all the answers are tallied up, the researcher can use a mathematical formula developed by Warner to calculate how many people cheated on their taxes.[2]

There are other ways of implementing the randomized response technique, but all of them involve a randomizing device such as a flipped coin and a set of questions on a show card. This technique has been found to yield more honest answers regarding sensitive behaviors and attitudes than direct questioning does. However, it does not allow the researcher to determine whether any particular respondent performed the behavior of interest. It can only reveal the proportion of all respondents who performed it.

Belief about Others' Attitudes.   Surveys often ask questions about facts, which on closer inspection turn out to be questions about what the respondent believes to be true. One should not believe answers to such questions when the respondents are not likely to possess the information needed to answer the questions. Asking people about the attitudes of others, for example, is not likely to be fruitful, since they are unlikely to know those attitudes. Studies of parents and high-school children, for example, have found that neither group has very accurate knowledge of the political views of the other. Parents are likely to think their children agree with them on politics even when that is not the case. At best these questions show how parents believe their children think or perhaps what parents want their children to think, not how they actually think. If the researcher wants to know someone's opinions on a matter, it is best to ask that person directly.

Predicting Behavior

Another task for which surveys are frequently used is predicting people's behavior. These predictions often are based on people's beliefs about what their actions are likely to be.

---

[2]S. L. Warner, "Randomized Response: A Survey Technique for Eliminating Evasive Answer Bias," *Journal of the American Statistical Association* 60 (1965): 63–69; James Alan Fox and Paul E. Tracy, *Randomized Response* (Beverly Hills: Sage, 1986). Several variants of this procedure have been developed to try to counteract the distrust of respondents who worry that they are being tricked; one common variant is to use for statement B on the show card a nonsensitive item, the probability of which is known, such as: "I was born in November."

Election Predictions. Perhaps the most widely known examples of this use are surveys conducted to forecast the outcomes of elections. Every four years the Gallup, Harris, and other polls track candidate popularity as the United States presidential campaign progresses in an attempt to predict the winner just before election day. Pollsters must contend with a 3 percent to 4 percent sampling error, so no poll can reliably predict very close races, but predictions of presidential election outcomes are usually remarkably accurate. As Table 7.1 shows, the Gallup Poll has been nearly perfect in forecasting the winners of recent American contests.

These predictions are based largely upon what people say they will do in the voting booth, and fortunately, people are good at predicting which candidate they will prefer on election day. However, people are not so good at predicting whether or not they will vote. Most people want to appear to survey interviewers as good citizens, so almost everyone says he or she expects to vote in the upcoming election, even though only about half of the nation's eligible voters actually participate in elections these days. In order to predict an election's outcome, a pollster must use only the predictions made by respondents who are most likely to make it to the voting booth. The challenge for the pollster is to figure out which respondents are likely to vote in the election and which are not.

Table 7.1   Gallup Poll Accuracy in Presidential Elections

Year	Election Winner	Gallup's Predicted Percentage for Election Winner	Actual Vote Percentage for Election Winner	Over-/Under-prediction of Winner's Vote in Percentages	Winner Prediction
1936	Roosevelt	55.7	62.5	−6.8	Accurate
1940	Roosevelt	52.0	55.0	−3.0	Accurate
1944	Roosevelt	51.5	53.3	−1.8	Accurate
1948	Truman	44.5	49.9	−5.4	WRONG
1952	Eisenhower	51.0	55.4	−4.4	Accurate
1956	Eisenhower	59.5	57.8	1.7	Accurate
1960	Kennedy	51.0	50.1	0.9	Accurate
1964	Johnson	64.0	61.3	2.7	Accurate
1968	Nixon	43.0	43.5	−0.5	Accurate
1972	Nixon	62.0	61.8	0.2	Accurate
1976	Carter	48.0	50.0	−2.0	Accurate
1980	Reagan	47.0	50.8	−3.8	Accurate
1984	Reagan	59.0	59.2	−0.2	Accurate

NOTE: "Accurate" is recorded when poll did not proclaim the wrong winner. Percentages are based on two-party vote, except in 1948, 1968, 1976, and 1980.
SOURCE: Adapted from The Gallup Report, August 1987, 33.

As might be expected, people are better at predicting their behavior a short time into the future than a long time into the future. Polls are therefore more accurate if the election is the next day than if the election is one month later. Election standings always change as the campaign progresses, in part because many people flirt with voting against their own party early in the campaign but vote for it in the end. Because popularity of candidates inevitably changes throughout the campaign, trying to predict the outcome of an election long in advance is unlikely to work.

American pollsters learned this lesson in an embarrassing way in 1948. It took a long time to interview large samples of respondents and to analyze the data in those days, so the last poll was conducted several weeks before the election. The results of the final poll suggested that Dewey would win the competition easily, a prediction pollsters made publicly. Unbeknownst to them, though, Truman's campaign caught on in the final weeks before the election, after interviewing had ended. As a result Truman won the election, and the pollsters' prediction was wrong. Now polling routinely continues until election eve.

Another factor that makes it difficult to predict the outcomes of elections is that many interviewees say they are undecided. Usually, these people split their votes fairly evenly between the two candidates, but this isn't always the case. Consider, for example, the 1980 presidential contest between Carter and Reagan. Polls conducted close to election day showed a fairly tight race, but many voters were undecided. In this case most of the undecided voters ended up voting for Reagan, so he won the contest in a landslide. Fortunately for the polling industry, that was an unusual event; the vote of the undecided is rarely so one-sided.

Different survey organizations rarely make identical predictions of election outcomes. This is partly because of sampling error, differences in wording of questions, and different interview dates. It is also due partly to how different organizations decide which people are likely to vote and what undecided voters will do on election day. When different pollsters make similar predictions, they are likely to be correct. But when the polls disagree with one another, it is safest to assume that none is exactly correct and that the truth lies somewhere near the average of their forecasts.

Sensitive Topics.   Predictions of behavior can also be inaccurate if one answer is seen as sensitive. For example, in 1982 surveys in California predicted that black Los Angeles Mayor Tom Bradley would win the governorship, but instead he lost by several percent. By all accounts, many white California Democrats were unwilling to tell interviewers that they were unwilling to vote for a black for governor.

Another factor that makes it difficult to measure people's predictions of their own behavior in emotionally charged situations is the bias of rationality.[3] The formality of the questions reduces the spontaneity of the interview; the one-to-one discussion eliminates the group influences that can incite action and violence; and the reasonable tone of the interviewer makes it harder to express unreasonable views. Thus, if one wants to know whether a person is likely to participate in an urban riot, survey interviewing may be too cool a methodology.[4] The artificial interview situation inhibits a range of emotional responses that occur in other settings. As a result, surveys may be least useful for the study of beliefs and future behaviors that are emotionally charged.

Measuring Attitudes

Nonattitudes.   Certainly the most common goal of surveys is to measure attitudes. However, as we discussed in Chapter 4, there is always the possibility that questions intended to measure attitudes instead measure *nonattitudes*. When respondents are asked questions on topics they have thought little about, the best answer is probably "I don't know." But instead of saying this, some respondents generate opinions on the spot, even though the responses they give are not indicative of preexisting, well-thought-out opinions. These answers represent what pollsters have come to call *nonattitudes*.

Evidence showing the prevalence of nonattitudes was reported by Schuman and Presser.[5] They conducted experiments in which some respondents were asked an attitude question and were explicitly invited to say "don't know" if they wished to (the filtered form of the question), whereas other respondents were not invited to (the unfiltered form). Whereas most people offered opinions in response to the unfiltered form, people low in education and those who said the issue was not important to them flocked to say "don't know" on the filtered

[3]Jean M. Converse and Howard Schuman, *Conversations at Random: Survey Research as Interviewers See It* (New York: Wiley, 1974)72–74.

[4]David Riesman, *The Academic Mind* (Glencoe, Ill.: Free Press, 1958),291.

[5]Howard Schuman and Stanley Presser, *Questions and Answers in Attitude Surveys*, (New York: Academic Press, 1981), 113–146.

form. These individuals offered opinions on the nonfiltered form, presumably because they felt it was inappropriate to say they didn't know.

There are at least three reasons why some respondents without opinions do not say so during survey interviews. First, respondents may not want to appear uninformed, which might occur if they say they don't know in response to lots of questions. It is easy and costs nothing to say you agree with a statement just read to you, whereas you might be embarrassed by suggesting to the interviewer that you have no idea what the question is about. A second reason for reporting nonattitudes may be that respondents feel that providing an answer is more polite and does the interviewer a favor.

A third reason why respondents sometimes report nonattitudes may be that researchers generally wish to obtain as many answers to their questions as they can, so they discourage respondents from saying they don't know. Closed-ended survey questions rarely include *don't know* on the list of responses, and researchers often instruct interviewers to probe don't-know responses to make sure the respondent really does not have an opinion. This probing is likely to suggest to respondents that it is better to offer an opinion than to say they don't know.

As a result, many responses do not reflect thoughtful consideration of the issue. People sometimes agree with statements rather than indicate a lack of opinion. They give neutral evaluations of a politician rather than admitting that they don't know who the person is. Or they concoct an opinion on the spot, even though they are not fully informed on a topic and their opinion is likely to change as they acquire new information. Thus, asking voters about presidential contenders long before an election may provide less than fully meaningful estimates of the candidates' potential to be elected. Answers to a question regarding a proposed new public policy may have little relationship to answers to the same question months later, after the issue has received widespread publicity. In these situations respondents are not at fault; researchers are asking questions before the public has crystallized its opinions.

Weakly held attitudes are not very useful for predicting people's behavior, a common goal for survey researchers. For example, survey-based predictions may overestimate support for civic improvements because questions usually do not force the respondents to take account of the costs of such projects. Respondents who say they support building a bridge may vote against it when they realize that taxes would have to be raised to cover the costs. Thus, a survey question may tap one attitude, though actual behavior may be based upon another, more complex attitude. For this reason social scientists should exercise caution when inferring behavior from survey reports of attitudes unless they have evidence indicating that the reports are not of non-attitudes.

Survey researchers have developed two ways to determine whether attitude reports generally reflect real attitudes or not. The first approach is based on the assumption that real attitudes predict behavior and nonattitudes do not. If an attitude report proves to be a useful basis for predicting an individual's behavior, it probably reflects a real attitude. The second approach is based on the assumption that real attitudes are stable over time, whereas a report of a nonattitude is likely to be different today than it was yesterday. In order to be sure not to measure nonattitudes, it is always best to include don't know filters in attitude questions and to test either the stability of attitude reports or their ability to predict behavior.

Disagreement about the Meanings of Words.   It is natural to read the report of a survey and to assume that respondents interpret the questions just the way you do. Sometimes, though, the attitudes or beliefs that analysts think they are measuring are not those that are in fact being reported.

Consider the case of ideology. Politicians, academicians, and journalists often use ideological terms such as *liberal* and *conservative* in their discussions of politics. These people view liberals as people who favor big government and who favor the welfare state, whereas conservatives are viewed as people who oppose big government and who favor free enterprise unconstrained by government regulations.

For many years, the Gallup Poll has asked Americans whether they consider themselves liberal or conservative. Almost one-third of respondents say they think of themselves as neither, which suggests that these people do not think of themselves in these terms. Because reports of liberalism/conservatism from the other two-thirds of respondents are quite stable over time, they seem not to reflect nonattitudes,[6] but it turns out that many of the respondents who call themselves liberals or conservatives do not mean what journalists and scholars assume. Most people think of liberals as people who spend money freely and think of conservatives as tightwads. This example illustrates how careful one must be when interpreting the results of attitude measures. Results that seem to mean one thing can in fact mean something quite different.

---

[6]Teresa E. Levitin and Warren E. Miller, "Ideological Interpretations of Presidential Elections," *American Political Science Review* 73(1979):751–71.

Intensity.   Another problem to watch in measuring public opinion is the intensity of peoples' attitudes. Some people may give an answer to a question but not really care much about it, while other people may care passionately about their view on the same question. In many cases it is important to measure the intensity as well as the nature of attitudes.

Take the issue of gun control. Surveys routinely show that a majority of Americans favor stricter gun control laws. Yet gun control legislation has had a very hard time getting passed in Congress. One reason is that the anticontrol people have much greater intensity in their attitudes than the procontrol people. Those opposed to gun control are more willing to finance and support large lobbying efforts to influence Congress, and they have on occasion cast single-issue votes against congressmen who supported gun control legislation. As a result, members of Congress have learned that votes for gun control can threaten their reelection to Congress, regardless of the majority support for gun control in public opinion polls. This is a case where public opinion polls should show the intensity of public attitudes as well as their direction.

MEASURING CHANGE

Imagine picking up the morning newspaper and seeing the headline "President's Popularity Increases." You begin to read the article and find that it reports the results of a recent survey in which respondents were asked whether they approved or disapproved of the president's handling of his job. The article says that 60 percent of Americans approve of the president's performance today, whereas 56 percent approved of his performance last month when a similar survey was conducted. Is the conclusion that presidential popularity has increased a valid one on the basis of this evidence? That is a very complex question.

Attitude Recall Data

You might imagine that the simplest way to assess whether attitudes have changed over time is to ask people. Respondents can be asked about their past attitudes as well as their current attitudes, and the difference can be attributed to attitude change. For example, people can be asked how they felt about legalized abortion last year and how they feel today so that changes in attitudes can be assessed.

Unfortunately, though, attitude recall data are frequently inaccurate; people typically underestimate the degree to which they have changed, thus overestimating their own consistency. When asked how they felt a year ago, they assume that they believed just what they do today, overestimating the similarity of their present attitudes to their attitudes before. It seems that people report what they think they should have thought instead of what they actually thought. For this reason, attitude recall data should be interpreted cautiously and should be avoided whenever alternative methods for measuring attitude change are available. Minimally, check whether people's recollections correspond with other evidence from the earlier period, such as surveys conducted at that time with different individuals, before accepting the recall data as valid.

Comparisons of Repeated Cross-Sectional Surveys

A much more useful way to determine whether public attitudes on a particular issue have changed over time is to survey the topic in question at different times and to compare the results. However, be careful when studying attitude change using this approach. What may seem to be an attitude change may reflect a change in methodology or the effect of sampling error. In order to evaluate whether an apparent change in attitudes is real, ask four questions:

- Did the same organization conduct both polls using the same interviewing methods?
- Was the same population sampled in the same manner on both occasions?
- Were the questions worded the same on both occasions?
- Is the size of the observed attitude change larger than could result from sampling variation alone?

We discuss each of these issues below.

Surveys Conducted by Different Organizations.   Survey organizations all have their own idiosyncratic procedures for drawing samples and for conducting interviews. Some use primarily older women interviewers, whereas others use many more young men when conducting telephone interviews. Even such seemingly simple decisions as how many times to call a phone number before giving up are made differently by different organizations. As a result, even if the sampling procedure used for two surveys was the same, the implementation of that sampling procedure or the interviewing procedure or both could be different. Changes in sampling or in the interviewing procedure can easily ruin the comparison.

Consider two telephone surveys on attitudes toward capital punishment conducted two weeks apart by two different organizations. In the first survey interviewers called homes three times before giving up, whereas in the second, the same phone number was called back six times. Imagine further that the first survey found more people to be favorable toward capital punishment than the second. This result could simply reflect the different call-back procedures. Wealthy people tend to be home less often than poor people, so the former are harder to get in touch with by telephone. As a result there were probably fewer wealthy people interviewed in the first survey than in the second. Because wealthy people tend to be less favorable toward capital punishment, their greater presence in the second survey could account for the apparent difference in results. Thus, the comparisons of the two surveys' results might reflect the fact that call-back procedures changed while attitudes remained constant.

Another example of this problem has to do with don't-know rates. Some survey organizations instruct their interviewers to discourage don't-know responses as much as possible and to encourage respondents to choose one of the alternatives offered by closed-ended questions. Other organizations tell their interviewers to accept don't-knows immediately and not to press respondents for substantive responses. Therefore, if one survey finds 15 percent of its sample saying they have no opinion about capital punishment, whereas a later survey done by a different organization finds 25 percent of people without opinions, it would be inappropriate to claim that people have become less opinionated on the issue, since the apparent change could actually be due to different interviewing practices.

Therefore, if different survey organizations conducted the surveys, their results should not be directly compared. If an analyst were able to obtain lots of information about the two organizations' interviewing procedures and found that they were identical, it would be legitimate to compare their results. However, it is rarely possible to obtain such detailed information and even rarer to find two organizations that use identical procedures. Thus, it is safest to compare only surveys done by the same firm.

Comparing Different Questions.   Even if two surveys are conducted by the same organization, it is inappropriate to compare their results if different questions were asked in the two surveys. Unfortunately, the survey literature is filled with examples of people trying to assess attitude change by using different questions at different times. For example, a researcher trying to determine whether whites' attitudes toward blacks are different in the 1980s than they were in the 1950s may compare current results to those of a poll conducted thirty years before. Most often the exact questions were not asked in both polls, so the researcher compares questions on the same topic even though they are phrased slightly differently.

Such comparisons are virtually meaningless. As you know from Chapter 4, even slight changes in a question's wording can produce dramatic changes in the distribution of answers to it. When substantial changes are made, it is impossible to anticipate what effects they will have on answers. Therefore, one can easily be misled about attitude change if one compares answers to different questions.

For example, the University of Michigan's Survey Research Center found that fewer people said they supported federal aid to education in the early 1960s than had done so previously. Some observers viewed this as evidence of changing attitudes. However, it is important to note that the wording of the question was revised in 1964. Before that time people were asked to indicate whether they agreed strongly, agreed but not very strongly, were not sure, disagreed but not very strongly, or disagreed strongly with the following statement: "If cities and towns around the country need help to build more schools, the government in Washington ought to give them the money they need."

In 1964, the question was changed to the following: "Some people think the government in Washington should help towns and cities provide education for grade and high school children; others think that this should be handled by the states and local communities. Have you been interested enough in this to favor one side or the other? (IF YES) Which are you in favor of?"

Even though the question was not changed a great deal, it is different in a number of ways. Perhaps most obviously, acquiescence bias might have led some people to agree to the old form of the question, whereas they are forced to make a choice in responding to the second. Therefore, at least some, if not all, of the differences between responses to these questions are probably attributable to the changes in the question, and not to changes in attitudes.

To make things more difficult, even if a question is worded exactly the same in both surveys, the social and political environment may have changed so much over time that the question means something different during the first interview than during the second. For example, in the 1960s if people were asked whether they favored or opposed racial integration, they probably thought of integration of restaurants, public transportation, and so on. However, if they are asked the same question in the 1980s, they are more likely to think of busing and other more contemporary issues. Answers to the same question may be different because it is interpreted differently. The longer the time between two surveys, the greater the chance for this type of change of interpretation to occur.

Successive Cross-sections.   A relatively safe procedure for studying attitude change is to compare surveys of the public conducted by the same organization using the same questions. Fortunately, some organizations have asked the same questions in many surveys over the years. Different samples were interviewed in each case, but the same population was sampled each time, and the sampling procedure was the same. The results for one survey of a cross-section of the public can therefore be compared with those for earlier cross-sections.[7]

Figure 7.1 shows an analysis of Americans' trust in government us-

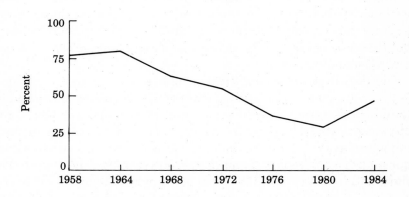

Figure 7.1 Trust in Government, 1958–1984.
Proportion of the public who feel they can trust the government in Washington to do what is right "always" or "most of the time."
(American National Election Studies codebooks.)

---

[7]There are several useful compendia of survey results over time. The University of Michigan's National Election Studies and Survey Research Center surveys are summarized in Philip E. Converse, et al., *American Social Attitudes Data Sourcebook 1947–1978* (Cambridge: Harvard University Press, 1980); and Warren E. Miller, Arthur H. Miller, and Edward J. Schneider, *American National Election Studies Data Sourcebook 1947–1978* (Cambridge: Harvard University Press, 1980). Similarly, the General Social Surveys are summarized in James A. Davis, *General Social Surveys 1972–82: Cumulative Codebook* (Chicago: National Opinion Research Center, 1982).

ing this strategy. These results are based on identically worded questions used in surveys by the University of Michigan's Survey Research Center. Therefore we can be confident that the trends shown here are not results of methodological artifacts. According to these results, Americans' trust in their government declined consistently during the 1960s and 1970s. Interestingly, the figure for 1984 suggests that this trend is reversing.

Be careful not to overinterpret minor fluctuations in successive cross-sections of this sort. As we saw in Chapter 3, no survey produces perfectly accurate results because of sampling error. A drop of 3 percent or more from one reading to the next might be totally attributable to such sampling error. Unfortunately, newspaper stories on presidential popularity polls frequently emphasize minor fluctuations, which could be due to random differences in sample selection rather than to real attitude change. When studying trends in attitudes, one should instead focus on major trends. Thus, the results in Figure 7.1 are useful because the trend is very clear and is therefore unlikely to be the result of sampling error.

Figure 7.1 provides a nice illustration of time-series analysis. However, it also shows the limits to such analysis. Studies of change over time can be relatively atheoretic. One can locate the timing of changes, but that does not reveal the reasons for those changes. Theory is required to interpret the changes.

One drawback inherent in comparing successive cross-section surveys is that the analyst can assess only net change and cannot estimate the degree of gross change. Imagine you conduct a survey and find that 40 percent of a national sample say they favor capital punishment and 60 percent say they oppose it. Imagine further that you asked the same question of a different national sample one year later. If between the times of the two surveys, 10 percent of the public became more favorable toward capital punishment and 10 percent became more unfavorable, while 80 percent did not change their attitudes, you would find the same distribution of attitudes at the time of the second survey: 40 percent in favor and 60 percent opposing. On the basis of this evidence, it would be fair to conclude that the distribution of attitudes in the nation did not change, but it would be wrong to conclude that no one's attitude changed. If one wishes to assess the extent of gross change in individuals' attitudes, a series of cross-sectional surveys will not do the trick. Instead, one must interview the same people on several different occasions.

Panel Studies

The best way to measure gross attitude change using surveys is to interview the same people a number of times. Repeated interviewing of the same respondents, referred to as a *panel*, reveals the amount of individual-level attitude change that occurred between the waves of the survey. For example, the University of Michigan's Center for Political Studies conducted a panel study in 1972, 1974, and 1976. Using those data, it is possible to assess how many people who voted for Nixon in 1972 also voted for Ford in 1976, how many switched to Carter, and how many did not vote. Similarly, one can examine the voting behavior in 1974 and 1976 of people who voted for McGovern in 1972.

Long-term panel studies have rarely been done because they are very expensive and labor-intensive. Since people often move from one address to another, it can be difficult to locate a respondent years after a first interview. Also, people are sometimes unwilling to be interviewed repeatedly, particularly if they were not interested in the subject of the interview in the first place. As a result, considerable *mortality* is common in panel studies, with smaller and smaller proportions of the original sample interviewed at each successive wave.

Another common problem in panel studies is that the wrong person is sometimes interviewed; instead of reinterviewing a man, an interviewer might mistakenly interview his wife at the second wave of a panel study. For example, in a 1960 panel survey conducted by the University of Michigan's Survey Research Center, 1 percent of the respondents are recorded as being a different sex at the postelection interview than at the preelection interview.In all likelihood, either a recording error was made at one of the waves or the wrong person was interviewed at the second wave. There is usually no way to correct for this since it is impossible to reconstruct what error occurred, but it reminds us that small amounts of error are present in all questions in surveys—even the seemingly obvious such as the gender of the respondent.

Panel sample mortality decreases the representativeness of the sample at later waves. The people who are found for reinterviews tend to differ in some respects from a random cross-section of the public. They tend to move their residence less often, which means they include fewer young people, and they tend to have more interest in and knowledge about the topic of the survey. Fortunately, it is possible to assess whether the part of a sample that was successfully followed up at later waves is unrepresentative of the original full sample. This can be done by comparing the first-wave answers given by respondents who were successfully reinterviewed with the first-wave answers given by those who were not. Unfortunately, most reports of studies analyzing panel data report results based only on respondents who were successfully reinterviewed and do not report how representative they were of the larger sample.

Another possible problem with panel designs is that the first interview may affect respondents' attitudes and behavior. For example, interviewing people for an hour about an upcoming election increases their interest in politics, and therefore more of them vote in the election than would have had they not been interviewed. Thus, because of the earlier interview of the panel sample, the behavior patterns apparent at the second wave of a panel survey may be slightly different from the behavior patterns of a representative national sample interviewed at the same time. In the case of voting the effect is not large, but it illustrates a possibly larger problem in some panel surveys.

Longitudinal Studies versus Cross-sectional Studies

A final point to make about measuring change is the importance of using longitudinal data when the focus is on change. Sometimes researchers try to make statements about change from a single cross-sectional study, but such conclusions are often incorrect. As a classic example, American surveys routinely show that the voting turnout rate of people with higher levels of education is greater than that of people with less education. It is tempting to conclude from that cross-sectional relationship that education leads to voting. However, that appears true only when one looks at a single cross-section survey. If compared across time, educational levels have increased dramatically in this country over the past century and even over the past thirty years while voting turnout has declined. A relationship found in a cross-sectional study may not hold longitudinally. Longitudinal data are necessary if change is the focus of the study.

In summary, conducting surveys to measure attitudinal and behavioral change is tricky business. Recall data are sometimes employed, but people's recall of their earlier views and actions is often faulty. Results of two surveys of different samples can be compared, but care must be taken to insure that the differences found are not due to changes in the questions or different sampling or interviewing procedures. Panel studies provide the best evidence of change, but they

are infrequently used because they are costly and difficult to implement. Cross-sections provide untrustworthy evidence of changes over
time.

MAKING SUBGROUP COMPARISONS

Surveys are frequently used to compare the attitudes, beliefs, and behaviors of subgroups. This may seem routine, but sometimes it has special implications for sampling. Say that one is interested in a subgroup
that is relatively small in size, such as blacks, Hispanics, or Jews. In a
representative national sample of two thousand people, one would not
obtain enough interviews in these categories to be able to compare
them accurately with the rest of the population.

One way to remedy this problem is to oversample a group of interest.
To assess blacks' attitudes, for example, it might be worth double-
sampling blacks. All of the interviews with blacks would be used to
make generalizations about blacks' attitudes. To describe the entire
sample, use only half of the black interviews, weighting the interviews
with blacks to their proper proportion.

Another approach is to combine samples in a *pyramiding* strategy.
Lacking enough Hispanics in one national sample to draw valid conclusions about their attitudes, it might be reasonable to combine a series of surveys, perhaps even taken over a period of years, so long as
those surveys contained similar questions and used similar sampling
and interviewing procedures. Thus, combining the 1972 through 1988
American National Election Studies might produce a large enough
sample of Hispanics to draw conclusions about their attitudes. Of
course, this strategy would not be useful if attitudes changed drastic-
ally over that period.

ASSESSING THE CAUSES OF BEHAVIOR

A final common goal for surveys is to understand why people say or do
certain things. It may seem reasonable simply to ask them. Unfortunately, though, people often do not know the reasons for their own actions, so their reports are often inaccurate.[8] Typically, the answers

---

[8]Richard E. Nisbett and Timothy Wilson, "Telling More than We Can Know: Verbal
Reports on Mental Processes," *Psychological Review* 84(1977):231–59.

people offer are rationalizations post hoc for behavior—their best guesses as to what the causes of their behavior might have been. Apparently people make up convincing explanations that appear rational to the interviewer. The explanations people offer may make sense and sound reasonable, but they often have nothing to do with the actual causes of behavior. It is therefore best not to ask people directly about the reasons for their behavior when the reasons are likely to be complex.

The better strategy for assessing the causes of behavior with surveys is to think through the different possible causes of the behavior, ask about those causes, and then analyze the results. Thus, surveys usually do not ask people why they voted as they did, but instead ask people about their feelings on the issues, the candidates, and the parties. Statistical analysis of these answers can reveal the relative importance of issues, candidates, and party in the vote decision.

SUMMARY

Surveys can be used to measure the prevalence of attitudes, beliefs, and behavior. Survey researchers have learned that measuring these variables can sometimes be difficult and that some ways to do so are better than others. Similarly, some ways of using surveys to assess change in attitudes, beliefs, and behavior are better than others. In this chapter we have described some of the advantages and disadvantages of particular survey designs for accomplishing these goals.

Questions

Assume that you are an expert in survey research and that you have been asked to evaluate the following survey results. What would you question about the studies?

1. A survey of high-school seniors found that a majority of young people have experimented with drugs.
2. A survey of members of Congress shows that a majority believe they should follow the wishes of their constituents rather than their own attitudes when the two are in conflict.
3. A survey finds when legislators in Western Germany and the United States were asked what their goals are, 20 percent more in West Germany gave ideological goals than in the United States.

PART II

Data Analysis

8

The Process of Data Analysis

The analysis of data gathered for a large research project can take years; it requires careful planning. In this chapter we describe a general approach to analyzing survey data. This involves three steps: 1) stating hypotheses in theoretical terms, 2) operationalizing the concepts in the hypotheses, and 3) testing the hypotheses.

STATING HYPOTHESES

Analysis of survey data can be either descriptive or explanatory. When the news media report poll results, they are often used only for description. For example, a poll may describe what proportion of the public supports the president, whether that support is increasing or decreasing, and whether some types of people are more likely to support the president than are others. Before examining the results of a poll, an investigator might formulate some hypotheses about the expected results. If support for the president is being studied, one might speculate on the basis of recent political events that support for the president is falling and is especially low among blue-collar workers as compared with white-collar workers. These are descriptive hypotheses.

In addition to describing, polls are often used for explanation: to understand the causes of people's beliefs, attitudes, and behavior. Usually, we seek to test generalizations that account for the attitudes and behavior of aggregates of individuals—generalizations derived from theories of human behavior. Thus, polling may be used to answer such questions as: What factors determined which candidate each citizen voted for in the last presidential election? Why do some people oppose capital punishment for convicted murderers, while other people favor it? Why do some people vote in presidential elections, while others do not? These are examples of questions requiring *explanations*.

Causal Explanations

When seeking explanations, social scientists attempt to find the *causes* of social phenomena. What is a cause? Causality has a number of meanings; in scientific usage, its meaning is similar to that of "producing."[1] One thing is the cause of another thing if a change in the first produces a change in the second. Therefore, it is appropriate to say that the weather causes human behavior. When it starts to rain, people put up umbrellas when they walk outside. Thus, a change in the weather produces a change in behavior.

Social scientists' causal hypotheses usually posit relationships between *variables*. A variable is something that varies from person to person or across situations. Variables often studied by social scientists include behavior, beliefs, attitudes, and background characteristics such as race, gender, educational attainment, family income, and religion. The variable that we wish to *explain* is called the *dependent variable*. For example, many studies of voting behavior seek to explain why some people vote Republican and others Democratic. In those studies voting is the dependent variable. The other variables used in hypotheses, called *independent variables,* are examined to discover whether they are causes of the dependent variable. In our example independent variables such as religion and race might be used to explain a person's vote. In short, a dependent variable is an effect, and an independent variable is a suspected cause. A hypothesis states that one variable may cause another.

A few variables that social scientists frequently study are almost always independent. These are demographic variables such as race, sex, and age. Social scientists are seldom interested in the causes of these variables, (although gender was treated as a dependent variable by geneticists who studied what makes some babies male and others female), so social scientists' hypotheses generally treat these variables as independent. In contrast, some variables are nearly always depen-

---

[1]Mario Bunge, *Causality* (Cambridge: Harvard University Press, 1959), 46-48; Hubert M. Blalock, Jr., *Causal Inferences in Nonexperimental Research* (Chapel Hill: University of North Carolina Press, 1964), 9.

dent in social scientists' hypotheses. Political scientists, for example, often study the cause of behavior such as voter turnout, vote choice, and political participation. Many other variables may be independent or dependent, according to the context in which they are studied. For example, party identification (that is, whether the person thinks of himself or herself as a Republican or a Democrat or an Independent) would be a dependent variable if we were studying the effect of income on party identification, but it would be an independent variable if we were analyzing the effect of party identification on a person's vote.

Explanation is not just a concern for academic social scientists. Politicians hire pollsters to provide campaign advice by explaining people's voting. Marketing firms want explanations of people's buying behavior. Public-policy analysts want explanations of people's responses to various welfare programs. These examples illustrate how explanation is always crucial to providing advice and evaluating solutions.

Necessary and Sufficient Conditions. In thinking about causation, many people find it useful to distinguish between necessary conditions and sufficient conditions. A *necessary condition* is required for an effect to occur, but by itself it does not guarantee that the effect will occur. For example, it is necessary in most American states to register in order to vote; one cannot vote in those states without first registering. However, some people who are registered do not vote, so registration is not a complete cause of voting.

By contrast, a *sufficient condition* is one that guarantees that the effect occurs, though the effect may also occur without it. Say we are studying the weather, in particular we are examining precipitation. The occurrence of snow is a sufficient condition of precipitation, since when it snows there is precipitation. However, precipitation can occur without snowing, as by raining, so it is not a necessary condition.

In some cases, we will find a condition that is both necessary and sufficient. In that case, the effect occurs *if and only if* the condition occurs. If the presumed cause is always followed by the presumed effect, and if that effect occurs only when that presumed cause precedes it, then we have identified a *necessary and sufficient condition.* Obviously, it would be ideal if we could always identify necessary and sufficient conditions for the dependent variables we are studying, but causation is not that simple. When causation is complicated, one may be able to identify necessary conditions, or sufficient conditions, but not both.

Multiple and Indirect Causes. A single independent variable almost never accounts fully for a dependent variable. Any given attitude or behavior is likely to have many causes that work simultaneously. Because of the typically complex effects of social science variables on one another, we usually try to identify causal processes rather than single causes.

Causal processes may work indirectly. For example, consider a social scientist studying cigarette smoking among adolescents. Most people believe that this behavior is caused by peer pressure. Put more formally, this hypothesis states that the smoking behavior of an adolescent's peers causes his or her smoking behavior. This causal influence may operate via the adolescent's beliefs about popularity. That is, adolescents whose friends smoke may believe that they will be more popular if they smoke. In contrast, adolescents whose friends don't smoke might believe that they will be more popular if they don't smoke. Therefore, it may be that peer smoking behavior causes an adolescent's beliefs about popularity, which cause his or her smoking behavior.

Arrow Diagrams. Causal processes can be represented by arrow diagrams (Figure 8.1). An arrow means that one variable is thought to affect the other; the direction of the arrow shows the presumed direction of influence. Such arrow diagrams are generally read from left to right and from top to bottom.

Figure 8.1 shows an example of a causal process by which some theories explain voting behavior. Evaluation of the candidates is portrayed as a cause of voting choice, and candidate evaluation is shown to have its own causes. Some causes are shown to have indirect effects, such as issues affecting the vote through their effect on the evaluation of candidates. Party identification is shown to affect the vote directly and also indirectly, through its effect on evaluations of the candidates.

This model posits *reciprocal causation,* whereby two variables cause each other. In this case evaluations of the candidates affect party identification, and party identification affects evaluations of candidates. Another possible reciprocal causal relation might be the claim that vote choice may be affected by party identification and may affect

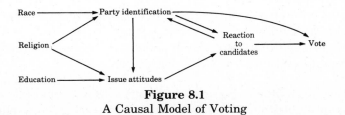

Figure 8.1
A Causal Model of Voting

party identification. This would occur if someone who has always considered himself or herself a Democrat happens to vote Republican in a series of elections and then begins thinking of himself or herself as a Republican.

When planning an analysis, it is often useful to draw such arrow diagrams. This exercise forces one to think in causal terms, to consider the full range of variables that should be included in an explanation, and to map out the presumed causal process.

Testing Causal Hypotheses

The relationship between two variables must pass four tests in order for causation to be possible. If any is not satisfied, then we know the variables do not have a causal relationship.

Association. First, a causal relationship between two variables is unlikely to exist unless there is some tendency for a change in one variable to be *associated* with a change in the other. Imagine, for example, that we were interested in the hypothesis that income causes educational attainment. That is, perhaps the amount of money a family earns determines whether or not children in that family go to college. In order for this hypothesis to be true, children in families with larger incomes must go to college more often than children in families with smaller incomes. If this is the case, we cannot be certain that income causes educational attainment. But if this is not the case, we can be relatively certain that income does *not* cause educational attainment.

Two variables can be related in a simple linear fashion or in a more complex way. In the simplest form of association, a one-unit change in one variable would always be associated with a certain number of units of change in the other variable. For example, such an association would exist if one additional year of education is always associated with an average increase of $800 in a person's annual income. However, such simplicity is rare in human society. A more complex possibility is that an increase from one year to two years of education may be associated with an average increase of only $200 in annual income, and an increase from twelve to thirteen years may be associated with an average increase of $1,400 in annual income. This is an example of a nonlinear association between two variables.

Temporal Order. Second, we can speak of causation only when the cause precedes the effect. Temporal succession of cause and effect is implicit in the notion of causation. That is, a change in the suspected cause must precede observed changes in the suspected effect. When surveys are used to test causal hypotheses, both variables are usually measured at essentially the same time, during the interview. Thus, it is impossible to assess whether changes in one variable occur before changes in another. Therefore, to test for temporal ordering in surveys, one must interview a sample many times and observe when changes in variables occur.

In many cases it is reasonable to assume that changes in one variable preceded changes in the other. We can ask people how many years they went to school and what their annual income is today because it is probably safe to assume that their formal education preceded the attainment of their current income level. However, when it is difficult to justify assumptions about temporal ordering, it is essential to use repeated surveys.

A change in one variable may at some times precede a change in the other and at other times follow it. This may signify that these two variables are unrelated, but it may also indicate that each of the two variables affects the other. In such cases of reciprocal causation, there is usually a clear back-and-forth interplay: a change in the first variable produces a change in the second, which, in turn, produces later change in the first, and so on.

Alternative Causes.   Even if two variables are found to be associated and changes in one always precede change in the other, it is possible that the one to change first does not cause the one that changes second. Instead, it could be that they are both caused by some third variable. For example, imagine that a researcher is interested in the relationship between the size of families' houses and how often they take vacations in Florida. The investigator finds that families that live in bigger houses tend to take vacations in Florida more frequently and that when families move from one house into a larger one, they tend to take a vacation in Florida soon thereafter. Would this prove that size of house causes vacation behavior? Of course not, because both house size and vacation behavior may be caused by family income. That is, every time a family receives a large salary increase, they may move into a larger house and then take a vacation in Florida. If this were the case, we would conclude that the relation between house size and vacation behavior is not causal but *spurious*.

It is therefore important to test alternative explanations for an observed relationship between two variables. This is done by positing reasonable alternative hypotheses and attempting to disprove them.

Unfortunately, because it is practically impossible to test every possible third variable cause, we can never completely rule out the possibility that an observed relationship between two variables is spurious. Thus, we can never be absolutely sure that a relationship is causal. However, ruling out many other variables allows one to become more confident about a causal hypothesis.

Causal Mechanism.   Another way to develop confidence in a causal hypothesis is to develop an understanding of the *causal mechanism* involved. If A seems to cause B, how might that happen? If we cannot think of a plausible causal mechanism relating the variables, then the apparent relationship might just be coincidence.

A classic example of a relationship between two variables without an apparent causal mechanism is the fact that the Republican party has usually won the presidential election in the years that the National League won the baseball World Series. This satisfies the first three necessary conditions of causation: there is association, the National League victory precedes the Republican victory, and there are no plausible third variable causes. Yet it is difficult to believe that a National League victory causes the Republicans to win the presidency. Since there is no plausible causal mechanism connecting the outcomes of the World Series and the presidential election, any apparent relationship is probably just coincidence. In cases when one can posit a causal mechanism, it is easier to have confidence that causation has been identified.

Summary.   To summarize, testing of a causal explanation requires four steps:

- Checking to see whether the variables are associated with one another
- Verifying that changes in the presumed cause precede changes in the presumed effect
- Eliminating alternative explanations
- Generating a plausible causal mechanism

OPERATIONALIZING CONCEPTS

In order to use survey data to test a theoretically justified causal hypothesis, one must operationalize the concepts in the hypothesis. That requires choosing survey questions to measure each variable addressed by the hypothesis. When doing so, it is important that the questions accurately measure variables that correspond to the theoretical concepts of interest. Investigators who design their own surveys accomplish that when writing the questions.

Secondary Analysis

Operationalization is more difficult for the secondary analyst, who analyzes a survey that was designed by someone else. Different researchers approach the same problem from different perspectives and with different philosophies and ideologies, so the secondary analyst may sometimes be dissatisfied with the original investigator's questions. Secondary analysts are often interested in hypotheses different from those of the original investigators. Consequently, some needed questions may be either missing or not asked in the most desirable way. Secondary analysis therefore often requires compromises, using the available questions that come as close as possible to those desired. In addition, the secondary analyst may sometimes have to use several surveys, testing with one study the hypotheses that cannot be adequately tested with another study.

The secondary analyst must be particularly concerned with the validity of the measures. He or she may be interested in one concept, while the questions in the survey address a different concept. Too often the secondary analyst employs the questions that come closest to his or her concepts without recognizing that the wrong concept is being measured. As a result, secondary analysis sometimes does not provide such sharp tests of hypotheses as does primary analysis, wherein the researcher devises survey questions to correspond identically to the concepts.

Level of Measurement

An important aspect of operationalizing concepts is ascertaining the level of measurement of the variables. Many different statistical tests can be made, and which statistics to compute depends partly on the types of variables being examined. Statisticians distinguish between three basic levels of measurement of variables: (1) nominal, (2) ordinal, and (3) interval. Each level requires a different type of statistical analysis.

Nominal Variables.   Nominal variables are made up of distinct categories that are not related in any numeric or orderly fashion. One example of a nominal variable is religion. A person may be Catholic, Protestant, Jewish, a member of another religion, or a member of no organized religion. There is nothing numeric about these categories, though coders may number the categories in order to enter data into a computer. Region is another nominal variable. One may live in the North, East, South or West, but there is nothing numeric about these categories. Even if such categories have been numbered in the coding process, arithmetic operations like averaging are not appropriate.

Ordinal Variables.   The second type of measurement occurs when ordered categories do not have any intrinsic numeric qualities. People may be asked if they "strongly agree, agree but not strongly, are neutral, disagree but not strongly, or strongly disagree" with a statement. These responses are intrinsically ordered from most favorable to least favorable.[2] However, the options do not have numeric properties, since it would be unreasonable to assume that the psychological differences between successive categories are the same. For example, the difference between strong and weak agreement to a statement may be more or less than the difference between weak agreement and neutrality.

Interval Variables.   Variables that are intrinsically numeric, like age and income, are known as interval variables. Interval measurement occurs when responses are numbers and when the distances between the successive numbers are equal. Such numbers can be manipulated arithmetically by addition and subtraction; averages can be calculated and more complex statistical techniques can be used.[3] Sur-

---

[2]Assigning numbers to categories in a systematic way does not suffice to make the variable ordinal. A variable is still nominal if the categories are not ordered along some dimension. For example, zip codes were assigned to areas in the United States according to systematic rules, but zip codes are only a nominal measure since low-to-high zip codes do not measure any dimension. (What does it mean, saying that your zip code is higher than someone else's?)

[3]Statisticians actually distinguish between numeric variables measured with a meaningful zero point and those without a meaningful zero point. The former are called *ratio variables* and the latter, *interval variables.* The examples in the text are ratio variables, while temperature, as measured by either the Fahrenheit or Celsius scale, is interval. The zero points for these temperature scales are not meaningful; they do not signify an absence of temperature, so they are interval rather than ratio scales. A numeric variable would be considered a ratio if it makes sense to say that one score is twice another (as for one person being twice as tall as another); other numeric variables are inter-

vey researchers who wish to use these statistical techniques often try to measure attitudes at the interval level, such as by using numbered response scales as described in Chapter 4.

The distinctions between nominal, ordinal, and interval measurement reappear continually in statistics, so it is important to understand the differences. Consider three possible questions concerning religion:

a. What is your religion? Are you Protestant, Catholic, Jewish, a member of another religion, or a member of no religion?

b. How religious do you consider yourself? Do you consider yourself very religious, somewhat religious, or not at all religious?

c. How many times a month do you usually go to religious services?

The first question is aimed at classifying people in terms of nominal categories. The second seeks to determine religiosity on an ordinal continuum. The third measures attendance at religious services in interval terms.

Choice of Measurement Level.   These three levels of measurement represent a hierarchical set. The highest level, interval data, can be divided into ordered categories and treated as ordinal data, a lower level. Similarly, ordinal data can be treated as nominal data, the lowest level. However, shifts in the opposite direction are generally not possible without special justification.[4]

Different types of statistics are appropriate for different levels of measurement. Throughout the remainder of this book, we refer to levels of measurement when we describe how to decide which statistical procedures are appropriate in particular situations.

It is useful to note that level of measurement does not matter for dichotomous variables—those with only two categories. Sex, major-party vote (Democratic or Republican), and whether or not a person voted are three examples of such variables. They can be treated as interval, ordinal, or nominal without any loss of meaning, though performing significance tests (as discussed in the next section) on them requires making assumptions about their distribution.

---

val. Statistics appropriate for analyzing ratio variables are also appropriate for analyzing interval variables, so we do not distinguish between the two in the text.

[4]Categorical variables can be treated as ordinal if a theory orders the categories along some dimension. For example, religion might be treated as ordinal if a theory orders the amount of ritual each religious denomination involves. Some analysts are willing to treat ordinal data as interval, though this entails some risk of fallacious conclusions.

TESTING HYPOTHESES

Once the variables for the analysis are selected, the analyst can test the hypothesis. When using a sample to test hypotheses about a population, the survey researcher must employ a very special logic.

The Logic of Null Hypotheses

Hypotheses are propositions that are deduced logically from theory; in the social sciences hypotheses are based on theories of human behavior. An hypothesis posits something about a variable, such as a mean value or its relationship to another variable. For example, theories of voting behavior suggest the hypothesis that political party identification causes voting behavior: identifying with the Democratic party leads people to vote for Democratic candidates, whereas identifying with the Republican party leads people to vote for Republican candidates.

When testing hypotheses like this one, avoid committing what logicians term *the fallacy of affirming the consequent*. Consider the claim that condition A causes condition B. Observing that condition B has occurred may seem to suggest that condition A should also exist. However, this argument is fallacious, because it may be that condition C also causes condition B. Observing that condition B has occurred does not indicate whether A or C caused it. For example, consider the claim "cities with heavy rain have high annual precipitation counts." Discovering that a city has a high precipitation count does not prove that it has heavy rain, because heavy snow also leads to high precipitation counts. Observing a high precipitation count does not indicate whether heavy rain or heavy snow is the cause.

Returning to the voting example, finding that Democrats voted for the Democratic candidate in a particular election more than the Republicans did does not prove the generalization that Democrats are more likely than Republicans to vote for Democratic candidates. It should be clear that verifying that Democrats did vote in a greater proportion for the Democratic candidate in the particular election than did Republicans does not prove that the research hypothesis (Democrats are *always* more likely than Republicans to vote for Democratic candidates) is correct. The research hypothesis states a generalization, and we have data on only one particular instance.

The rules of logic permit a different type of proof. *Denying the conse-*

quent is a valid form of argument. Consider again the claim "condition A causes condition B." If this claim is true and if condition B has not occurred, it is certain that condition A has not occurred. If cities with heavy rain have high precipitation counts, then a low precipitation count for a city proves that it does not have heavy rain. Similarly, finding that Republicans voted in a greater proportion for the Democratic candidate in an election than did Democrats would show that the claim that more Democrats than Republicans always vote for Democratic candidates is false. The rules of logic are different for proof and disproof, and as a result, science proceeds by a series of disproofs rather than by direct proofs.

Because one cannot prove a research hypothesis but only disprove it, scientists have developed the notion of the null hypothesis. The null hypothesis is usually the opposite of the research hypothesis. In our example the null hypothesis is "Republicans are as likely as Democrats to vote for Democratic candidates." Most often the null hypothesis states that there is no relationship between two variables or that one variable does not affect another variable. After stating a null hypothesis, researchers try to disprove or *reject* it. Disproving a null hypothesis offers some support for the research hypothesis.

Remember, however, that disproving the null hypothesis does not prove the research hypothesis. At best, by offering evidence that the null hypothesis is not true, we show that the research hypothesis may be true. In spite of this warning, many researchers speak of "accepting" the research hypothesis. We shall use this terminology as well, but readers should bear in mind that accepting the research hypothesis does not mean that one has proven it to be true.

Types of Error

When a researcher decides whether or not to reject a null hypothesis, two types of error can be made (Table 8.1). First a true null hypothesis may be rejected by mistake. Falsely refecting a true null hypothesis is known as *Type I error*. Second is to accept a null hypothesis when it is false. Accepting a false null hypothesis is known as *Type II error*. Social scientists strive to avoid both types of error.

The two types of error are related. The more stringent the criterion for rejection of the null hypothesis, the fewer true null hypotheses we will mistakenly reject (less Type I error), and the more false null hypotheses we will keep by accident (more Type II error). The same crite-

Table 8.1   Error Conditions When Accepting or Rejecting a Null Hypothesis, Depending on Whether the Null Hypothesis Is True or False

	H_0 true	H_0 false
accept H_0	Correct	Type II Error
reject H_0	Type I Error	Correct

rion that protects us from wrongly rejecting a true null hypothesis (wrongly accepting a research hypothesis) also causes us to err more often by accepting a false null hypothesis. Thus there is a tradeoff between these two types of error.

Scientists generally view Type I error as the more serious. In medicine, for example, one would not want to change treatment if the new treatment were not a real improvement over a safe, widely used treatment. Therefore, one would not want to take a large chance of falsely rejecting a true null hypothesis of no difference between the treatments. If one has to make a mistake, continuing with the old treatment when the new one is better is preferable to switching from a widely used treatment to one that may prove worse. Therefore, a slight chance of Type I error and a larger chance of a Type II error is preferred to the reverse.

In science new studies sometimes contradict previous results, but we should not toss out the established wisdom in a field on the basis of weak evidence. The null hypothesis in this situation is that the previous results are correct. If the findings of the new research challenge those results, we have to decide whether the evidence is strong enough to publish the new findings. The new findings could be wrong, in which case publishing them would constitute rejecting a true null hypothesis (Type I error). Or the new conclusion might be right, in which case not reporting it would constitute accepting a false null hypothesis (Type II error). The usual conservative procedure in statistics is to take only a small chance of making a Type I error, even if doing so entails a large chance of Type II error. Thus, we are stringent in publishing new results, even if that occasionally means not publishing some correct findings. Presumably, if the null hypothesis is incorrect, some later study will reject the null hypothesis more conclusively, so there is no lasting harm in avoiding Type II error.

Statistical Inference

When testing a null hypothesis, a researcher must decide how big a chance of making a Type I error he or she is willing to take. Usually in the social sciences investigators are willing to take a 5 percent chance. That is, tests are set up so that there is only a .05 probability of rejecting a true null hypothesis. The likelihood of a Type II error is usually ignored in this procedure. Sometimes researchers employ more stringent levels, such as the .01 level or even the .001 level, but usually .05 is sufficient.

To illustrate this approach to testing a hypothesis, imagine that 54 percent of a survey sample favors a proposed government program. A researcher might wish to test the hypothesis that there is majority support for this program, that is, to know whether the true proportion in favor is more than 50 percent. The null hypothesis corresponding to this hypothesis is that the true proportion in favor is 50 percent or less. Thus, disproving the null hypothesis would indicate that there is majority support for the program. We compute a *test statistic* to determine whether the null hypothesis should be rejected. The test statistic can be used to determine the probability that the observed proportion is 54 percent, if the true proportion in the population is 50 percent or smaller. If the probability is less than 5 percent, we would reject the null hypothesis. Otherwise, we would accept it.

The test of a hypothesis described above is only one way to draw a statistical inference. Another is the confidence interval. When using this method, one determines an interval in which the population value is likely to fall given an observed proportion. For example, if an investigator obtained a sample proportion of 54 percent with a sampling error of 7 percent, there is a 95 percent chance that the true population value is 54 percent − 7 percent and 54 percent + 7 percent. More precisely, in 95 out of 100 samples of the same size, the sample mean would be within 7 percent of the true population mean. From this perspective the researcher would decide that the result is not significantly different from 50 percent, since the 95 percent confidence interval extends from 47 percent to 61 percent, which includes 50 percent.

Whichever method is used, the question usually being asked is whether a result is likely to hold for the population of interest. If you find 54 percent of the sample favoring the proposed program, does it mean that a majority of the population favors it? Phrased more technically, is 54 percent significantly greater than 50 percent? As we saw in Chapter 3, whether 54 percent is significantly greater than 50 percent depends on how large the sample is. A larger sample is more likely to be representative of the population, so larger samples have smaller sampling errors which allow one to detect smaller differences between observed proportions and hypothesized ones.

Even if a result is statistically significant, researchers often argue about whether it is substantively significant. Even if our sample is so large that 54 percent is statistically significantly greater than 50 percent, we still may feel that the 4 percent difference is not significant in a substantative sense. After all, 54 percent is so close to 50 percent that it would be more appropriate to describe the public as evenly split on the program than to say that a majority favors it. Deciding what is important is not just a technical statistical issue; it depends on the researcher's substantive understanding of what is being studied. Statistical inference is useful for determining how to interpret a set of results, but one must always assess substantive significance as well.

In designing an analysis the researcher must decide whether to employ significance tests and what types to employ. When dealing with large samples, researchers often decide not to employ formal significance tests and instead simply describe the sample results.

SUMMARY

Analysis design consists of the three steps described in this chapter: the specification of the hypotheses to be tested, the operationalization of the specific concepts, and the selection of appropriate statistical tests. These steps must be carefully meshed. Variables must properly operationalize the concepts in the hypotheses, and statistical techniques must be appropriate for the variables and their measurement level. These three steps for analysis design should be followed whether analyzing primary survey data or doing secondary analysis of surveys others have taken.

The chapters that follow explain common statistical analysis procedures. An analysis usually begins by counting and rendering into percentages the responses to single questions (Chapter 9) and then examines relationships between pairs of variables (Chapters 11, 12, and 14). Often alternative hypotheses are tested by seeing whether two-variable relationships are different for people who differ on other variables (Chapters 13 and 14).

Questions

1. Construct a model of the causal process that determines a person's income. Use age, education, and parent's social class as predictors. What other explanatory variables might be useful? (To avoid some definitional problems, assume a restriction to people over twenty-five years of age.)
2. Construct a model of the causal process than determines a person's political party preference. Use parent's social class, parent's party preference, and the person's social class as predictors. What other predictors might be included in the model?
3. Construct a model of the causal process that determines a person's attitude toward legalized abortion. Include the person's religion, the person's age, and the extent to which the person has traditional values as predictors. Consider what additional predictors might be included.
4. What level of measurement is each of the following variables?
   a. The number of states the Republicans won in the last presidential election
   b. A person's marital status, coded as *married, never married, separated, divorced,* or *widowed*
   c. Whether a person reads the daily newspapers every day, frequently, occasionally, seldom, or never

9

Single-Variable Statistics

The first step in analysis of survey data is to examine one variable at a time. This can consist of tallying up the responses to a particular question or calculating the average age of respondents. In this chapter we present the procedures for analyzing single-variable statistics along with procedures for changing and combining variables.

FREQUENCY DISTRIBUTIONS

The simplest display of results for a single variable is a list showing the number of people giving each answer to the variable—the distribution of the frequency of each response. This information is sometimes called *marginals* because the frequency distribution is often printed in the margin of the codebook. Table 9.1 displays some hypothetical data in the form of a frequency distribution.

The table shows a majority of respondents supporting the idea of government health insurance. Of 1,303 people, 863 are said to support government health insurance; 863 is clearly bigger than 440, the number that are said to oppose government health insurance. This summarizes the results nicely, except that it does not indicate whether 863 is a very large majority of 1,303 or not.

Percentage Distributions

It is usually more effective to present the frequency distributions in percentage form. For example, the proportion said to support the

Table 9.1   Attitudes on Government Health Insurance

"Would you support or oppose having the federal government take over health insurance in this country?"

Support	863
Oppose	440
	1,303

SOURCE: Hypothetical.

program in Table 9.1 is $(863 \div 1,303) \times 100 = 66.2$ percent. The proportion opposing it is $(440 \div 1,303) = 33.8$ percent. Table 9.2 again reports exactly the same data as does Table 9.1; however, this time the display is in percentages. The percentage table shows at a glance that government health insurance commands support from approximately a two-thirds majority.

The number of cases (often called N) is listed under the percentages in Table 9.2 so that the reader knows how much confidence to place in the results. Two-thirds is a large majority, but we have much greater confidence that the results reflect the nation's attitudes accurately when we know that there were 1,303 respondents rather than just thirty or forty. Listing the number of cases also allows the reader to compare the numbers of people who gave each response.

Missing Data

Unfortunately, survey results are never as cut and dried as those in Tables 9.1 and 9.2; extra categories may be needed. For example, some respondents may say they would support the program only as long as private insurance was still permitted; in other words, it *depends*. Many people have not thought about the problem, and many will admit they have *no opinion*. Sometimes the interviewer forgets to read a question or the respondent terminates the interview before the

Table 9.2   Attitudes on Government Health Insurance

"Would you support or oppose having the federal government take over health insurance in this country?"

Support	66.2%
Oppose	33.8%
Total	100.0%
(Number of cases)	(1,303)

SOURCE: Hypothetical.

Table 9.3   Attitudes on Government Health Insurance

"Would you support or oppose having the federal government take over health insurance in this country?"

Support	863
Depends	223
Oppose	440
No opinion	350
Not ascertained	18
Total	1,894

SOURCE: Hypothetical.

interviewer has managed to ask this particular question. If so, the respondent's attitude on this issue is *not ascertained*.

If we included these categories in the frequency distribution, we might obtain the results shown in Table 9.3. How do we summarize opinion in this table? The largest problem is the lack of answers from the no-opinion and not-ascertained categories.

Not Ascertained. "Not ascertained" shows that the question was not asked of everyone. Therefore, the people in that group could certainly be treated as having missing data and be dropped from the table. Replacing the remaining numbers with percentages would give us Table 9.4. Note that the number of cases on which Table 9.4 is based is less than the number on which Table 9.3 is based because the not-ascertained category has been subtracted.

Incidentally, why do the percentages in Table 9.4 add to 100.1 percent rather than 100.0 percent? Because we have rounded each percentage to one digit after the decimal point, and the rounded percentages sum to 100.1. It is common in such tables for percentages to add to 99.9 percent or 100.1 percent instead of 100.0 because of the effects of

Table 9.4   Attitudes on Government Health Insurance

"Would you support or oppose having the federal government take over health insurance in this country?"

Support	46.0%
Depends	11.9%
Oppose	23.5%
No opinion	18.7%
Total	100.1%
(Number of cases)	(1,876)

SOURCE: Hypothetical.

rounding off to the nearest tenth of a percent. Similarly, if the percentages are rounded to the nearest whole percent the total might be 99 percent or 101 percent. This error due to rounding should not be of any concern.

Table 9.4 gives an honest rendition of the results. More hypothetical respondents support government health insurance than oppose it. But many have intermediate views, and many have not made up their minds yet. Those supporting the program are not a majority, but they could form a majority by attracting some of those with no opinion or accommodating those who say it depends.

No Opinion.   The "no opinion" category shows to what extent opinion has crystallized on the question. A large number of people saying they don't know suggests that most of the public has not made up its mind on an issue. However, it is still interesting to know the distribution of opinion among those who have made up their minds. One might ask: of those who had an opinion and answered the question, how many support government health insurance? This means treating the no-opinion category as a missing-data category and excluding it from the table. Thus we get Table 9.5.

Of those with an opinion, a majority support the government health insurance plan and fewer than 30 percent oppose it. Table 9.5 does not tell how many people are undecided on the issue, but it does summarize the views that were stated. Present a table without the no-opinion category when the assumption is that undecided respondents will eventually be distributed in about the same way as who now have opinions. In other words, a table like 9.5 is based on the assumption that about 56.6 percent of the people with no opinion will eventually support government health insurance. Although that is the most likely assumption, there are several other assumptions that also prompt one not to report the no-opinion category. Imagine a policy maker who takes a survey to

Table 9.5   Attitudes on Government Health Insurance

"Would you support or oppose having the federal government take over health insurance in this country?"

Support	56.6%
Depends	14.6%
Oppose	28.8%
Total	100.0%
(Number of cases)	(1,526)

Source: Hypothetical.

help with a decision that must be made soon so it is safe to ignore respondents who have no opinion. Another example is provided by a survey taken the day before an election. It is doubtful that those who have no opinion about the candidates will take part in the election.

There are certain circumstances under which the no-opinion category should not be omitted. Dropping the no-opinions would be misleading if there were reason to suspect that these respondents did or will have a particular opinion. For example, one might not want to drop the no-opinions on a question concerning racial issues if there was reason to believe that it was a covert racist answer—the respondent claimed to have no opinion rather than give the interviewer a racist answer. This is rarely a serious problem, although it often makes sense to consider whether "no opinion" has a concealed meaning. Also, "don't know" may be a meaningful answer, as on questions of political information such as how many justices there are on the United States Supreme Court. The don't-knows are not missing data, but rather an indication of the fact that the respondent did not know the correct answer, hence may be uninformed about politics. It would thus be a mistake to drop that category from a summary table. Another circumstance in which one should not drop the missing-data category is when the proportion of respondents falling into the category is quite large in comparison with the proportion endorsing the substantive categories. That usually indicates some problem with the questions, and the reader should be made aware of it.

Note that Tables 9.1 through 9.5 are all based on exactly the same set of responses, those listed in full in Table 9.3. The tables differ in only two respects: (1) whether the results have been expressed as percentages or numbers of cases, and (2) which categories have been omitted. Table 9.2, 9.4, or 9.5 could be published as "The Distribution of Public

Table 9.6   Attitudes on Government Health Insurance

"Would you support or oppose having the federal government take over health insurance in this country?"

Support	56.6%
Depends	14.6%
Oppose	28.8%
Total	100.0%
(Number of cases)	(1,526)
(No opinion)	(18.7%)
(Total number of cases)	(1,876)

Source: Hypothetical.

Opinion on Government Health Insurance," yet the three tables give somewhat different views. When you read a poll result, it is worth checking whether intermediate categories (like *depends*) and the missing-data categories were included or not.

As another means of displaying the same data, Table 9.6 gives the distribution of opinions plus an indication of how many respondents offered no opinion. This may be the most helpful way to display the results.

Graphic Displays

A final way of presenting frequency distributions is graphically. Graphic presentations usually are the most effective mode of presentation. Readers who find frequency tables hard to understand usually can understand graphs easily. To paraphrase the old saying, a picture is worth a thousand numbers.

Several graphic forms have been developed for displaying frequency distributions. Figures 9.1 through 9.3 present three common forms. The pie chart in Figure 9.1 displays how many people gave an answer by the area in the circle for each category. Nearly twice as many people support government health insurance as oppose it, according to these

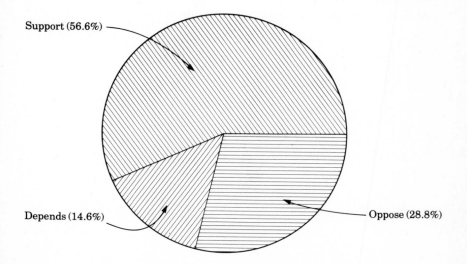

Figure 9.1
Pie Chart of Attitudes on Government Health Insurance
Source: Hypothetical

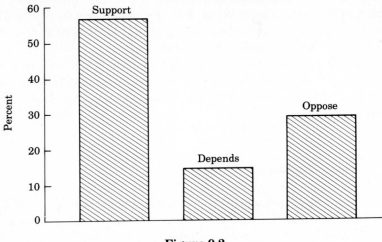

Figure 9.2
Bar Chart of Attitudes on Government Health Insurance
Source: Hypothetical

hypothetical data, and that is represented by the relative areas for the supporting and opposing groups.

The bar chart in Figure 9.2 represents how many people gave an answer by the height of the bar for each category. The height bar for "support" is nearly twice as tall as that for "oppose" to show how many more people support government health insurance than oppose it.

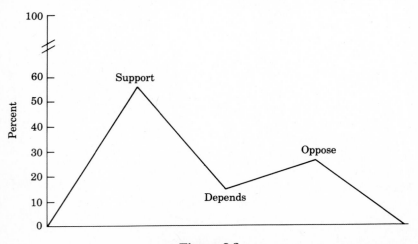

Figure 9.3
Frequency Polygon of Attitudes on Government Health Insurance
Source: Hypothetical

The frequency polygon in Figure 9.3 also uses height to represent the frequency of responses. The response categories are ordered along the horizontal axis, and the height of the line above each category shows how popular it is. The frequency polygon is usually used for interval and ordinal data, while the bar and pie charts are used for nominal data.

Interpreting Frequency Distributions

We must not take the percentages in such tables and graphs to be perfect descriptions of opinions. They are affected by many factors other than the attitudes being measured. One factor discussed in Chapter 3 is sampling error, the error that occurs when a sample of people is not perfectly representative of the population. It depends mainly on the sampling procedures and the sample size. With 1,526 interviews, there is a sampling error of approximately 3 percent or 4 percent, which means that the percentage in our example of the population supporting government health insurance is between about 53 percent and 60 percent. Even with this sampling error, it would be clear that the program had majority support of those with opinions.

The second important factor (also discussed in Chapter 4) is the wording of the question. We should not take the observed distribution of responses too literally because they depend on the wording of the questions (or code categories). What if the question on health insurance had been, "Would you prefer government health insurance or private health insurance in this country?" It is not unreasonable to expect a 10 percent to 20 percent difference due solely to the question wording. Sometimes there is no difference at all between the results of different wordings, but one should never assume that wording does not matter. Thus, Table 9.6 should be interpreted as showing public support for government health insurance, but we should not give too much emphasis to the 56.6 percent level of that support.

Consider another example. Table 9.7 gives the frequencies of responses to the presidential vote question from the 1984 National Election Study. These results can be arranged in a more concise manner than in Table 9.7 by presenting only the percentages of people who voted for the two major party candidates. Since a large number of respondents say they did not vote, it is important to include that fact in some way. In Table 9.8, percentages have been calculated, and categories like don't-know have been eliminated. Obviously, there are other reasonable ways of presenting these data; however, Table 9.8 conveys

Table 9.7   1984 Reported Vote for President

Category	Frequency
Reagan	801
Mondale	575
Refused to say	9
Other	13
Don't know	4
Not ascertained	47
Inappropriate	
Voted, but not for	
president	15
Did not vote	525
Not reinterviewed	
after the election	268
Total	2,257

NOTE: The category *inappropriate* was separated into subgroups shown here on the basis of other survey variables.
SOURCE: 1984 American National Election Study.

the points that probably interest most readers: (1) the percentage voting for each of the two major candidates and (2) the percentage not voting.

In general, when constructing frequency distributions, it is most important to include sufficient information to illustrate the important substantive point. Often what you want to show with the data will determine how much detail (and, in fact, which details) should be included in a table. Readability is usually improved by showing percentages rather than raw frequencies, although the number of cases underlying the percentages should be given so the reader can reconstruct the raw frequencies if necessary.

MEASURES OF CENTRAL TENDENCY

It is easy to examine Table 9.8 (or any of the preceding tables in this chapter) to get a quick impression of the distribution of public atti-

Table 9.8   Reported Vote for President

Reagan	58.2%
Mondale	41.8%
Total	100.0%
(Number of cases)	(1,376)
(Not voting)	(27.6%)
(Total number of cases)	(1901)

SOURCE: 1984 American National Election Study.

Table 9.9   Ideal Family Size

"How many children would you consider the right number
for a family?"

None	10.5%
One	22.1%
Two	35.2%
Three	21.6%
Four	5.8%
Five	3.1%
Six	1.6%
Eight	0.1%
Total	100.0%
(Number of cases)	(1,404) .

SOURCE: Hypothetical.

tudes. Consider, however, Table 9.9, with its rather large number of substantive categories. One can examine the full set of percentages, but it would be useful to summarize the results more compactly. When the responses are tallied and a frequency distribution produced, responses may be summarized statistically, for example to report the average response or give some idea of how unified the public is in its attitudes. This gets us into the realm of statistics.

The simplest type of summary measure is the *central tendency*, which indicates how the typical person behaves or what the typical value of a variable is. However, summary measures that are appropriate to the analysis of some variables are inappropriate for analysis of others. For example, we could calculate from Table 9.9 the average number of children mentioned as the ideal, but we could never calculate the "average religion" of respondents. Although the average may be a useful concept in analyzing some variables, it cannot and should not be calculated for others. What measures are appropriate depends mainly on the level of measurement of the variables as discussed in Chapter 8.

The Mean

The most familiar measure of central tendency is the arithmetic average, known technically as the mean. A mean can be calculated only for interval-level variables. To compute it, add up the values of the variable for each case and divide that by the number of cases. Thus, if a survey found that 6 people attended religious services 0, 1, 3, 3, 5, and 8

Table 9.10 Central Tendency Measures

(A) Interval Variable: Frequency of Attendance of Religious Services

	Times per Month	Frequency	(Times × Frequency)
x_1	0	1	$(0 \times 1) = 0$
x_2	1	1	$(1 \times 1) = 1$
x_3, x_4	3	2	$(3 \times 2) = 6$
x_5	5	1	$(5 \times 1) = 5$
x_6	8	1	$(8 \times 1) = 8$
Total		6	20

$$\text{Mean} = \overline{X} = \frac{\sum_{i=1}^{N} x_i}{N} = \frac{20}{6} = 3.33$$

(B) Ordinal Variable: Religiosity

	Proportion	Cumulative Proportion	
Very religious	40%	40%	
Somewhat religious	35%	75%	(50% point)
Not at all religious	25%	100%	

Median: Somewhat religious

(C) Nominal Variable: Religion

	Proportion
Protestant	45%
Catholic	30%
Jewish	5%
Other	10%
None	10%

Mode: Protestant

SOURCE: Hypothetical.

times per month respectively, add these numbers together to get a sum of 20 and divide by 6 (the number of people) to get a mean of 3.33. The average number of times that these people went to church is 3.33. Table 9.10A illustrates the above calculation.

We needed a more concise way of describing the information in Table 9.9. The mean should help. Although the mean for Table 9.9 takes longer to calculate than that for Table 9.10A, the process is exactly the same. After adding up the number of children mentioned by each of the 1,404 respondents and dividing that number by 1,404, a mean of 2.06 results.

It is useful to understand some of the mathematical notation that is used to describe the mean. We often speak of the observations of the variable X as x_1 (the first person's value), x_2 (the second person's value), $x_3, \ldots, x_N$. We would say that there are N observations of x, where N is the number of people. The sum of those N observations of x can be written:

$$x_1 + x_2 + x_3 + \cdots + x_N = \sum_{i=1}^{N} x_i$$

This is to read as "the sum of the x-sub-i's, where i ranges from 1 to N." The mean of $\overline{X}$, often written $\overline{X}$, can be expressed:

$$\overline{X} = \sum_{i=1}^{N} x_i/N$$

Alternative Measures

The average is appropriately calculated only for interval data; other measures are available for ordinal and nominal data. If a variable is ordinal, we can examine the median—the middle position. If 40 percent of the sample indicate that they consider themselves very religious, 35 percent somewhat religious, and 25 percent not at all religious, then the middle person in the sample considered himself or herself somewhat religious. That is the median response (Table 9.10B). Technically, the median response should have half of the responses below it and half above it. Frequently, though, the median falls in a large group of other responses, so that the numbers of responses above and below are not exactly equal. In these instances the median is the category that comes closest to being in the middle of the distribution.

If a variable is nominal, we can locate the mode—the category that occurs most frequently. If more people in the United States consider themselves Protestants than Catholics, Jews, members of other religions, or members of no religion, then the modal religion is Protestant (Table 9.10C).

Choice of Central Tendency Measure

Sometimes the mode and median are also used for numeric variables. For example, Table 9.9 on ideal family size might best be summarized by saying that both the modal number and the median number of children desired is two. The mean number of children desired in this case is also quite close to two—it is 2.06. In some instances the mean can be distorted by a few extreme values of the variable that are outside the normal range of the values. Say, for example, that a few people said that twenty children would be ideal; that might raise the mean a great deal. In such a situation, the median or the mode would be a much more reasonable measure of the average person's preference.

While the mode and the median can be used for numeric data, the mean should not be used for nonnumeric data, and the median should not be used for nominal data. Thus, for a nominal variable like region, one might find which region of the country most people live in (the mode), but it would not make sense to speak of the mean region or the median region even if numbers had been assigned to the regions in the coding process.

The mean can be used for dichotomous variables. Say, for example, that gender has been coded 0 for male and 1 for female, and say that 55 percent of the sample is female. Then the mean of sex would be 0.55. Thus, calculating the mean on a dichotomous 0/1 variable correctly shows what proportion of people fall into the 1 category.

Incidentally, if you are using a computer for data analysis, do not automatically feel you can use a statistic just because the computer printed it. People who write computer programs often have the computer automatically print a wide range of statistics and expect the researcher to decide which are appropriate. Thus, we must not assume that we have a true interval-level measurement on a variable just because the computer calculated a mean for it.

Finally, in computing any of these measures of central tendency, always be sure that the missing data have been excluded. For example, a set of data might have the symbol 99 coded for a person who was accidentally not asked a question (not ascertained). That 99 should not be allowed to affect the calculation of, say, the average number of children a person wants!

MEASURES OF DISPERSION

Social scientists often seek to account for differences among people. The variance is a measure of how different the scores are for interval variables. Not everyone has the same score, so there is variance. If everyone had the same score, it would be the mean and there would be no variation. Variation is a measure of how dispersed the cases are from the mean. Since the mean is a measure of central tendency, it is near the middle of the cases; the variance tells us how scattered the cases are

Table 9.11 Variance of Age

Age	Frequency	(Age − Mean)	(Age − Mean)^2
20	1	$(20 - 24.33) = -4.33$	$-4.33^2 = 18.75$
23	1	$(23 - 24.33) = -1.33$	$-1.33^2 = 1.77$
30	1	$(30 - 24.33) = 5.67$	$5.67^2 = 32.15$
Total	3	0.01	52.67

$$\overline{X} = 24.33 \qquad s^2 = \frac{\sum\limits_{i=1}^{N} (x_i - \overline{X})^2}{N} = \frac{52.67}{3} = 17.56$$

SOURCE: Hypothetical.

around the mean. The smaller the variance, the closer the cases are to the mean; the larger the variance, the more widely they are scattered.

One might imagine measuring the dispersion around the mean by subtracting it from each value and summing those differences. However, one would find that the sum would always be zero (within rounding error), because the sum of the differences for the cases above the mean is the same as the sum of the differences for the cases below the mean (with the opposite sign). This can be seen in the third column of Table 9.11.

There are at least two ways of handling this problem. One is to take the absolute value of the differences, and the other is to square them. Although it would make little difference for present purposes, statisticians prefer working with the squared values when they generalize the variance concept to more than one variable. Therefore, the variance is customarily defined as the average squared deviation from the mean:[1]

$$s^2 = \frac{(x_1 - \overline{X})^2 + (x_2 - \overline{X})^2 + \ldots + (x_N - \overline{X})^2}{N} = \frac{\sum\limits_{i=1}^{N} (x_i - \overline{X})^2}{N}$$

Table 9.11 illustrates this calculation. The mean is subtracted from each person's score; the resulting differences are squared, summed, and then divided by the number of people. For the first person, the

---

[1]Note that the denominator of the variance in this equation is N because this is the variance for a population. Some versions of the formula have $N - 1$ in the denominator; technically, those refer to samples. Usually, the sample size is so large that the numeric difference between the two formulas can be ignored. When we are specifically discussing a sample, we will use the $N - 1$ version; otherwise, we shall use N.

mean of 24.33 is subtracted from the score of 20. That yields a deviation of −4.33, which, when squared, is 18.75. Similar calculations for the second and third persons give squared deviations of 1.77 and 32.15. These squared deviations sum to 52.67. The variance is 52.67 divided by 3 (the number of people), which is 17.56.

Since we squared the differences between each value and the mean before we added them, the measurement scale of the variance is the square of that of the original variable. It is hard to know what to make of a variance of 17.56 squared years in our example, so it makes more sense to move back to the original unit of measure. As a result, statisticians suggest that it is more meaningful to look at the square root of the variance. The result is the *standard deviation*. In our example the square root of 17.56 is 4.19. We would speak of these people as having a mean age of 24.33 with a standard deviation of 4.19 years.

It is useful to see how the variance and standard deviation contrast instances of small and large variation. The example in Table 9.12 illustrates two sets of data on income with the same number of people (five) in each set and the same mean income ($10,000) but with quite different dispersions. Group A has a variance of 20,000, while group B's variance is 12.5 million. The standard deviations for the two groups are 141 and 3,535 respectively. Both the variances and the standard deviations report what is obvious in the original data: the income for group A are substantially less dispersed than those for group B.

At this stage you might wonder how these dispersion measures are used and why they are important. It would be premature to explain at this point, but we shall repeatedly make use of them in dealing with statistical inference and correlation/regression (see Chapters 10 and 14, respectively).

Two final cautions. First, the variance and the standard deviation can be computed only for interval variables because the data must be

Table 9.12   Income of Two Groups

Group A	Group B
$9,800	$5,000
$9,900	$7,500
$10,000	$10,000
$10,100	$12,500
$10,200	$15,000
$\overline{X} = \$10,000$	$\overline{X} = \$10,000$
$s^2 = 20,000$	$s^2 = 12,500,000$
$s = 141$	$s = 3,535$

SOURCE: Hypothetical.

actual numbers. For ordinal and nominal data, there are no standard measures of dispersion, but one can still look at graphic displays of each variable to see how much dispersion exists. Second, one occasionally encounters variables with little or no variance; that is, the responses are all nearly the same. These variables are not useful in data analysis. Since social scientists usually wish to explain variation, there is little to explain in these instances. Also, variables with no variance have no explanatory potential. As an example, there is no reason to try to explain the vote for president of Republicans in 1984, because more than 95 percent of the Republicans voted for Reagan.

COMPUTER ANALYSIS

Social science data analysis is now routinely performed on computers. We are giving little attention to this aspect of data analysis in this book, since there is so much variability in computer systems. However, it is useful to introduce the topic here, with some attention to single-variable statistics as an example of computer analysis.

Computers range from large mainframes with enormous capacity generally available only in large organizations such as corporations or university computer centers, to small desktop personal computers. Social science data analysis was originally done exclusively on mainframe computers, but it is shifting increasingly to personal computers.

In order to analyze a set of survey data, it is necessary to obtain access to it. When the analysis is on a mainframe computer, this usually amounts to being told how to access the desired data. For example, it is common to store surveys on magnetic tape, which is similar to tape used on tape recorders. If the data are on tape, the analyst must find out how to access the tape and how to locate the survey on the tape (since there usually are several data sets on the same tape). When using a personal computer, the data can generally be handed to the analyst on a small diskette.

The analyst also must obtain the codebook for the study. The codebook will indicate what variables are in the data set and what each is called. For example, it might be necessary to refer to V788 to access presidential vote, or the data might be set up so that one can simply refer to PRESVOTE or a similar shortened name. It is also important to inspect the codebook for relevant sampling information about the study. If the sampling procedure in the study is unusual, the analyst may have to take special steps. For example, some studies purposely oversample some groups, such as double-sampling blacks so there are enough blacks in the sample to provide valid estimates of their attitudes. Such studies include a special *weight* variable (which counteracts the oversampling), which has to be specified in the analysis when valid estimates are desired for the complete sample.

The next step is to use a statistical analysis program. Most installations maintain several such programs on their mainframe computers. Common statistical analysis programs for mainframes include SPSS-X (Statistical Package for the Social Sciences, version ten), SAS (Statistical Analysis System), and BMD (Bio-Medical). Statistical analysis programs also exist for personal computers; three of the more common programs are MINITAB, SPSS, and SYSTAT. Using these programs requires instructions on how to operate the computer, how to access the program, how to feed the data into the program, and how to use the specific analysis program.

As a brief example consider the SPSS-X procedure for finding the frequency of people who have given each response for a question. The example shown below would produce the frequencies for presidential vote and race (V1083) for the previously saved file ELEC84.

```
TITLE VOTE AND OTHER FREQUENCIES
GET FILE = ELEC84
FREQUENCIES VARIABLES = V788,V1083/
    BARCHART/
    STATISTICS = MEAN
FINISH
```

The first line TITLE is used to label the output of the program so the analyst can tell different analyses apart. The second GET FILE tells the program the name of the data file. The third FREQUENCIES indicates the type of analysis that is to be done *and* the variables to be analyzed. The next BARCHART asks for a graph of the distribution of each variable. STATISTICS requests that the mean be calculated for each variable. The FINISH line completes the SPSS-X run.

The specific instructions for data analysis differ from computer to computer and from program to program, but this example shows several common aspects: labels for program output, telling the program how to access the data file, indicating the type of analysis desired and what variables to analyze, choosing particular options to tailor the analysis to one's needs, and choosing which statistics to employ from long lists of available statistics.

The important thing to remember about computer analysis is that computers are only tools. They are useful tools because they can process huge amounts of data quickly and accurately. However, they cannot decide what analysis is appropriate for a set of data, nor can they interpret the results. The analyst must still decide what procedures to use, what statistical tests are appropriate given the level of measurement of the data, and whether weighting is required by the sampling design. In some cases the program may print out many different statistics (such as the mean, median, and mode), and the analyst has to decide which are appropriate for the data. Computers are very useful, but the analyst must still make sure the analysis makes sense.

MODIFYING VARIABLES

So far we have assumed that the variables in the data can be used as is. However, it is frequently necessary to modify variables prior to analysis. The variables in the data file may not be identical to those that the analyst wants to study. The concepts in the theory suggest certain types of operational indicators, which can be derived from (but are not identical to) the variables in the data file. In these cases it is necessary to change the variables prior to generating the desired set of tables, correlations, or controls. In this section, we shall review procedures for changing variables through recoding, index construction, and scaling.

Recoding

Modifying a Variable.   The first case of this type is one in which variable recoding is required. For example, the data may include a variable named party identification that shows to which political party the respondent feels closer. The variable may be coded:

0. strong Democrat
1. weak Democrat
2. Independent leaning to Democrat
3. Independent leaning to neither
4. Independent leaning to Republican
5. weak Republican
6. strong Republican
7–9. missing data

But the theory being investigated may pertain to strength of partisanship rather than its direction. For example, the theory may be that the longer one has identified with a party, the stronger is that identification. The dependent variable for that relationship is strength of partisanship without a direction component. Ideally, strength of partisanship would be coded as follows:

>   0. strong identifier
>   1. weak identifier
>   2. independent leaner
>   3. pure independent
> 7–9. missing data

By a process of combining categories, strength of partisanship can be determined from the party identification variable available in the data set:

> new 0 = old 0 or old 6
> new 1 = old 1 or old 5
> new 2 = old 2 or old 4
> new 3 = old 3
> new 7 = old 7
> new 8 = old 8
> new 9 = old 9

The new category 0 (strong identifier) includes those coded 0 (strong Democrat) or coded 6 (strong Republican) on the original list. Similarly, the new category 1 (weak identifier) consists of those coded 1 (weak Democrat) or 5 (weak Republican) on the party variable. The other categories have been transformed in the same way. Conceptually, there is nothing complicated about this single-variable recoding, though it is important that the computer program have an easy way of doing it.

Most statistical computer programs can transform variables in this manner, though they differ in the way they accomplish the recoding. Once a variable is recoded, the new variable may be used in any table or analysis (or other recoding) in which any of the original variables might have been used.

Combining Two Variables.   A more difficult but nevertheless useful type of recoding is *bivariate recoding*, in which two variables are recoded together to yield the variable that is of interest. For example, one might have a theory that older citizens vote against their party less often than younger ones. The study would have a variable showing the party the person identifies with (coded as in the previous example) and a variable showing how the person voted, but no variable showing whether or not the respondent voted with his or her party. If we need this last variable, we would have to construct it from party identification and vote.

To do so, list the desired categories for the new variable, being sure to include all necessary missing data codes:

1. vote with party
2. vote against party
9. no party, no vote, or missing data on either question

Say that the vote is coded:

1. Democrat
2. Republican
5. did not vote
8. don't know
9. missing data

The appropriate recoding:

new 1 (vote with party)   = party identification 0, 1, or 2 and vote 1 (Democrat voting Democratic) and
= party identification 6, 5, or 4 and vote 2 (Republican voting Republican)

new 2 (vote against party) = party identification 6, 5, or 4 and vote 1 (Republican voting Democratic) and
= party identification 0, 1, or 2 and vote 2 (Democrat voting Republican)

new 9 (missing data)   = party identification 4, 7, 8 or 9 (independent or missing data on party) and
= vote 5, 8, or 9 (did not vote or missing data on vote)

The result of the recoding is a new variable we might call defection, showing whether or not the person defected from the party with which he or she identifies.

Indices

The recoding process can be built up beyond two variables. New variables can be some combination of several variables. This is especially useful when a survey includes a battery of questions measuring a complex concept. As Chapter 4 indicated, this strategy makes the results less dependent on the wording of particular questions than when only a single question is used. A special way of combining such questions is building additive indices.

For example, a survey might ask people four questions concerning whether or not they obtained news about the election campaign from television, radio, newspapers, and magazines. For some purposes one would want to keep the differentiation among the four different media, for example to see whether those who rely on television differ in their behavior from those who rely on newspapers. For other purposes it would be useful to know from how many media the person obtains news. People who pay attention to several media could differ in their behavior from those who employ only a single news medium. Therefore, we would want a count of how many news media the person employs.

Say that each variable is coded:

>   1. employs this medium
>   0. does not employ this medium
>   9. missing data

We might make an index from the four separate media variables by adding up each person's scores on the four separate variables. A person who employs all four media would get a score of 4; 3 would mean the person employs any three media, and so on.

Missing Data.   Missing data can be handled in several ways. One might give a missing-data code to anyone with missing data on any one of the four questions. Or, more likely, we might decide not to count the 9s when adding the variables, but to give a respondent a score of 9 on the index if he or she has missing data on all four questions.

The result if we used the second approach to handling the missing data would be a variable coded:

>   4. employs four media
>   3. employs three media (possibly missing data on the fourth)
>   2. employs two media (possibly missing data on others)

1. employs one medium (possibly missing data on others)
0. employs no media (possibly missing data on some)
9. missing data on all four media

This would be an additive index of the four media questions, with a minimum assignment of cases to missing data. Remember when analyzing this variable, the 9 signifies missing data rather than nine media used.

More Than One Dimension.   One problem with additive indices is that different variables may be tapping wholly different concepts. Consider, for example, category 2 on our media index. Respondents who employ only the print media—newspapers and magazines—would receive a score of two on the index, as would respondents who employ only broadcast media—television and radio. These two types of people would have the same score for two very different forms of behavior. It is not difficult to imagine that very different types of people employ only print media or only broadcast media. One would expect, for example, the broadcast-media people to have received less total information about a political campaign than if they had read detailed articles in the print media. In other words, in this example the index may be measuring two different underlying concepts or *dimensions*—a broadcast-media dimension and a print-media dimension. Because there may be more than one dimension, we cannot expect all the respondents coded 2 on the index to be similar. A researcher must therefore be careful to create indices using variables that all tap the same concept.

Guttman Scaling

Clearly it is of value to know if an index is *unidimensional* (composed of only one dimension). Guttman scaling was developed to determine whether a set of variables measures a single concept or dimension and thus whether they can be combined. It should be emphasized from the outset that Guttman scaling is only one way to assess the unidimensionality of a set of variables. There are other meanings of unidimensionality that Guttman scaling does not measure. However, Guttman scaling is still useful in beginning to suggest what dimensionality is and why it is important to check the dimensionality of a set of variables.

We will use our example above to illustrate scaling. Say television is the easiest medium to use, so most people use it first; radios are the next easiest, newspapers the next, and magazines the hardest. If media use were unidimensional, no one would employ a more difficult medium without first employing all of the easier ones. No one would use newspapers for campaign news unless he or she used radio and television. Those who used magazines would use all of the other media. Thus, if media use were perfectly unidimensional in the Guttman sense, these are the only patterns that would appear:

4. uses all media
3. uses television, radio, newspapers
2. uses television, radio
1. uses television
0. uses no media
9. missing data

Table 9.13 illustrates the same notion in a slightly different form. Each column gives data from a set of respondents. The columns headed by the letters A through E correspond to the perfectly cumulative categories. Below these columns are shown the ordinal scores (4, 3, 2, 1, 0) of the persons in each category on a Guttman scale. If only the cumulative patterns A through E appeared in the data, then a perfect Guttman scale would be formed. The appearance of the other possible response patterns (such as W through Z) is counted as an "error"—that is, as a divergence from the perfect Guttman scale.

Measuring the Extent of Cumulation.   To determine the extent to which a set of questions form a Guttman scale, it is necessary to count the number of errors that occur in the responses. The number of errors for a pattern is the least number of responses that must be changed in order to obtain a valid pattern. Consider, for example, pattern W. Since that pattern most closely matches valid pattern A (except that the person does not watch television), it scores 4 with one error. X most closely resembles valid pattern E, so it is scored 0 with one error. Sometimes an error pattern is equally close to more than one valid pattern. Thus pattern Y can be scored 4 with two errors, 2 with two errors, or 0 with two errors. Scoring where data are missing is often possible, as with pattern Z, which is said to fit pattern A without errors. Note that altogether there are four errors present, given the frequency of each response pattern in Table 9.13. The proportion of the total number of responses that fit the valid patterns is known as the *coefficient of reproducibility*. Its calculation is illustrated beneath Table 9.13.

When the coefficient of reproducibility is 1.00, each person's responses are perfectly reproducible from the person's score on the scale.

Guttman originally suggested that a reproducibility of at least .90 should be required for a good scale. However, experience with that criterion suggests that it is too low and that a criterion of .95 might be more realistic. The coefficient of scalability shows how much better a scale's reproducibility is than the minimum reproducibility that would be expected given the marginal frequencies of the responses to each question in the scale. The point behind this measure is that if, say, 90 percent of the respondents give the same answer on a question, then at most 10 percent of the responses on that question can produce scale errors (since there would be no error if all the respondents were identical). Consequently, we can find the lowest limit of the coefficient of reproducibility given the numbers of respondents that answered the questions in each way. We could then compute the improvement of the actual reproducibility over that minimum value. The coefficient of scalability is the ratio of the actual improvement to the maximum potential improvement.

For example, while the coefficient of reproducibility for Table 9.13 is .99, it could not possibly be lower than .68, given the marginal distributions of the answers. The actual improvement in reproducibility is .99 − .68 = .31, while the maximum potential improvement is 1.00 − .68 = .32. Thus the actual improvement is 97 percent (.31/.32) of the potential improvement, and the coefficient of scalability has a value of .97. Generally the coefficient of scalability should be at least .60 for a good scale.

Because the scoring and error-counting procedures outlined so far are difficult and time-consuming, a simpler and quicker procedure is often substituted. This second procedure is used in most computer programs for Guttman scaling. While both procedures are usually referred to as Guttman scaling, they do give slightly different results. For example, pattern W would receive a score of 3 for the fast procedure because the respondent uses three media: pattern W differs from the valid pattern with three media used (B) by using magazines (one error) but not television (a second error). Thus pattern W would be given a score of 1 (since one medium is used) but with two errors, and pattern Y would be given a score of 2 with two errors. Also, in order to speed calculation, patterns containing missing data are dropped from the analysis in the second procedure. This rapid Guttman scaling procedure does produce some scores that differ from those produced by classical Guttman scaling, but the two sets of scores are highly correlated with each other. They also have similar correlations with other variables.

Table 9.13 Media Use Scale

Medium Used	Valid Patterns					Error Patterns				Total
	A	B	C	D	E	W	X	Y	Z	
Television	yes	yes	yes	yes	no	no	no	no	yes	
Radio	yes	yes	yes	no	no	yes	no	yes	?	
Newspapers	yes	yes	no	no	no	yes	yes	no	yes	
Magazines	yes	no	no	no	no	yes	no	yes	yes	
Frequency	20	19	19	19	19	1	1	1	1	100
Score	4	3	2	1	0	4	0	?	4	
Number of errors	0	0	0	0	0	1	1	2	0	4
Number of yeses	4	3	2	1	0	3	1	2	?	
Second error count	0	0	0	0	0	2	2	2	?	6

Guttman's method: Number of errors = 4

Number of responses = (Number of people)
× (Number of items) − Amount of missing data
= (100) × (4) − 1 = 399

$$CR = \text{Coefficient of reproducibility} = 1 - \frac{\text{(Number of errors)}}{\text{(Number of responses)}}$$

$$= 1 - \frac{4}{399} = .99$$

MMR = Minimum marginal reproducibility = .68

$$\text{Coefficient of scalability} = \frac{CR - MMR}{1 - MMR} = \frac{.99 - .68}{1.00 - .68} = .97$$

Alternate method: 6 errors, 396 responses; Reproducibility = .98

NOTE: "?" is used to represent missing data.

The quick procedure yields an error count that is about twice as high as the classical Guttman count, which immediately lowers the reproducibility. Under this error-counting procedure, a .90 reproducibility would be considered good.

Number of Dimensions. The essential difference between an index and a scale is that index construction simply adds together the scores on the individual questions, while scaling is concerned with the pattern of responses. According to the Guttman scaling logic, if the responses do not fit a cumulative pattern, then they do not measure the same underlying concept or dimension and should not be combined into a Guttman scale. Sometimes it makes sense to drop a variable that is not cumulative with the remaining variables. Other times it might be possible to construct two separate dimensions, such as one for print media and one for broadcast media.

It should be remembered that whether a set of questions can be formed into a Guttman scale is an empirical question. A scale with a sufficiently high coefficient of reproducibility may or may not be useful and valid. In fact, researchers are sometimes interested only in whether a set of questions constitute a Guttman scale. In such a circumstance, the researcher might argue that a set of questions on governmental policy all represent the same dimension. For example, a researcher might argue that attitudes toward a set of policies represent a liberal-conservative dimension because they form a Guttman scale. In other situations the researcher forms the scale as the first step in a more complex scheme of analysis. For example, individuals could be scored on a liberal-to-conservative scale so that these scores can be related to income and education.

Often it is impossible to account for a set of attitudes with a single Guttman scale. For example, if we had a set of questions on international and domestic policy, we might find that those who are liberal on domestic issues are not necessarily liberal on international issues. Separate Guttman scales would then be needed for domestic and international issues. We would say that there are two dimensions underlying the data. In other circumstances more than two dimensions may be required.

Incidentally, there are several ways besides Guttman scaling to examine the dimensionality of data. These procedures can handle interval variables as well as ordinal measures and dichotomous data. However, the other scaling procedures are more complicated than we can consider in this introductory book.

SUMMARY

Statistical analysis of a single variable begins with generating its frequency distribution and possibly displaying it graphically. The next step is computing an appropriate measure of central tendency, usually the mean for numeric variables, the median for ordinal variables, and the mode for nominal variables. The variance and standard deviation are measures of dispersion for numeric variables.

We often require different forms of variables than are available in the data set. Simple recoding often suffices to construct the needed variables. Additive indices are also useful. However, when several variables are combined into an index, it makes sense to check first whether they all pertain to the same dimension. Guttman scaling is one test of such dimensionality.

Data analysis should involve more than single-variable statistics. However, inspection of these statistics for each variable should be a routine part of any data analysis. They give the researcher an extra chance to check for errors in the data that might escape detection in a multiple-variable analysis. Additionally, they help the researcher understand the variables to be used in further analysis.

Questions

Partisanship

Republican	250
Independent	350
Democrat	400

1. The total number of cases in this table is _____ .
2. What proportion of the people are Republican? _____ .
3. What proportion are Democrat? _____ .
4. What proportion are independent? _____ .
5. What categories have probably been omitted from this table? _____ .
6. What is the partisanship of the average American according to these data? _____ .
7. Five people gave the incumbent president the following thermometer ratings: 95, 85, 80, 75, and 65. Find the mean thermometer score, the variance, and the standard deviation for the group.
8. You want to determine whether young people are more likely to consider themselves political independents than are older people. However, the only available measure of partisanship is coded (0) strong Democrat, (1) weak Democrat, (2) independent leaning to Democrat, (3) pure independent, (4) independent leaning to Republican, (5) weak Republican, (6) strong Republican. Construct a new variable coded (1) independent (including independent leaners), (2) partisan.
9. You want to determine whether strength of partisanship is related to whether a person votes a split ticket (votes Republican for some offices and Democrat for others). However, the only measures of voting are presidential vote, coded (1) Democrat, (2) Republican, (3) not vote; and congressional vote, coded: (1) Democrat, (2) Republican, (3) not vote. Construct a new variable coded: (1) straight ticket, (2) split ticket, (3) skipped voting for at least one race.
10. You hypothesize that a person's level of education affects his or her amount of campaign participation. However, the available questions on

participation are separate questions on attendance at political meetings, coded (1) yes, (0) no, (9) missing data; working for a party or candidate, coded (1) yes, (0) no, (9) missing data; and giving campaign contributions, coded (1) yes, (2) no, (9) missing data. How would you construct an additive index from these questions to yield an overall measure of campaign participation?

11. If the above questions on campaign participation formed a Guttman scale, with party meetings being the most frequent activity and campaign contributions being the least frequent activity, then what response patterns would fit the scale perfectly?

10

Statistical Inference for Means

When studying a sample, it is important to be sure that the results are not due to chance. If the sample is small, the odds that it is atypical are great. Another sample of the same size might give very different results. Consequently, one does not want to overgeneralize on the basis of small samples. In this chapter we describe procedures for statistical inference that are used for small simple random samples to determine what inferences to the target population safely can be made.

PROBABILITY THEORY

In order to understand statistical inference, it is necessary to be familiar with probability theory.

The Meaning of Probability

We often speak of the probability of an event, such as the probability of drawing a red card if one randomly selects one card from an ordinary deck of playing cards. What is a probability? It is a number between 0 and 1 that is associated with an event. These numbers are assigned so that they indicate how likely it is that the event will occur under certain conditions. A common interpretation of probabilities (although not the only interpretation) relates to the *relative frequency* of events. For example, the relative frequency of red cards in a deck is the ratio of the number of red cards (26) to the total number of cards in the deck (52): 26/52 = .50; the probability of drawing a red card from a full deck is .50. By similar logic, the probability of drawing a black card from the deck is also .50, the probability of drawing a heart is .25, the probability of drawing a diamond is .25, the probability of drawing an ace is 4/52 = .08, and so on.[1]

If we draw one card from the deck, replace it, shuffle, draw again, and keep doing this sampling with replacement a large number of times, the proportion of times that we draw a red card will be very close to .50. Thus, probabilities can refer not only to the relative frequency of events but also to long-term rates of occurrence of events.

Two events are described as mutually exclusive if both cannot occur at once. For example, drawing a red card and drawing a black card are mutually exclusive events, because when one card is drawn it cannot be both red and black. Probabilities of mutually exclusive events can be added up, so the probability of drawing either a red card or a black card is .50 + .50 = 1.00, or certainty. Similarly, drawing a heart and a diamond are mutually exclusive events, so the probability of drawing either a heart or a diamond is .25 + .25 = .50, the probability of drawing a red card. Probabilities of events that are not mutually exclusive cannot be added together. For example drawing a heart and drawing an ace are not mutually exclusive because drawing an ace of hearts would satisfy both events at once, so the probability of drawing either a heart or an ace (16/52) is the proportion of cards that are either hearts or aces or both. This does not equal the sum of their separate probabilities: (13/52 + 4/52 = 17/52).

A set of events is called *exhaustive* if all possible outcomes are accounted for by the events. Drawing a red card and drawing a black card are exhaustive events because any card drawn from the deck satisfies one event or the other.

A *probability distribution* states the probabilities of a set of mutually exclusive and exhaustive events. For example, the probability distribution associated with the color of a card in an ordinary deck of playing cards is .50 for a red card and .50 for a black card. Similarly, the probability distribution for the suit of a card in an ordinary deck of playing cards is .25 for a heart, .25 for a diamond, .25 for a club, and .25

---

[1]There are two common interpretations of probabilities in addition to relative frequency. One is *long-term frequency*, such as deciding that a coin is biased when it lands heads up 75 percent of the time in a series of 1,000 coin flips. The other is a *subjective interpretation*, as when people guess the likelihood that the vice president will succeed the president.

for a spade. Note that the probabilities sum to 1.00 in each case because the events are mutually exclusive and exhaustive.

The Normal Probability Distribution

Some theoretical probability distributions are particularly important in statistics. The most important one is the *normal distribution*. The shape of the distribution follows a precise mathematical equation that is graphed in Figure 10.1. The horizontal axis shows the value of the variable, and the vertical axis is the relative frequency of each value.

The horizontal axis of Figure 10.1 is calibrated in standard deviation units from the mean, called *z scores*. Recall from Chapter 9 that the standard deviation is a measure of the dispersion of the values of the variable. Z scores are computed according to the following formula:

$$z = (X - \overline{X})/s$$

where $\overline{X}$ is the mean value of the variable X and s is its standard deviation. For example, if the mean of a variable is 10 and its standard deviation is 5, then a score of 15 is one standard deviation above the mean ($z = +1$); a score of 20 is two standard deviations above the mean ($z = +2$), a score of 5 would be one standard deviation below the mean ($z = -1$), and so on. A z score of 0 always represents the mean of the variable.

If a variable has a normal distribution, then its mean is at the center of the normal curve. Values of the variable closest to the mean occur

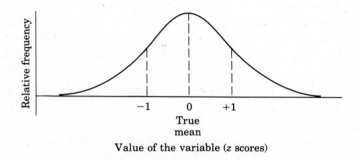

Figure 10.1
The Normal Distribution

most frequently, while values farthest away occur least frequently. For example, if our variable is a set of test scores with a normal distribution, scores near the mean occur more frequently than scores far above or below the mean.

Areas under the Normal Curve.   The normal curve is constructed so that the area between it and the horizontal axis is one unit. The area under the curve is interpreted as a probability. For example, the probability of a value of a variable falling between the lowest possible value on the horizontal axis and the highest possible value on the horizontal axis is the area under the entire curve, or 1.0—certainty.

Because the mean is at the center of the distribution, the probability of a value being higher than the mean equals the area under the curve to the right of the mean, or half the total area under the curve—.50. The curve is symmetric, so the probability of a value being lower than the mean is exactly the same as the probability of its being above—.50.[2]

The probabilities of other values of the variable can also be obtained by examining the normal curve. For example, the probability of obtaining a value more than one standard deviation below the mean is .16; that is, the area under the curve to the left of one standard deviation unit is .16. Because the curve is symmetrical, the probability of obtaining a value more than one standard deviation above the mean is also .16. Thus, the probability of obtaining a value no greater than one standard deviation unit either side of the mean is:

$$(1.0 - .16) - .16 = .68.$$

Let us consider an example. Imagine that scores on the Graduate Record Examination (GRE) are normally distributed with a mean of 500 and a standard deviation of 100. The probability of a score under 400 (the mean of 500 minus one standard deviation) would be .16, the probability of a score above 600 (500 + 100) would be .16, and the probability of a score between 400 and 600 (plus or minus one standard deviation unit around the mean) would be .68. These values are shown in

---

[2]What about the probability of obtaining *exactly* the mean value? The normal curve is used with continuous numerical variables such as length. There is virtually zero probability of a pencil being exactly three inches long. It might be 3.00012358 inches, but the chances of it being any particular value is infinitesimal. Therefore, we can disregard the possibility of the variable having a value exactly equal to the mean. More generally, the normal curve shows the probability of values falling into particular ranges, not the probability of specific values.

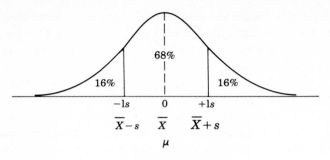

Figure 10.2
One Standard Deviation Range for the Normal Distribution

Figure 10.2. This does not mean that you have a .16 chance of scoring below 400 on the GRE. Instead it means that 16 percent of the students taking the exam score below 400, so the probability that a randomly chosen individual has a score below 400 is .16.

Note that the values in the tails of the distribution (the parts farthest from the center) are particularly unlikely. Extreme values are much less likely than moderate values. In fact, the probability of obtaining any range of values declines as the range moves away from the mean either below (to the left) or above (to the right). The probability of obtaining a value more than 1.96 standard deviation units below the mean is only .025, as is the probability of obtaining a value more than 1.96 standard deviations above the mean. Therefore, the probability of obtaining a value not more than 1.96 standard deviation units from the mean in either direction is $(1.0 - 0.25) - .025 = .95$ (see Figure 10.3). In the GRE example, this corresponds to a .95 probability of obtaining a score between 304 [which is $500 - (1.96 \times 100)$] and 696 [which is $500 + (1.96 \times 100)$]. The chance of obtaining extreme scores below 304 and above 696 is only .05.

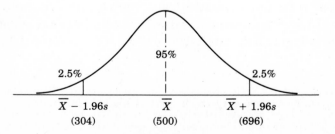

Figure 10.3
Ninety-Five Percent Range for the Normal Distribution

Table 10.1 Areas under the Normal Curve. (Entries show the probability of obtaining a z value above z_0. Areas are found by symmetry for negative values of z_0.)

Area $= \Pr(z \geqslant z_0)$

$0 \quad z_0$

z_0	\multicolumn{10}{c}{Second Decimal Place of z_0}
	0.00	0.01	0.02	0.03	0.04	0.05	0.06	0.07	0.08	0.09
0.0	.5000	.4960	.4920	.4880	.4840	.4801	.4761	.4721	.4681	.4641
0.1	.4602	.4562	.4522	.4483	.4443	.4404	.4364	.4325	.4286	.4247
0.2	.4207	.4168	.4129	.4090	.4052	.4013	.3974	.3936	.3897	.3859
0.3	.3821	.3783	.3745	.3707	.3669	.3632	.3594	.3557	.3520	.3483
0.4	.3446	.3409	.3372	.3336	.3300	.3264	.3228	.3192	.3156	.3121
0.5	.3085	.3050	.3015	.2981	.2946	.2912	.2877	.2843	.2810	.2776
0.6	.2743	.2709	.2676	.2643	.2611	.2578	.2546	.2514	.2483	.2451
0.7	.2420	.2389	.2358	.2327	.2297	.2266	.2236	.2207	.2177	.2148
0.8	.2119	.2090	.2061	.2033	.2005	.1977	.1949	.1922	.1894	.1867
0.9	.1841	.1814	.1788	.1762	.1736	.1711	.1685	.1660	.1635	.1611
1.0	.1587	.1562	.1539	.1515	.1492	.1469	.1446	.1423	.1401	.1379
1.1	.1357	.1335	.1314	.1292	.1271	.1251	.1230	.1210	.1190	.1170
1.2	.1151	.1131	.1112	.1093	.1075	.1056	.1038	.1020	.1003	.0985
1.3	.0968	.0951	.0934	.0918	.0901	.0885	.0869	.0853	.0838	.0823
1.4	.0808	.0793	.0778	.0764	.0749	.0735	.0721	.0708	.0694	.0681
1.5	.0668	.0655	.0643	.0630	.0618	.0606	.0594	.0582	.0571	.0559
1.6	.0548	.0537	.0526	.0516	.0505	.0495	.0485	.0475	.0465	.0455
1.7	.0446	.0436	.0427	.0418	.0409	.0401	.0392	.0384	.0375	.0367
1.8	.0359	.0351	.0344	.0336	.0329	.0322	.0314	.0307	.0301	.0294
1.9	.0287	.0281	.0274	.0268	.0262	.0256	.0250	.0244	.0239	.0233
2.0	.0228	.0222	.0217	.0212	.0207	.0202	.0197	.0192	.0188	.0183
2.1	.0179	.0174	.0170	.0166	.0162	.0158	.0154	.0150	.0146	.0143
2.2	.0139	.0136	.0132	.0129	.0125	.0122	.0119	.0116	.0113	.0110
2.3	.0107	.0104	.0102	.0099	.0096	.0094	.0091	.0089	.0087	.0084
2.4	.0082	.0080	.0078	.0075	.0073	.0071	.0069	.0068	.0066	.0064
2.5	.0062	.0060	.0059	.0057	.0055	.0054	.0052	.0051	.0049	.0048
2.6	.0047	.0045	.0044	.0043	.0041	.0040	.0039	.0038	.0037	.0036
2.7	.0035	.0034	.0033	.0032	.0031	.0030	.0029	.0028	.0027	.0026
2.8	.0026	.0025	.0024	.0023	.0023	.0022	.0021	.0021	.0020	.0019
2.9	.0019	.0018	.0018	.0017	.0016	.0016	.0015	.0015	.0014	.0014

SOURCE: Generated by the authors, using the cdform function in SPSS-X.

Since it is difficult to read the area from a curve such as shown in Figure 10.1, statisticians have constructed tables from which the area can be read more easily. Table 10.1 gives the probabilities of particular ranges of values under the normal curve. To read the table, choose a number of standard deviation units (z) above the mean. The table shows what proportion of the area under the normal curve is above that z value. For example, to find the area above the mean, look under .00 standard deviations above the mean, and you will find in row .0 and column .00 the number .5000, indicating that half the area is above the mean. To find the area above one standard deviation unit, look under z of 1.00—row 1.0 and column .00—and you will find the number .1587, which we rounded to .16 for Figure 10.2 and in the above example. To find the area above .45 standard deviations above the mean, use row .4 and column .05 to find the value .3264.

The normal-curve table can also be used to obtain the z values (number of standard deviation units above the mean) associated with certain areas. To find the z value for which there is only a .025 probability of higher values, find .025 in the body of the table—it is in row 1.9 and column .06, so the z value is 1.96. Similarly, to find the z value for which there is only a .005 probability of higher values, find .005 in the body of the table—it is in row 2.5 and between columns .07 and .08, so the z value is about 2.575. (More precise tables indicate it is actually 2.576.)

The table gives probabilities only for positive z's. However, the symmetry of the normal curve permits the same table to be used for negative z's. If you want to know the proportion of the area under the curve less than $z = -1.28$, you would look under row 1.2 and column .08 to get the value .1003.

The Importance of the Normal Distribution.   The normal curve is important for a number of reasons. Some variables have normal distributions, although most social-science variables do not have normal distributions. Researchers often assume that the errors in measurements for a variable have a normal distribution. That assumption considerably simplifies the mathematics in some statistical proofs. The normal distribution often serves as a good approximation to other distributions, such as the number of heads in fifty tosses of a coin. Finally, and most important, even when a variable does not have a normal distribution, the mean of that variable for a large sample can be regarded as having come from a normal distribution of sample means. This result is known as the *central-limit theorem.*

The Central-Limit Theorem

Sampling Distribution.   In order to explain the central limit theorem, we need some additional terminology. In a population there

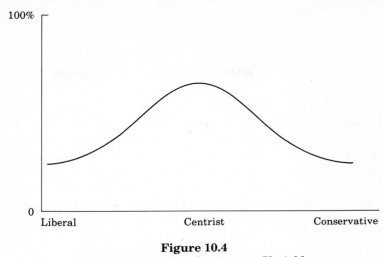

Figure 10.4
The Population Distribution on a Variable
Source: Hypothetical

is a distribution of cases on a variable, such as the one shown in Figure 10.4. In a random sample of cases from that population there is a distribution of sample values on the variable — the sample distribution. We can graph that distribution in a fashion similar to that used in Figure 10.4, and we can calculate the mean for that sample.

Say we calculate the mean for a second independent random sample, a third, and so on for a large number of samples. If we look at the means of all these samples together, we have a distribution of sample means, known as the *sampling distribution of means*, or often simply as the *sampling distribution*.

According to the central-limit theorem, for very large numbers of large samples, the sampling distribution of means is approximately normal; that is, it is approximately the same shape as the normal distribution. As an example, assume GRE scores have a true mean of 500 and a standard deviation of 100 in the population. We give this test to one sample of people and get a mean of 510 for that sample. Another sample might have a mean of 485, and so on. If our samples are large and we take a lot of them, these means would have a normal distribution. That distribution of sample means is what we call the sampling distribution.

Standard Error.   The mean of the sampling distribution is the same as the population mean of the variable. The standard deviation of the sampling distribution is called the *standard error of the mean*:

$$s_m = \sqrt{s^2/(N-1)} = s\sqrt{(N-1)}$$

For a sample of 26 students for the GRE example above, the standard error would be 20 (the standard deviation of 100 divided by the square root of 26 − 1).

We now know that GRE sample means have a normal distribution with a mean 500 and a standard error of 20. Recall our earlier results on the probability of values with a normal distribution. There is a .68 probability of a value being within one standard deviation of the mean; hence there is a .68 probability of the sample mean being between 480 and 520 for a sample of 26. There is only a .05 probability of a value being farther than 1.96 standard deviations away from the mean, so there is only a .025 probability of the sample mean being below 460.8 [which is 500 − (1.96 × 20)] and a .025 probability of it being above 539.2 [which is 500 + (1.96 × 20)].

You may be wondering why we are using 20 for our calculation of the range of sample values for the mean in this last example but used 100 in the earlier example. In the earlier example we were examining the distribution of cases, so we used the standard deviation (100). When we examined the distribution of possible means in the more recent example, we used the standard error of the mean (20), an estimate of the standard deviation of the sampling distribution.

Note that the larger the sample, the smaller the standard error. As a result, the bounds on the sample means will be narrower for larger samples. If the sample in the GRE example were of 101 students, the standard error would be 10. There would be a .68 probability of the sample mean being between 490 and 510 and only a .05 probability of the sample mean being either below 480.4 or above 519.6. A sample has to be nearly four times as large to cut the standard error in half. This is what we should expect: There should be less chance of a large sample giving an atypical mean (a mean far away from the population mean) than of a small sample giving an atypical mean.

The *law of large numbers* makes this point more generally. For random samples, the larger the sample size, the more likely that the sample mean is very close to the population mean. A small sample can have an atypical mean, but it is less likely that a large sample will. Of course, if the sample is large enough to include the entire population, there is no difference at all between the sample mean and the population mean.

We have noted the standard error's dependence on the sample size. The standard error of the mean also depends on the standard deviation of the variable. The more dispersed the observations, the less confidence one can have that the observed mean is the correct one. Conversely, if there is little dispersion in the observations, one can have more confidence in a sample of the same size.

Assumptions.   The central-limit theorem makes no assumptions about the shape of the variable's distribution. Even if a variable has a distribution that is very different from the normal curve shape (as in Figure 10.5, where the variable is bimodal and so takes on only very small or very large values but never moderate values), the means of large samples will be very close to the population mean, and the distribution of means of the samples will approximate a normal distribution. Thus the central-limit theorem makes the normal distribution important for data analysis, even if the variables themselves do not have normal distributions.

The central-limit theorem requires that the population variance of the variable be known. Rarely are we in a position to know the true population variance for a variable. For large samples this is no problem; the normal distribution still holds even when we must estimate the population variance with the sample variance. For small samples the distribution of means sampling has a shape that is near that of the normal distribution but that is not exactly the same. The distribution of means for small samples has the shape of the *t-distribution*. We shall present this distribution in greater detail later in this chapter. Statistical inference with the *t*-distribution is very similar to statistical in-

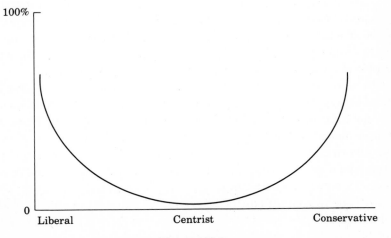

Figure 10.5
A Bimodal Distribution of Opinion
SOURCE: Hypothetical

ference with the normal distribution except that there is a slightly greater chance for extreme means.

So far we have assumed that the population mean is known. We have looked for the probability of an atypical sample mean given a known population mean. In practice the population mean is not known, and it is too costly to take repeated samples in order to get a sampling distribution of means. Usually, we have only a single mean and its standard deviation. In statistical inference we reverse the central-limit theorem. We act as if our one sample mean represents a sample from a normal distribution of means. The central-limit theorem indicates that if the population mean were known, a sample mean far away from it would be unlikely. Even if the population mean were not known, it should be rare for the population's mean to be far away from the sample mean. Therefore, we make inferences about the population mean on the basis of the sample mean.

STATISTICAL INFERENCE

There are actually several different approaches to statistical inference. We begin by describing the classic one: hypothesis testing.

Hypothesis Testing

As an example of hypothesis testing, assume that we know that scores on the GRE have a normal distribution and a standard deviation of 100. We take a sample of 26 from your university and obtain a mean of 541. We know that the national average on the test is 500. Does the sample show that your school differs from the national value?

The null hypothesis is that the population mean for your school is 500. The hypothesis-testing procedure is therefore useful. As shown in the last section, the standard error for this example is 20. Thus, our sample mean is more than two standard error units away from the null hypothesis mean. If the null hypothesis were correct, the probability of a sample mean more than two standard error units away would be less than .05, so we can reject the null hypothesis at the 0.05 level. Your school's mean is significantly different from the national mean of 500.

Incidentally, the use of the significance level of .05 is arbitrary. With the .05 level, there is only a 5 percent probability of obtaining the observed results by chance, and this is usually considered decent betting odds in statistical inference. However, fields such as medicine often demand more stringent testing, and therefore use .01 or even the .001 level. Some exploratory studies are less stringent, using the .1 level. The example here would not be found significant if the .01 or .001 levels were being used, but is significant at the .1 and .05 levels. If one chose the significance level after conducting the test, it would be possible to manipulate which results are found significant, so it is important to choose the significance level before inspecting the results. The .05 level is the most conventional in surveys, so we use it through the remainder of the text.

Critical Ratio. To perform hypothesis testing more formally, one would compute a *test statistic* known as the *critical ratio*, or *z*. The critical ratio is the difference between the sample mean (X) and the null-hypothesis mean (which we denote by the Greek letter mu, μ) divided by the standard error of the mean: $z = (X - \mu)/s_m$. The normal curve table gives the *z* values required for different levels of significance. *Statistical significance* at a particular level means that the probability of rejecting a true null hypothesis is less than or equal to that level. The *z* value required for significance at the .05 level is 1.96. In our example the *z* value is $(541 - 500)/20 = 2.05$. Since it is greater than 1.96, we reject the null hypothesis. If *z* were less than 1.96, we would not reject the null hypothesis.

Critical Region. An equivalent procedure for hypothesis testing involves setting up a *critical region* of values (or *rejection region*); a sample mean in the region would justify rejection of the null hypothesis. For the normal distribution there is a 5 percent (or .05) chance of obtaining a value more than 1.96 standard errors from the population mean. When the population mean for the GRE is 500 (the null hypothesis) and the standard error is 20, there is a .05 chance of a sample obtaining a mean GRE below 460.8 [$500 - (1.96 \times 20)$], or above 539.2 [$500 + (1.96 \times 20)$]. Therefore, the critical region in which we would reject the null hypothesis is below 460.8 and above 539.2. The critical region corresponds to the darkened area in Figure 10.6. In our example above the sample-mean GRE was 541; hence, we would reject the null hypothesis.

The critical region immediately indicates what action to take for any sample's mean. We would not reject the null hypothesis if the sample's mean GRE were 535; if the sample's mean GRE were 455, we would reject the null hypothesis; and so on. Thus, the critical-region calculation provides all the information of the critical-ratio test and is simple to use.

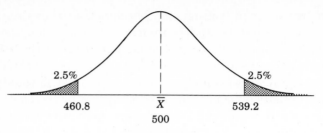

Figure 10.6
Critical Region at the 0.05 Level

Probability Value

The critical ratio and the critical region share a disadvantage: They are tied to a particular level of significance (the .05 level in our example). A researcher who wants to use a different level of significance from one used in a published research report would be unable to quickly employ the new level. An alternative is to calculate the probability value for the sample mean.

The probability-value approach is an equivalent method of hypothesis testing. The normal-curve table shows the probability of different z values. In our example we had a z value of 2.05. Table 10.1 indicates that there is only a .02 chance of obtaining a z value above 2.05 by chance. There is also a .02 chance of obtaining a z value below -2.05 by chance. So the overall probability of a sample producing a mean at least 2.05 standard error units from the population mean is .02 + .02 = .04, the probability value or p value. The p value is the probability that the null hypothesis is true. If p is less than .05, we say that the result is significant at the .05 level.

If we decided to use the .05 significance level, we would reject the null hypothesis, since p is less than .05. This is entirely consistent with the results of the critical-ratio and critical-region procedures. However, the p value permits other researchers who believe the .01 level is more appropriate to decide not to reject the null hypothesis. The probability-value procedure relieves some of the arbitrary character of significance levels, so many researchers prefer to report probability values instead of hypothesis tests.

Note that if our data did not contradict the null hypothesis, we would accept the null hypothesis. We could never prove the null hypothesis because we can never prove that the population's mean GRE is 500 (or any other value) on the basis of a sample. At most, we can say that the sample is not inconsistent with such a possibility. As we argued in

Chapter 8, science proceeds by a series of disproofs rather than proofs. This is part of the reason that Type II error is deemphasized. After all, if the null hypothesis is wrong, a later study is likely to disprove it conclusively.

Many researchers are dissatisfied with the asymmetry between the two types of error. Others desire more information about the population mean than just whether or not an arbitrary null hypothesis is rejected. As a result, hypothesis testing is not very popular in some social-science fields. An alternative way of reporting statistical inferences is establishing confidence intervals for the unknown population mean. This approach is based on the same statistical theory as hypothesis testing, but yields a range of possible values for the mean rather than a test of whether or not the mean has a specific value.

Confidence Intervals

If we are willing to accept a 5 percent chance of making an error, we can construct a *confidence interval*. This is a range of values in which we can be 95 percent sure that the true population mean falls. If we took a large number of random samples and constructed confidence intervals for all of them, 95 percent of them would contain the population mean. The 95 percent confidence interval extends 1.96 standard errors on either side of the sample mean.

In our example the sample mean for your university was 541 and the standard error was 20. Therefore the confidence interval ranges from 501.8 [541 $-$ (1.96 $\times$ 20)], to 580.2 [541 $+$ (1.96 $\times$ 20)]. On the basis of our sample of only 26 cases, we should be able to conclude at a high level of confidence (95 percent) that the population-mean GRE for your university is between 501.8 and 580.2 (Figure 10.7).[3]

The calculation of the confidence interval is similar to the calculation of the critical region. Both involve a radius of 1.96 times the standard error. The critical region was centered on the null-hypothesis value, 500 in our example, and indicated which sample means would lead to rejection of the null hypothesis (those below 460.8 and those above 539.2). By contrast, we do not require a null hypothesis in order to compute a confidence interval. It is centered on the sample mean (541 in our example). It indicates the region (501.8 to 580.2) in which

---

[3]Because the national mean of 500 does not fall into this 95 percent confidence interval, we see once again that the mean for your school is significantly greater than the national mean.

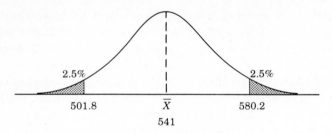

Figure 10.7
Ninety-Five Percent Confidence Interval for the Mean

the population mean is 95 percent likely to fall. Note that our earlier null-hypothesis value of 500 does not fall within the confidence interval. The two procedures always lead to identical conclusions with the type of test described so far. That is not the case in making directional tests, described in the next section.

Directional Tests

In the hypothesis-testing procedure considered above, the sample mean can be either above or below the hypothesized mean. In some situations, however, the researcher is interested in only one of those possibilities. Say, for example, that the GRE is known to have a mean of 500 for the population of college seniors. If we had a sample of students from elite universities, we might be interested only in whether their abilities are significantly greater than those of the population. We would strongly believe that the mean for the population of students from which our sample was selected could not be less than 500. We want to test the null hypothesis that the mean for the population of elite universities was 500 or less against the research hypothesis that the mean is greater than 500.

Our previous significance testing involved *nondirectional tests*, or *two-tailed tests*, in which we were interested in whether our sample deviated significantly in either direction from the population mean. We looked at the probability of a sample mean at least 1.96 standard errors less than the population mean as well as the probability of a sample mean 1.96 or more standard errors above the population mean. The probability of these two extreme conditions together was .05. In *directional*, or *one-tailed*, tests, only one of these possibilities is of interest. There is a .025 chance of obtaining a sample mean 1.96 standard errors above the population mean. So to operate at the .05 level of significance, we have to modify the value 1.96. The normal-curve table indicates that there is a .05 chance of obtaining a z value greater than 1.645. Therefore, for the same level of significance, in directional tests, we substitute $+1.645$ for $+1.96$ and -1.96.

We can use any of our earlier hypothesis-testing procedures for a directional test. First, we can calculate a critical ratio and see if it is greater than 1.645. Second, we can establish a critical region greater than 1.645 standard errors above the null hypothesis mean. Third, we can use the normal-curve table to find the probability of a z value more extreme than our obtained z value and then see if it is less than .05. However, if we chose to construct a 95 percent confidence interval, we would still construct it 1.96 standard error units around the sample mean, so the confidence interval would not be identical to directional hypothesis testing.

Since the sample mean of 541 in our example was significant at the .05 level with a nondirectional test, it would also be significant with a directional test. After all, if the z value or critical ratio is greater than 1.96, then it certainly is greater than 1.645. Assume instead that the sample-mean GRE is 535. We would not reject the null hypothesis with a sample-mean GRE of 535 for a nondirectional test. What about a directional test? For 535, the z value would be 1.75. That is greater than 1.645; therefore, we would reject the null hypothesis that the population mean is 500 or less. With a sample of 26, a sample-mean GRE of 535 would be enough to show that there is a 95 percent chance that the population mean is greater than 500. The critical region (Figure 10.8) for this test would involve rejecting the null hypothesis for sample means above 532.9 $[500 + (1.645 \times 20)]$. If the null hypothesis were true, the probability of sample-mean GRE of 535 would be .04 (the value in Table 10.1 for a z of 1.75); hence, we would reject the null hypothesis at the .05 level.

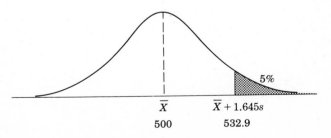

Figure 10.8
Critical Region for Nondirectional Test

Thus, a mean that is not significant in a nondirectional test can be significant in a directional test. Since nondirectional tests are more conservative, it is wrong to use directional tests if you have no idea which direction to test until after seeing whether the sample mean is above or below the hypothesized mean. However, in some situations one direction may make no sense or the researcher may be certain of the direction. In these cases directional tests should be used.

The *t*-Distribution

The previous discussion has assumed that the population standard deviation is known. We rarely know the population standard deviation; we can only estimate it on the basis of a sample. However, the sampling distribution of means is not exactly normal when dealing with an estimated standard deviation. Instead, it has the *t-distribution*. That distribution has a shape (Figure 10.9) that looks very much like the normal distribution except that extreme values are slightly more likely. To complicate matters further, there is not one *t*-distribution but several, depending on the sample size. We define the *degrees of freedom* for a *t*-distribution as the sample size minus one. In significance testing and for establishing confidence intervals, we use the *t*-distribution for the appropriate degrees of freedom instead of the normal distribution. It happens, though, that with a large number of cases the *t*-distribution is virtually identical to the normal distribution. Therefore, the normal distribution can still be used for samples of 120 or more. We switch to the *t*-distribution only for smaller samples.

We now return to the nondirectional null hypothesis of a mean GRE of 500. Say that a sample of 26 leads to a mean of 541 with an estimated standard error of 20. In that case the appropriate test would involve the

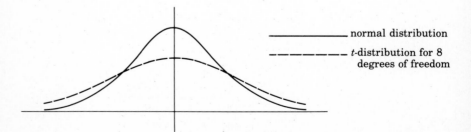

Figure 10.9
A Comparison of *t*-Distribution and Normal Distribution

t-distribution based on $(N - 1 =)$ 25 degrees of freedom. Table 10.2 shows that a value of 2.06 would be required for significance in this instance rather than the 1.96 used for the normal distribution. Our t value would be 2.05 [(541 − 500)/20], less than the 2.06 required for significance at the .05 level. Therefore, we would not reject the possibility that the mean GRE is 500. Table 10.2 also shows that a value of 1.71 is required for a directional test for 25 degrees of freedom. Because the t value in this instance (2.05) is greater than the value required at the .05 level (1.71), we reject the null hypothesis for the directional test, hence conclude that the mean GRE is greater than 500.

Conclusions

If all this seems complicated, it is in practice fairly straightforward. First, consider whether the sample size is large (120 or greater). If it is, use the normal distribution. If it is small and if the population standard deviation is known, use the normal distribution. If the sample size is small and the population standard deviation is not known, use the t-distribution.

Next decide whether to use a directional or nondirectional test. Nondirectional tests are preferred because they are more conservative. In situations where one direction makes no sense, the test should be directional. Then determine the value required for significance with the distribution that you have chosen.

If several significance tests are run, there is a high probability that at least one will be significant by chance alone. The person who runs 100 significance tests and reports the 5 that turn out to be statistically significant at the .05 level is forgetting that 5 out of 100 tests will be significant by chance. Looking at all the possible tests to see which are significant can thus lead to incorrect conclusions.

COMPARING TWO MEANS

So far we have described how to test whether an observed sample mean is different from a specified value. In this section we describe how to test whether two observed sample means are different.

To illustrate the problem, say that a simple random sample of eighteen colleges, divided into private and public colleges, have mean GREs as shown in Table 10.3. The average GRE score for the public colleges in 520 and that for the private colleges is 525, so there is a differ-

Table 10.2 Critical Ratios for the *t*-Distribution. (Entries show the *t* ratio required for significance.)

Pr d.f.	0.05 Directional	0.05 Nondirectional	0.01 Directional	0.01 Nondirectional
1	6.314	12.706	31.821	63.657
2	2.920	4.303	6.965	9.925
3	2.353	3.182	4.541	5.841
4	2.132	2.776	3.747	4.604
5	2.015	2.571	3.365	4.032
6	1.943	2.447	3.143	3.707
7	1.895	2.365	2.998	3.499
8	1.860	2.306	2.896	3.355
9	1.833	2.262	2.821	3.250
10	1.812	2.228	2.764	3.169
11	1.796	2.201	2.718	3.106
12	1.782	2.179	2.681	3.055
13	1.771	2.160	2.650	3.012
14	1.761	2.145	2.624	2.977
15	1.753	2.131	2.602	2.947
16	1.746	2.120	2.583	2.921
17	1.740	2.110	2.567	2.898
18	1.734	2.101	2.552	2.878
19	1.729	2.093	2.539	2.861
20	1.725	2.086	2.528	2.845
21	1.721	2.080	2.518	2.831
22	1.717	2.074	2.508	2.819
23	1.714	2.069	2.500	2.807
24	1.711	2.064	2.492	2.797
25	1.708	2.060	2.485	2.787
26	1.706	2.056	2.479	2.779
27	1.703	2.052	2.473	2.771
28	1.701	2.048	2.467	2.763
29	1.699	2.045	2.462	2.756
30	1.697	2.042	2.457	2.750
40	1.684	2.021	2.423	2.704
60	1.671	2.000	2.390	2.660
120	1.658	1.980	2.358	2.617
∞	1.645	1.960	2.326	2.576

Source: Based on Thomas A. Wonnacott and Ronald J. Wonnacott, *Introductory Statistics*, 2nd. ed. (New York: Wiley, Copyright © 1972), p. 481. Reprinted by permission of John Wiley & Sons, Inc. and Biometrika trustees.

Table 10.3   GRE Scores by Type of College

Public	Private
510	515
509	514
511	516
520	525
519	524
521	526
530	535
529	534
531	536
$\overline{X}_1 = 520.00$	$\overline{X}_2 = 525.00$
$s_1^2 = 67.33$	$s_2^2 = 67.33$
$s_1 = 8.21$	$s_2 = 3.21$

$$\overline{X} = 522.50$$
$$s^2 = 73.58$$
$$s = 8.58$$

SOURCE: Hypothetical.

ence of 5 in the average GRE for the two types of colleges. The important statistical question is whether that difference is real or whether it could be due to chance. Might the difference of 5 be due to the fact that we have examined only a sample of colleges rather than examining the entire population of colleges? Or is the difference of 5 statistically significant? A difference-of-means test is required to answer these questions.

Hypothesis Testing

To determine how to test the statistical significance of the difference between two means, recall how the significance of a single mean was tested above. A critical ratio was computed; the ratio was the difference between the observed and hypothesized means divided by the estimated standard error of the mean: $(\overline{X} - \mu)/est\ s_m$. The test for the significance of a difference of means is similar in form. A critical ratio is computed. The numerator is the observed difference of means instead of the difference between an observed mean and its hypothesized value. The denominator must also be an estimated standard error of the difference: $(est\ s_{\text{diff}})$. Thus, the critical ratio is $(\overline{X}_1 - \overline{X}_2)/(est\ s_{\text{diff}})$.

What is an *estimated standard error of the difference* and how is it computed? The significance of the observed difference of means depends on the dependent variable's variance. In Table 10.3 the observed difference of means is $525 - 520 = 5$. Whether a difference of 5 is large depends on how much variance there is in the GRE scores. If the GREs have little variance, then 5 may be a large difference. If the GREs have great variance, then 5 may be a small difference. More precisely, the significance of the observed difference of means depends on the dependent variable's variance within each category. If there is little variance in mean GREs among private colleges and little variance in mean GREs among public colleges, then 5 may be a large difference. If the mean GREs in either (or both) type of college have great variance, then 5 may be a small difference. The difference between types of colleges is considered large only if it is large with respect to the differences within each type.

As was shown above, statistical testing requires knowing something about the sampling distribution of the statistic to be tested. In this case we need to know about the sampling distribution of the difference between two means. The sample represented in Table 10.3 gives the difference of means for one possible sample. A different sample would probably yield a different difference of means. If we took a very large number of same-size samples of a population and examined the difference between means from sample to sample, we would have a sampling distribution for the difference between two means. If the sample size were large, the distribution would be normal. If not, it would be approximated by the t-distribution. In any case it is the standard deviation of that distribution that is useful for inferential statistics, and it is called the *standard error of the difference of means*.

For separate independent samples from two groups whose population variances are unknown, the standard error of the difference is

$$est\, s_{\text{diff}} = \sqrt{s^2{}_{m_1} + s^2{}_{m_2}}$$

or, using our formula for the standard error of the mean:

$$est\, s_{\text{diff}} = \sqrt{\frac{s_1{}^2}{N_1 - 1} + \frac{s_2{}^2}{N_2 - 1}}$$

If we make the assumption that the variances of the two populations are equal but unknown, we can use both samples' standard deviations to estimate the one underlying population standard deviation:

$$est\, s_{\text{diff}} = \sqrt{\frac{N_1 s_1{}^2 + N_2 s_2{}^2}{N_1 + N_2 - 2}} \sqrt{\frac{1}{N_1} + \frac{1}{N_2}}$$

$$= \sqrt{\frac{\sum (X_{1i} - \overline{X}_1)^2 + \sum (X_{2i} - \overline{X}_2)^2}{N_1 + N_2 - 2}} \sqrt{\frac{1}{N_1} + \frac{1}{N_2}}$$

where X_{1i} is the GRE for the i-th private college, X_1 is the private college mean, and X_{2i} and X_2 are similarly defined for public colleges. The first term is the combined or "pooled" estimate of the standard deviation of the dependent variable.

Returning to the example, the pooled estimate of the standard deviation is

$$\sqrt{\frac{9(8.21)^2 + 9(8.21)^2}{9 + 9 - 2}} = \sqrt{\frac{606 + 606}{16}} = \sqrt{\frac{1212}{16}} = 8.70$$

Therefore, the estimated standard error of the difference is

$$est\, s_{\text{diff}} = 8.70 \sqrt{\frac{1}{9} + \frac{1}{9}} = 8.70(.47) = 4.10$$

The critical ratio for a 5-unit difference is then $5/4.10 = 1.22$. To determine whether this is statistically significant, we employ a t-test using 16 degrees of freedom ($N_1 + N_2 - 2$). According to Table 10.2, a critical ratio of at least 2.12 would be required for statistical significance at the .05 level with 16 degrees of freedom, so the difference is not significant at .05. That is, there is more than a 5 percent probability of obtaining the observed difference by chance if the two types of colleges have the same average GRE. Therefore, we conclude that the data do not demonstrate that public and private colleges have significantly different GREs.

Confidence Intervals

It is also possible to construct a confidence interval for the difference between two means. The confidence interval is the observed difference $\pm\ t(est\, s_{\text{diff}})$, where the estimated standard error of the difference is computed as above.

For the example in Table 10.3, there are 18 cases, so the number of degrees of freedom for the t-value is $18 - 2 = 16$. According to Table

10.2, a t-value of 2.12 corresponds to a 95 percent confidence interval with 16 degrees of freedom. Because the estimated standard error of the difference was found to be 4.10, the confidence interval is the observed difference $5 \pm 2.12 (4.10)$, or 5 ± 8.69, or -3.69 to 13.69.

In other words, we expect that 95 percent of the time the means for the two types of colleges will differ by as much as 8.69 due to random fluctuations in the sample. We conclude, therefore, that the means in Table 10.3 may differ as much as they do by chance alone. Another way to say this is to note that the confidence interval includes zero, so we cannot be sure that the two population means differ from one another.

The confidence interval tells you the maximum amount of difference that may be due to chance. Generally speaking, differences larger than that are statistically significant, and smaller ones are not. An observed difference less than t times ($est\ s_{\text{diff}}$) may represent no actual difference between the two population means. Thus, in the present example the observed difference in means would have to be larger than 8.69 (or smaller than -8.69) to be statistically significant.

Assumptions

The t-distribution has been used so far in this section because of the small sample sizes. For large samples the normal distribution is used.

Also, if the population variance is known, then the population standard deviation is substituted for the pooled standard deviation in the formula for the standard error of the difference.[4] Where population variances are both known and different:

$$s_{\text{diff}} = \sqrt{\frac{s_1^2}{N_1} + \frac{s_2^2}{N_2}}$$

Where population variances are equal and known:

$$s_{\text{diff}} = s \sqrt{\frac{1}{N_1} + \frac{1}{N_2}}$$

Even using the t-distribution, it is necessary that the populations be normally distributed and that the population variances be nearly

---

[4]Actually, it is not quite that simple; $N - 1$ in the denominator should be replaced by N.

equal. Fortunately, these assumptions can be violated without harm if the same sizes are large (for the assumption of normality) and of equal size (for the assumption of equal variance).

Finally, it would be wrong to do a large number of t-tests (or confidence intervals) at the .05 level and report only those that are statistically significant. After all, 5 percent of the tests will be significant by chance alone. Even more than 5 percent will be significant by chance if the tests are not independent of one another, as if we separately tested the significance of the difference in mean tax rates between religious and nonreligious private colleges, religious and public colleges, nonreligious and public colleges. When comparing several means, procedures for analysis of variance (which are beyond the scope of this book) must be used.

SUMMARY

When dealing with samples, it is necessary to check whether one's results are statistically significant, particularly when the samples are small. According to the central-limit theorem, the sampling distribution of means has a normal distribution, regardless of the distribution of the variable, with a standard error that depends on the standard deviation of the original variable and the sample size. This result is used to test the significance of sample results. In testing of the null hypothesis the deviation of the sample mean from the null hypothesis mean in standard deviations is compared with the value required for statistical significance at the chosen significance level. Alternatively, the probability value of a particular standardized deviation from the null hypothesis mean can be obtained from the normal-curve table. Confidence intervals can be used to find regions of values in which the population mean is likely to fall. In dealing with small samples with unknown variances, the t-distribution is used rather than the normal distribution. Finally, related tests can be used to test the significance of the difference between a pair of means.

Questions

1. According to the normal-curve table, what proportion of the area under the normal curve is above $z = .50$?
2. Say that a variable has a normal distribution with a mean of 75 and a standard deviation of 10.

    a. What is the probability of a value being above 95?

    b. What is the range within which 95 percent of the cases will fall?

3. Say that a variable has a normal distribution with a mean of 75 and a standard deviation of 10, and say that a sample of 101 is taken.

    a. What is the standard error of the mean?

    b. Would a sample mean of 78.5 be significantly different from a hypothesized mean of 75 at the .01 level?

    c. What is the 99 percent confidence interval for a sample mean of 78.5?

4. Say that a variable has a normal distribution with a mean of 75 and a standard deviation of 10, and say that a sample of 26 is taken.

    a. What is the standard error of the mean?

    b. Would a sample mean of 78.5 be significantly different from a hypothesized mean of 75 at the .05 level?

    c. What is the 95 percent confidence interval for a sample mean of 78.5?

5. Say that a variable has a t-distribution with a mean of 75 and a standard deviation of 10, and say that a sample of 26 is taken.

    a. What is the standard error of the mean?

    b. Would a sample mean of 78.5 be significantly different from a hypothesized mean of 75 at the .05 level?

    c. What is the 95 percent confidence interval for a sample mean of 78.5?

11

Two-Variable Tables

Academic researchers are interested in more than describing popular attitudes and behavior. They are also interested in understanding what causes attitudes and behavior. As we have said, one studies the causes of an attitude or behavior by examining what other variables are associated with it. This chapter begins our description of how to study relations among variables by discussing how to study a pair of nominal or ordinal variables.

CONTINGENCY TABLES

A common way of studying the relation between two nominal or ordinal variables is to construct a *bivariate frequency distribution*, which is also called a cross-tabulation, cross-tab, or contingency table. Table 11.1 is an example of a cross-tab constructed from hypothetical data.

Cross-tabs are very informative if read correctly, but they are often misread. The table shows that more people were hurt crossing the street at the corner than were hurt jaywalking. In fact, 60 percent of those hurt crossing the street crossed at the corner. Is it more dangerous to cross at the corner? A quick glance at the data would seem to suggest that it is. However, intuition tells us that it is more dangerous to jaywalk — and so does the table, if we read it correctly. Note that ten times as many people crossed at the corner as jaywalked and that only one and a half times as many people were hurt at the corner. Clearly, your chances of being hurt are greater if you jaywalk.

Table 11.1   Pedestrian Accidents by Location of Pedestrian

	Crossing at Corner	Jaywalking	Total
Safe	1,997,000	198,000	2,195,000
Hurt	3,000	2,000	5,000
Total	2,000,000	200,000	2,200,000

SOURCE: Hypothetical.

This example illustrates how survey data can be used to mislead people. Imagine that a group of people wanted a law that would eliminate all crosswalks. They could argue that people should not cross the street at the corner because 60 percent of accidents occur there. Without seeing the entire table, it is easy to accept such a false conclusion. A real-life example of this has to do with speed limits. Many people argue that when the speed limit on highways was lowered to 55 in the 1970s, the number of deaths per year due to traffic accidents dropped dramatically. These advocates claimed that this showed that a lower speed limit saves lives. However, some critics argued that after the speed limit was lowered, people drove less frequently on highways. In fact, they said, the number of traffic deaths per highway mile driven did not change when the speed limit was lowered. This shows why it is important to look at the entire contingency table and read it carefully.

Percentage Tables

It is generally easier to interpret a table if the data are expressed in percentages rather than raw frequencies, like those in Table 11.1. Since we are interested in the danger of crossing the street at the corner relative to that of jaywalking, we would like to compare the proportion of jaywalkers hurt with the proportion of people who crossed at the crosswalk who were hurt. We can begin to do so by calculating the percentage of people who crossed at the corner who were hurt and the percentage who were safe. Next we calculate the percentage of people who jaywalked who were hurt and the percentage who were safe. Then we can compare the jaywalkers' percentages with those of crosswalk users. In this way we can assess the relation between the location at which one crosses the street and the likelihood of being hurt. As Table 11.2 illustrates, 1 percent of those who jaywalked were hurt, and only 0.15 percent of those who crossed at the corner were hurt. Crossing at the corner is almost seven times as safe as jaywalking.

This hypothetical example illustrates some of the comparisons that

Table 11.2   Pedestrian Accidents by Location of Pedestrian

	Crossing at Corner	Jaywalking
Safe	99.85%	99.00%
Hurt	0.15	1.00
Total	100.00%	100.00%
(N)	(2,000,000)	(200,000)

SOURCE: Hypothetical.

can be made with data in table form. It is usually better to compare percentages than raw numbers as long as the percentages are calculated correctly. For example, the statement that 60 percent of those hurt were crossing at the corner was correct but misleading. The percentages should be calculated so that they add up to 100 percent for each category of the independent variable. Recall that independent variables are used to explain the dependent variable. In the present example the dependent variable is whether one is hurt crossing the street; the independent variable is where the person crossed the street. In Table 11.2 percentages were calculated within categories of the independent variable. Calculating percentages this way allows a researcher to assess how much effect the independent variable might have on the dependent variable.

COMPARING PERCENTAGES

Researchers examine tables to determine how much effect one variable has on another. This requires calculating the percentages in the right direction and comparing those percentages. In this section we explain how the size of a relation between two variables is gauged from a table. Our examples are based on data from the 1984 American National Election Study.

Percentage Differences

Table 11.3 reports 1984 data on voter turnout separately by race. One would construct such a table in order to study the causes of turnout rates—the proportion of people who go to the polls and cast a vote. That is the dependent variable. Our independent variable in this instance is race because we suspect that racial differences may cause turnout differences. (It is difficult to imagine turnout causing racial differences).

Table 11.3   Turnout by Race, 1984

(A) Column Percents

	Whites	Blacks
Voted	75%	66%
Did Not Vote	25	34
Total	100%	100%
(Number of Cases)	(1719)	(215)

(B) Row Percents

	Voted	Did Not Vote	Total	Number of Cases
Whites	75%	25	100%	(1719)
Blacks	66%	34	100%	(215)

SOURCE: 1984 American National Election Study.

The table shows that 75 percent of whites reported voting in the 1984 presidential election as compared with 66 percent of blacks.

Percentage Direction.   Note how Table 11.3 was figured according to the rule described above. We could have calculated the proportion of voters who were white and the proportion who were black. Instead, we figured the percentages within the categories of the independent variable. Race is the independent variable, one category of which is whites. We calculated the percentages of whites who voted and who did not. Then similar calculations were done for blacks.

Two forms of the cross-tabulation are shown in Table 11.3. Note that Table 11.3A has the independent variable as the column variable and that Table 11.3B has the independent variable as the row variable. Either way the interpretation of the table is the same. Generally tables with the independent variable as the column variable are easier to read. An exception to this rule is made when one of the independent variables has a lot of categories; then it is put on the rows because it is easier to fit the table onto a piece of paper. Regardless of the choice, adopting a consistent table format within a paper or article is recommended. Always be sure to figure percentages within categories of the independent variable.

Direction of Comparison.   Because we calculated percentages within the categories of the independent variable, we can compare the percentages across categories to assess the effect of the independent variable (race) on the dependent variable (turnout). In the present example 75 percent of whites voted and 66 percent of blacks voted. Subtracting the second percentage from the first, we find a 9 percent difference. This is sometimes summarized by saying that the turnout rate for whites is 9 *points* higher than that for blacks. The 9 percent difference is presumed to be the effect of race on turnout.[1] The percentages must be calculated correctly in order for the percentage difference to show the effect of the independent variable on the dependent variable.

Size of the Percentage Difference.   Table 11.3 also reports the number of cases in each category of the independent variable. There are 1,719 whites and 215 blacks in the sample. These values are large enough to permit a great deal of confidence that the observed percentages are very close to the actual percentages of whites and blacks who voted in the 1984 election. This is so because the sampling error with 1,719 whites and 215 blacks is smaller than the 9 percent difference in the turnout rates. Thus the large sample size in this table allows us to state that the 9 percent difference is probably very accurate. If there were only 40 people in each category, we should place little trust in the percentages.

How strong is the relationship between race and turnout? There could have been 100 percent difference if all whites had voted and no blacks had voted; there could have been no difference if whites and blacks had voted in equal proportions. The 9 percent difference found in the table falls near the low end of this 0-to-100 continuum. It obviously shows a relatively weak relation.

Survey data on attitudes rarely reveal large percentage differences. A 60 percent difference would be enormous, and most researchers would consider a 30 percent difference large. A 5 percent to 10 percent difference is relatively small; it may even be the result of sampling error if the sample size is around 1,500. A quick way to determine whether a percentage difference is greater than sampling error is to consult a table like Table 11.4. It shows the maximal sampling errors for percentage differences between two groups of specified sizes. If an observed percentage difference is smaller than its associated sampling error, a researcher cannot be confident that it did not occur by chance. However, if a percentage difference is greater than its sampling error, a researcher can be confident that the two groups really differ on the dependent variable. For example, if there were 1,000 whites and 1,000

---

[1]The variable *turnout* is actually based on respondents' reports of their voting behavior. Unfortunately, some respondents report voting when they actually did not. Consequently, turnout figures derived from surveys are usually somewhat higher than actual turnout percentages.

Table 11.4   Maximal Sampling Errors for Differences in Proportions

Size of Other Sample or Group	Size of One Sample or Group					
	3,000	1,000	700	500	300	200
3,000	4	5	6	7	8	10
1,000		6	7	8	9	11
700			8	8	10	11
500				9	10	12
300					11	13
200						14

NOTE: The figures in the table are maximal because they represent the sampling errors for proportions in the range of 35 percent to 65 percent. The sampling errors decline when the proportions are more extreme, especially when the proportions are below 10 percent or above 90 percent.
SOURCE: Donald P. Warwick and Charles A. Lininger, *The Sample Survey* (New York: McGraw-Hill, 1975), p. 313. Reprinted by permission of the publisher.

blacks, the sampling error is no greater than 6 percent. That is, there are just 5 chances out of 100 of getting a difference as large as 6 percent by chance alone.[2] The values in Table 11.4 are a special application of the difference-of-means test presented in the previous chapter, this time applied to differences in proportions and percentages.

Even if a percentage difference is very close to its sampling error, one need not discount it as due to chance if it is consistent with data from other surveys. For example, all the surveys during elections prior to 1984 show that a greater percentage of whites than blacks voted. Therefore, we can have some confidence that whites were more likely than blacks to vote in 1984 even though the observed 9 percent difference is close to its sampling error.

Missing Data

The problems with missing-data categories described in Chapter 9 must be faced with cross-tab tables. Researchers generally omit categories that represent no data when computing percentage tables. For example, in Table 11.3 people whose race was not determined by the interviewer were omitted. As in Chapter 9, though, the decision about whether to omit a category of respondents must be based upon whether the category of missing data is substantively important. If it is important, it should be included. When data are missing due to interviewer failure to determine race or to ask a particular question, they

---

[2]The error for percentages below 35 and above 65 is smaller than shown in Table 11.4. More complete tables are given in Donald P. Warwick and Charles A. Lininger, *The Sample Survey* (New York: McGraw Hill, 1975), 313.

are usually omitted. On the other hand, some researchers prefer to include don't-know responses to attitude questions.

Even when missing data are included in a table, though, they are generally omitted from the percentages. However, the decision about whether to include a category in percentages must again be made on the basis of the substantive significance of the category. In Table 11.3, people who were neither white nor black were omitted because there were very few cases in some of the categories. If we were interested in thoroughly analyzing the relation of turnout to race, we would want to include the data for the other races as well.

There is a problem with missing data in cross-tab tables that does not arise with one-variable distributions. In the present case a respondent must have a value on each of the two variables in order to contribute to our understanding of the relation between the two variables. If a person is missing a value on either one, he or she must be excluded from the table.

Larger Tables

Table 11.3 is relatively simple, since both race and turnout have only two categories. Table 11.5 shows a more complex analysis, the relationship between party identification and vote in the 1984 American presidential election. Here we wish to explain the respondents' votes, so voting behavior is the dependent variable. A person's party identification is presumed to be a cause of voting behavior; therefore, it is the independent variable.[3] In this table there are five categories of party identification and two categories of vote.

Table 11.5   Vote in 1984 by Party Identification

Presidential Vote	Strong Democrat	Weak Democrat	Independent	Weak Republican	Strong Republican
Reagan	11%	32%	66%	94%	97%
Mondale	89	68	34	6	3
Total	100%	100%	100%	100%	100%
(Number of cases)	(265)	(256)	(421)	(211)	(216)

SOURCE: 1984 American National Election Study.

---

[3]It is often difficult to be sure that the independent variable is the cause of the dependent variable, particularly when both are measured in the same survey. In this example some respondents might first decide whether to vote Republican or Democrat and then

Because Table 11.5 is more complex than the preceding tables, it provides more information than a two-by-two table such as Table 11.3. Table 11.5 tells us a number of things. First, party identification is associated with voting behavior. Second, the difference between strong and weak Democrats is larger than the difference between strong and weak Republicans. While 89 percent of the strong Democrats voted for Mondale, only 68 percent of the weak Democrats did so. The percentage vote for Mondale continues to fall as one moves toward the Republican end of the spectrum: 34 percent of independents, 6 percent of weak Republicans, and 3 percent of strong Republicans. Note that the difference between strong and weak Democrats is 21 points, whereas the difference between strong and weak Republicans is only 3 points. We can therefore tentatively infer that (1) party identification may affect voting behavior, and (2) strength of party identification may have affected Democrats more than Republicans in 1984.

Note that looking at relationships rather than simple percentages reduces the impact of certain types of errors. For example, say that Republicans were oversampled: assume that in 1984 the sample had twice as many Republicans as it should— 854 instead of the 427 reported in Table 11.5. As Table 11.6 shows, our total percentage vote for Reagan would be distorted in this case, but the relationship between party identification and vote might be the same as in Table 11.5. Thus, the relationship between two variables is minimally affected by oversampling or undersampling on the independent variable.

As the number of categories of variables in a cross-tab table increases, summarizing the patterns of relationship in the table becomes more difficult. Graphs are sometimes employed to solve this prob-

Table 11.6   Vote in 1984 by Party Identification, with Double-Sampling of Republicans

Presidential Vote	Strong Democrat	Weak Democrat	Independent	Weak Republican	Strong Republican
Reagan	11%	32%	66%	94%	97%
Mondale	89	68	34	6	3
Total	100%	100%	100%	100%	100%
(Number of cases)	(265)	(256)	(421)	(422)	(432)

Source: Hypothetical.

report that as their party identification. Thus voting would cause party identification. Because the dominant theory of voting behavior is that partisanship precedes vote decision for most respondents, we take that view and construct our analyses accordingly.

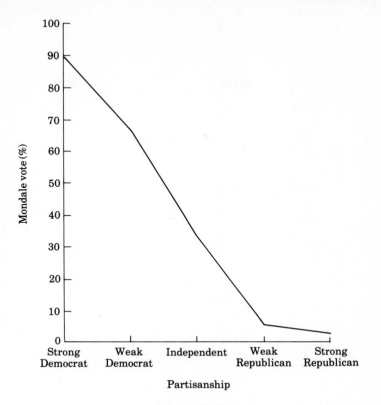

Figure 11.1
Mondale Vote by Party Identification
(Based on 1984 American National Election Study.)

lem. For example, Figure 11.1 presents the figures in Table 11.5 in a graphic fashion. Obviously, the figure does not present all of the information in the table. Rather, it makes the important pattern easy to read.

INTERPRETING RELATIONSHIPS

Group differences are almost always smaller than we expect them to be. As an example, consider survey evidence on differences in attitudes between social groups. Our stereotypes lead us to assume that everyone in a group thinks alike and that two groups differ a lot from one another. In fact, attitude differences between men and women, between blacks and whites, and between young and old are usually relatively small. As Table 11.7 shows, in 1984 social-group differences on many

Table 11.7 Group Attitude Differences in 1984 (in percentages)

Question	Age			Sex			Race		
	18–24	> 24	Difference	Women	Men	Difference	Blacks	Whites	Difference
Government should provide more services, even if that increases spending	44	32	12***	39	31	8***	62	32	30***
Government should help blacks and other minorities	38	29	9***	32	31	1	59	28	31***
Government should help improve social and economic position of women	43	37	6**	41	35	6***	64	36	28***
Government should guarantee everyone a job and a good standard of living	42	30	12***	37	30	7***	66	29	37***
U.S. should become less involved in internal affairs of Latin American countries	55	54	1	60	49	11***	68	53	15***
Decreased defense spending	38	30	8***	34	30	4**	46	31	15***
We should try to cooperate more with Russia, rather than being tougher with Russia	43	32	11***	36	34	2	44	34	10**

* p < .05
** p < .01
*** p < .001

SOURCE: 1984 American National Election Study.

political issues were small. Racial differences overwhelm gender gaps and generational cleavages. Sex and age have only limited effects on attitudes, with attitude differences being no larger than 12 percent. Racial differences on some questions are larger, but only three issues have differences as large as 25 percent.

This table uses a common notation system to show which differences are statistically significant. One asterisk indicates the difference is significant at the .05 level; two asterisks shows that there is less than one chance out of 100 of getting that large a difference by chance alone, and three asterisks shows the probability of such a large difference is less than one in 1,000.

Thus, Table 11.7 shows where large differences emerge and shows that differences do not exist where we might expect them.[4] This analysis illustrates one of the valuable effects of survey data—correcting our stereotypes by demonstrating that differences between social groups in terms of attitudes are relatively small in contemporary America.

SUMMARY

Cross-tab tables are used to determine whether there is a relation between two nominal or ordinal variables. Percentage tables can be read most easily, and the percentages must be figured within categories of the independent variable. It is important to remember that even if a relationship between two variables is found in this fashion, that does not prove that the independent variables caused the dependent variable. The role of other variables in affecting the dependent variable must be examined before one can assess causality with any confidence. As we shall see in Chapter 13, taking additional variables into account can change the apparent importance of the two-variable relation shown in a cross-tab. Thus, examining such tables is only the beginning of statistical analysis.

---

[4]One reason the differences between groups are not large is that groups overlap. For example, you might expect that young people, women, and blacks support large defense expenditures less than older people, men, and whites. But what about white women? Older blacks? Young whites? The expectations for these overlapping groups are contradictory, and that lessens the overall differences between young and old people, between women and men, and between whites and blacks. When many people fall into groups with contradictory tendencies, social-group differences are muted.

Questions

U.S. Relations with Soviet Russia

Education	Less Militant	Status Quo	More Militant	Total
College	30%	30%	40%	100%
High school	35%	30%	35%	100%
Grade school	40%	30%	30%	100%

Source: Hypothetical.

1. The independent variable in this table is _____ .
2. The dependent variable in the above table is _____ .
3. Are the percentages in the correct direction in the above table?
4. The 40 percent in the college row and more militant column means that:
    a. 40 percent of the respondents are people with a college education who want a more militant stand toward Russia.
    b. 40 percent of those wanting a more militant stand have a college education.
    c. 40 percent of the college-educated want a more militant stand.
    d. 40 percent of the college-educated who want a more militant stand voted in the last election.
5. Does the table suggest that those with more formal education want a more militant stand or less militant stand toward Russia, as compared with those with less formal education?
6. Is the relationship between formal education and position on relations with Russia large or small?
7. What simple piece of information is missing from the table but is necessary to evaluate the importance of these results?

12

Measures of Association

In the last chapter we described cross-tab tables — a simple way to determine whether two variables are associated with one another. Associations between variables vary in strength, some are strong, others weak. Therefore, once a researcher has determined that two variables are related to one another, it is useful to determine how strongly they are related. Researchers compute *measures of association* in order to do so. A measure of association is a single number that summarizes the information in a cross-tabulation in simpler form.

LOGIC OF MEASURES OF ASSOCIATION

Two Models of Association

What is meant by *association* between variables? The usual way to think of a relationship is in terms of *covariation* — the extent to which a change in one variable is accompanied by a change in another variable. If two variables vary or change together, either in the same direction or in opposite directions, we say they covary and are associated or related. If an increase in the independent variable is always accompanied by an increase in the dependent variable, we call it a *perfect positive relationship*. Similarly, a *perfect negative relationship* is one in which an increase in the independent variable is always accompanied by a decrease in the dependent variable. We say that *no relationship* exists if the dependent variable is equally likely to increase, decrease, or remain the same when the independent variable increases.

Another common way to think of a relationship is in terms of *predictability*. How well can a person's category on the dependent variable be predicted from his or her category on the independent variable? In a perfect positive relationship, knowledge of the value of the independent variable permits perfect prediction of the value of the dependent variable. If there is no relationship, knowledge of the value of the independent variable does not provide any information with which to predict the value of the dependent variable.

In most respects the covariation model and the prediction model are the same; throughout the introductory material in this chapter, we do not draw distinctions. Later we will discuss the differences between these models.

Extreme Relationships

Table 12.1 illustrates a perfect relationship for both the predictive and covariation models. The predictor variable here is education, and the dependent variable is the respondent's answer to a survey question asking what social class he or she belongs to. According to these hypothetical data, people with a grade-school education consider themselves to belong to the working class; those with a high-school education consider themselves to belong to the middle class; those with a college education consider themselves to belong to the upper class. Knowing a person's education level allows a researcher to predict perfectly the person's class identification. As education increases, so does

Table 12.1   Perfect Relationship Between Education and Class

Class	Education		
	Grade School	High School	College
Working	100%	0%	0%
Middle	0	100	0
Upper	100	0	100
Total	100%	100%	100%
N (total 2,611)	(510)	(1,342)	(759)

tau-b = 1.00 d_{rc} = 1.00   gamma = 1.00
lambda$_{rc}$ = 1.00   tau-c = .920

NOTE: The coefficients of correlation (tau-b and so forth) will be explained later in the chapter. The reader will be referred to this table.
SOURCE: Hypothetical.

Table 12.2 Negative Relationship Between Education and Class

	Education		
Class	Grade School	High School	College
Working	0%	0%	100%
Middle	0	100	0
Upper	100	0	0
Total	100%	100%	100%
N (total 2,611)	(510)	(1,342)	(759)

$$\text{tau-}b = -1.00 \qquad d_{rc} = -1.00 \qquad \text{gamma} = -1.00$$
$$\text{lambda}_{rc} = 1.00 \qquad \text{tau-c} = -.920$$

subjective social class. Consequently, there is a perfect positive relationship between education and subjective social class for both models. The relationship is positive because as education increases, so does subjective social class.

We would say that the relationship is negative if as education increases, subjective social class decreases. Table 12.2 illustrates a hypothetical perfect negative relationship. This relationship is perfect, in the predictive sense, in that class can be predicted perfectly from education. But this relationship is negative because *higher* education is associated with *lower* subjective social class. In reality, education and social class have a positive relationship like that in Table 12.1 (the higher the education, the higher the class), only weaker. Table 12.2 is provided merely as an example of what a negative relationship would look like.

By way of contrast, Table 12.3 illustrates no relationship between two variables. Of those with grade-school education, 30 percent con-

Table 12.3 No Relationship Between Education and Class

	Education		
Class	Grade School	High School	College
Working	30%	30%	30%
Middle	50	50	50
Upper	20	20	20
Total	100%	100%	100%
N (total 2,611)	(510)	(1,342)	(759)

$$\text{tau-}b = .000 \qquad d_{rc} = .000 \qquad \text{gamma} = .000$$
$$\text{lambda}_{rc} = .000 \qquad \text{tau-c} = .000$$

sider themselves to be part of the working class, as do 30 percent of those with a high-school education and 30 percent of those with a college education. Of those with a grade-school education, 50 percent consider themselves to be part of the middle class, and the same holds true for the higher education levels. Finally, 20 percent of each education group considers itself to be part of the upper class. A higher education does not lead to a higher subjective social class according to these hypothetical data. Instead, the two variables are unrelated—people with little or no education are as likely to consider themselves members of a particular class as those with more education. Education and class are *statistically independent* here, meaning that the proportions reading down each column are identical. Because knowledge of a person's education provides no information about his or her class, this is an example of no relationship.

Subjective social class and education are unlikely to be totally unrelated, as in Table 12.3, and they are unlikely to be perfectly related, as in Table 12.1. Instead the relationship is probably somewhere between those shown in the tables. Since most relationships between variables are neither perfect or null, it is useful to summarize how strong they are.

Features of Measures of Association

Measure of association indicate how strong a relationship is—how close to perfect or null. In order to convey the information with a single number, the following conventions are usually followed:

- The absolute value of a measure of association equals 1.0 if there is a perfect relationship between two variables.
- The measure equals 0 if there is no relationship.
- The larger the measure's absolute value, the stronger the relationship.
- A value greater than zero represents a positive relationship.
- A value less than zero represents a negative relationship.

It is meaningful to talk about the direction of a relationship only when the categories of both variables are ordered in some way. Therefore, the distinction between positive and negative relationships is made only when the variables involved are ordinal or interval and not when they are nominal.

Caution is required in dealing with the sign of the measure of association. It indicates the direction of the relationship between the vari-

Table 12.4   Reversed Education Variable

Class	Education		
	Grade School	High School	College
Working	0%	0%	100%
Middle	0	100	0
Upper	100	0	0
Total	100%	100%	100%
N (total 2,611)	(759)	(1,342)	(510)

tau-b = -1.00 d_{rc} = -1.00 gamma = -1.00
lambda$_{rc}$ = 1.00   tau-c = $-.920$

Source: Hypothetical.

ables *as they are coded.* For example, a researcher might set up a table involving education so that the first category is college, the second is high school, and the third is grade school (Table 12.4). Is this a positive or negative relationship? The measure of association for Table 12.4 as presented will have a negative sign. Substantively, the table represents a positive relationship between education and class, as does Table 12.1. The measure of association is negative here because the categories of education have been reversed. If you verbalize the structure of the table—"greater educational background is associated with higher social class identification"—you will clearly understand the table regardless of the sign of the measure.

It is easy to get confused about the direction of a relationship between two variables. It is therefore a good idea to verbalize the structure of cross-tab tables before looking at measures of association. Also, one should always set up tables so that the categories of row variable increase as they go down the page, and the categories of the column variable should increase as they go from left to right. If a measure of as-

Table 12.5   Actual Relationship Between Education and Class in 1984

Class	Education		
	Grade School	High School	College
Working	70.0%	58.5%	35.5%
Middle	30.0	41.5	64.5
Total	100.0%	100.0%	100.0%
N (total 2,164)	(474)	(786)	(904)

tau–b = .267 d_{rc} = .234   gamma = .451
lambda$_{rc}$ = .249   tau–c = .303

Source: 1984 American National Election Study.

sociation is negative even though the substantive relationship is positive (or vice versa), either the columns or the rows can be reversed and the sign changed.

Table 12.5 illustrates the relationship between education and subjective social class as based upon data from the 1984 National Election Study. There are only two class categories in this table because only a handful of people considered themselves to be members of the upper class. The relationship in Table 12.5 is positive—higher education is associated with higher class identification. The relationship is neither perfect nor null, so a measure of association summarizing it will be some number between zero and one.

Alternative Measures

There are many different measures of association that might summarize the relationship shown in Table 12.5. Different measures have been developed because researchers have different needs at different times. Specifically, one basis for deciding which measure to use is the level of measurement (interval, ordinal, or nominal) of the variables involved. Different arithmetic operations are appropriate for the different levels of measurement. In this chapter we will describe measures of association appropriate for ordinal and nominal data.

ORDINAL MEASURES

The three most commonly used measures of association at the ordinal level are *tau, d*, and *gamma*. They have a great deal in common and usually have similar values, although each has its own purpose. Unfortunately, there is no simple rule to determine the appropriate statistic to use, nor is one or the other always best. In fact, there is no general consensus among researchers on which measure is best.

A Covariation Measure

Kendall's tau (τ hereafter referred to as *tau*) is probably the most frequently used ordinal measure of association. It measures the extent to which a change in one variable is accompanied by a change in another variable. It precisely fits the covariation model discussed earlier. Since tau measures covariation, or how two variables vary together, it always has the same value regardless of which variable is the independent variable and which is the dependent. Therefore, tau is called a *symmetric measure*.

Having calculated a value of tau, the researcher must judge the importance of that value. We know that 1.0 is a perfect relationship and that 0.0 indicates no relationship at all, but it is usually useful to specify how strong the relationship is. As a rough guideline, we would call a tau above .7 high, a tau between .3 and .7 moderate, and a tau between 0 and .3 small. In fact, values higher than .3 are rare in survey research, so correlations of even .1 are reported as important. Much depends upon the state of knowledge in the field and whether the proper predictors are known. Ideally, only correlations of .3 or stronger should be emphasized, but smaller relationships can sometimes be of interest—in such cases it is important to recognize that a relationship is small.

There are actually two forms of tau. Tau-*b* can obtain a value of 1.0 only if there are an equal number of categories of each of the two variables (such as when there are two partisanship categories and two vote categories). Tau-*c* corrects for unequal numbers of variable categories and can attain a value of 1.0 if there are unequal numbers of independent-variable and dependent-variable categories. Only tau-*b* need be calculated if the variables have the same number of categories. In fact, if tau-*c* is used when the variables have the same number of categories, as in Table 12.1, it will not always produce a value of 1.0 when there is a perfect relationship. As a result, tau-*b* seems to us to be the more generally useful measure.

The tau-*b* value for Table 12.5 is .27, showing a small relationship between education and class. The tau-*c* value for the same table is .30, which is close enough to suggest a similar conclusion. Since there are an unequal number of rows and columns in this table, some would consider tau-*c* more appropriate.

Note that we report the tau values with two digits after the decimal point. Computers often provide more digits (such as .30274), but reporting those additional digits is unnecessary. Given the amount of error in any set of survey data, more than two-digit accuracy should not be taken seriously.

A Measure of Difference Between Percentages

Somer's *d* (hereafter referred to as *d*) is another ordinal measure of association. It is a generalization of the logic of differences between percentages that we used to compare categories of the independent variable in Chapter 11. There, since the independent and dependent variables each had two categories, a single percentage-difference figure could be derived from a cross-tab table in a simple fashion. Things become more complex when variables have more than two categories. Somer's d summarizes percentage differences under these conditions. The value of d is an indicator of how large is the change in the dependent variable for a change in the independent variable. For the data in Table 12.5, d is .23, which indicates a weak relationship.

Recall that when the data in a table are presented in percentages, the percentages should be calculated within the categories of the independent variable; otherwise the comparisons are not informative of causal relationships. Since d is based on the same logic, it is calculated according to whether the column or the row variable is the independent variable. Statistics like d, which have different values depending on which variable is independent, are called *asymmetric measures*. Since there are two d values for any table, a system is needed to distinguish them: d_{rc} is used to indicate the value of d when the row variable is dependent; d_{cr} denotes the opposite—the column variable is dependent.

Computer data analysis programs generally calculate both d_{rc} and d_{cr}. The researcher must decide which is correct for the specific table being analyzed. For Table 12.5, $d_{rc} = .23$ and $d_{cr} = .30$. It would be fallacious to report both values, since only one of the variables is dependent. Here, subjective social class—the rows—is the dependent variable; hence, d_{rc} is the appropriate measure. It can be shown that there is a relationship between Somer's d and tau-b discussed above: tau-b^2 = $d_{rc}d_{cr}$. As a result, the value of tau-b for a table always falls in between the values of d_{rc} and d_{cr}. Tau-b for Table 12.5 is .27, between d_{rc} = .23 and $d_{cr} = .30$.

A Measure for Scale Relationships

Goodman and Kruskal's gamma (γ) is another measure of association for ordinal variables. Instead of measuring the effects of independent variables on dependent variables, a researcher might want to know whether two variables measure the same underlying dimension, as discussed in Chapter 9. Suppose we suspect that interest in a political campaign and concern about the outcome are two measures of the same underlying dimension, which we call political involvement. We might hypothesize that people who are not involved in politics will also show little interest and little concern; people with great involvement will show substantial interest and concern; people with medium involvement will show high concern but low interest. It is hard to imagine anyone highly interested in a campaign having little concern about the outcome.

Table 12.6 illustrates this hypothesis. If this hypothesis is correct, concern and interest are both measures of involvement, but interest is a better indicator than concern—people with medium involvement can show high concern, but only those people with high involvement can show high interest. Notice that this leaves one cell of the table empty. Gamma seeks to measure this type of relationship. Gamma is 1.0 for Table 12.6 because there is a perfect relationship between interest and concern (with only high-concern types showing interest).

The logic of gamma is based on the notion of *concordant* and *discordant* pairs in a cross-tabulation of two variables. Two respondents are considered a concordant pair if the person with a higher score on one variable also has the higher score on the other variable; two respondents are considered a discordant pair if the person with the higher score on one variable has the lower score on the other variable. The formula:

$$\gamma = (C - D) / (C + D)$$

where C is the number of concordant pairs and D is the number of discordant pairs. The numerator is the excess of concordant over discordant pairs, while the denominator is the total number of pairs of respondents who respond differently to the two questions. Thus, gamma is the excess of concordant over discordant pairs of respondents relative to the total number of respondents who respond differently to the two questions.

In order to illustrate how to calculate gamma, let us begin with a table with two rows and two columns (Table 12.6). Compare one person in

Table 12.6 Scale Relationship Between Interest and Concern

Concern Over Outcome	Interest in Election	
	Low	High
Low	300	0
High	400	300
Total		(1,000)

tau-*b* = .429 d_{rc} = .429 d_{cr} = .429   gamma = 1.00

the upper left cell with one person in the bottom right cell. The person who scored higher on one variable also scored higher on the other variable, so these two people constitute a concordant pair. The total number of concordant pairs, C, is then the product of the number of people in the top left cell and the number in the bottom right cell, or 300 × 300 = 90,000 in Table 12.6. Next compare one person in the top right cell with one person in the lower left cell. The person who scored higher on one variable scored lower on the other variable, so these two people constitute a discordant pair. The total number of discordant pairs, D, is then the product of the number of people in the upper right cell and the number in the bottom left cell, or 0 × 400 = 0 in Table 12.6. Gamma for Table 12.6 is therefore (90,000 − 0)/(90,000 + 0) = 90,000/90,000 = 1.0. As this example illustrates, gamma will equal 1.0 in all two-by-two tables with one zero cell.

In larger tables the calculation is a generalization of that given here. Two sums of products are generated. First, each cell of the table is multiplied by the total frequency of all cells below and to the right of that cell, and those products are summed to get the value of C. Then, each cell of the table is multiplied by the total frequency of all cells below and to the left of that cell, and those products are summed to get the value of D. After those two sums of products are computed, gamma is computed according to the formula given above.

When studying the relationship between two ordinal variables, gamma measures how often knowing the relative ordering of a respondent on one variable allows you to predict his or her relative ordering on the second variable. Numerically, it is the number of correct predictions (that is, the number of pairs of respondents with the same order on the two variables) minus the number of incorrect predictions, divided by the total number of predictions. In this sense gamma indicates the amount that prediction error was reduced by knowing the person's score on the independent variable.

Gamma is never smaller than tau, and it tends to produce much higher values. In Table 12.6, tau-b is .43, and gamma is 1.0. This feature of gamma makes it attractive to researchers who want to report relationships that appear to be strong. Some researchers argue that gamma is a measure of predictive association for ordinal data, and therefore they prefer gamma to tau.[1] However, because of the predic-

---

[1]For this argument, see Herbert L. Costner, "Criteria for Measures of Association," *American Sociological Review* 30(1965):341−53. The view in the text is developed in Herbert F. Weisberg, "Models of Statistical Relationship," *American Political Science Review* 68(1974):1638−55.

tion rule used by gamma and because of the special circumstances under which gamma can have a value of 1.00, we do not recommend its use except when a researcher believes that two variables may reflect the same underlying dimension, as described above.

A Measure of the Correspondence of Rank Ordering

One additional ordinal measure deserves mention. Some ordinal variables are *rank orders*, such as the rank order of people from richest to poorest or from most conservative to most liberal. Spearman's rho (r_s) is used to measure the association between two variables that constitute rank orders. Table 12.7 illustrates an example. In the income column, 1 stands for highest income and 5 for the lowest. In the ideology column, 1 stands for most conservative and 5 for least conservative. The calculation for Spearman's rho is shown at the bottom of the table. The data show a strong tendency for people with more income to be more conservative, since rho is large and positive (.70). Spearman's rho can be used only when all respondents are rank-ordered on both variables. When the data consist of ordered categories of people, such as conservatives, moderates, and liberals, Kendall's tau is more useful.

Choice of Measure

When one does not have rank-order variables, which of the measures of association should be used: tau, d, or gamma? One is generally

Table 12.7   Calculation of Spearman's Rho

Person	Income	Ideology	Difference	Difference Squared
A	1	1	0	0
B	3	2	1	1
C	2	4	−2	4
D	4	3	1	1
E	5	5	0	0
Sum			0	6

$$N = \text{number of people} = 5$$

$$r_s = 1 - \frac{6(\text{sum of squared differences})}{N(N^2 - 1)} = 1 - \frac{6(6)}{5(5^2 - 1)}$$

$$= 1 - \frac{36}{120} = .70$$

SOURCE: Hypothetical.

correct in using tau. One might use d instead, but tau is used more generally. Use gamma only if your model of a perfect relationship is a scale. The most important thing is to understand the table; statistics should aid in that understanding rather than act as a substitute for it. Once you understand the table, you may want to use a measure of association to summarize the amount of relationship in the table.

These ordinal measures do not agree on what constitutes a perfect relationship. What is perfect according to one is not necessarily perfect according to another. However, these measures do agree on what constitutes no relationship. If one ordinal measure for a particular table is zero, the others will also be zero. Also, these measures all have the same sign for any particular table. Thus, the choice between them will have only small consequences for your interpretation.

Use of Ordinal Statistics

The statistics described above should be used only with ordinal variables. One must use care when employing them, because many variables have categories that cannot be ordered in a meaningful fashion and are therefore not ordinal. For example, say that voting behavior in a presidential election is divided into the following categories: *voted Democratic, voted Republican,* and *did not vote.* Did-not-vote prevents this from being an ordered set of categories—it is not meaningful to suggest that voting behavior ranges from voting Democratic to not voting, with voting Republican somewhere in the middle—so it would not be appropriate to apply ordinal statistics. In order to apply ordinal statistics in this case, people who reported that they did not vote could be omitted, and the statistics could be computed using only respondents who voted for either the Democratic or Republican candidate. Then ordinal statistics would be meaningful. More generally, missing data must always be excluded before computing any measure of association.

So far we have stressed using ordinal measures for ordinal variables. All ordinal measures of association assume that as one variable increases, the other will consistently increase or consistently decrease. This is called a *monotonic relationship* between two variables. Difficulties arise if the second variable increases for a while and then decreases, or vice versa. Table 12.8 illustrates a relation in which the independent variable, education, is not monotonically related to the dependent variable. Tau-b and gamma for this table are near zero. However, we can perfectly predict the value of the dependent variable

Table 12.8   Predictive Relationship Between Education and Class

Class	Education		
	Grade School	High School	College
Working	100%	0%	0%
Middle	0	0	100
Upper	0	100	0
Total	100%	100%	100%
N (total 2,164)	(474)	(786)	(904)

tau-b = .060 d_{rc} = .060   gamma = .060
lambda$_{rc}$ = 1.000   tau-c = .058

SOURCE: Hypothetical.

from the value of the independent variable. These ordinal measures of association suggest that the variables are not related to one another, which is not true.

Therefore, one should not necessarily apply ordinal-level measures to ordinal variables. One should apply ordinal measures of association only when examination of a cross-tab table reveals that the relationship between the variables is monotonic. If a researcher wished to examine the relationship between age and turnout, he or she would probably not expect to find a monotonic relationship. Instead, turnout probably increases with age until about retirement age, when it may begin to decrease with age. In this case ordinal-level measures are inappropriate, because although the categories of the variables are ordered, the expected relationship is not monotonic.

NOMINAL MEASURES

If one or both of the variables in a cross-tab table have more than two categories that cannot be ordered, then there is no choice but to treat the variable as nominal and to apply nominal-level measures of association.

A Predictive Measure

The most useful nominal measure of association is lambda (λ). Lambda is asymmetric; it has different values depending on whether the row or column variable is the independent variable. It conforms to the predictive model of a relationship, but it derives a very direct em-

Table 12.9   Presidential Vote by Race in 1984

Vote	Black		White		Total	
	Percent	Frequency	Percent	Frequency	Percent	Frequency
Reagan	9%	12	63%	774	58%	786
Mondale	91	117	37	446	42	563
Total	100%	129	100%	1,220	100%	1,349

$N = 1,349$

tau-b = .323	d_{rc} = .541	gamma = .888	lambda$_{rc}$ = .87

SOURCE: 1984 American National Election Study.

pirical interpretation from the predictive measure described above. The value of lambda is the proportion by which error in predicting the value of the dependent variable is reduced by knowing the value of the independent variable. That is, lambda tells you how much better your prediction of the dependent variable is if you know the value of the independent variable. Measures of association that have this property are called *proportional reduction in error* (PRE) measures.

Table 12.9 displays an example of the use of lambda. Both raw frequencies and percentages are shown there. If we did not know the independent variable, race, how would we guess that person voted in 1984? Well, more people voted for Reagan (786) than voted for Mondale (563), so we would be correct more often if we guessed for Reagan. How often would we be wrong? We would be wrong 563 times out of 1349. The proportion of errors will be 563/1,349. If we knew the voter was black, how would we guess he or she voted? For Mondale, of course. How often would we be wrong? Twelve times out of 129. If we knew a voter was white, we would guess he or she voted for Reagan, and we would be wrong 446 times out of 1,220. Hence, if we knew the value of the independent variable, we would have been wrong 458 (12 + 446) times out of 1,349. The proportion of error if we knew the independent variable was 458/1349. Lambda, the proportion by which we reduced our original error, is equal to the original proportion (563/1,349) minus the proportion of error if we knew the value of the independent variable (458/1,349), all divided by the original proportion of error (563/1,349):

$$\frac{\dfrac{563}{1,349} - \dfrac{12 + 446}{1,349}}{\dfrac{563}{1,349}} = \frac{563 - 458}{563} = \frac{105}{563} = .187$$

Another way to think of lambda is that it measures the improvement in prediction due to knowing the independent variable. The number of errors we would make not knowing the race of the respondents is 563. If we knew their race, we would make only 458 errors (12 + 446). Hence we would reduce the number of errors by 105. Because it is easier to interpret measures of association if they range from zero to one, we divide the improvement (105) by the maximum that we could have improved, 563. By doing so, we produce a measure of association that varies between zero and one.

Dichotomous Variables

Variables with only two categories may be considered either nominal or ordinal. The categories of sex cannot be ordered, but because there are only two, ordinal and nominal measures of association are equally appropriate. A table involving two dichotomous variables is shown in Table 12.9. The value of d_{rc} is easy to interpret here (91 percent − 37 percent = 54 percent difference). Gamma is very high because few blacks voted for Reagan; if no blacks had voted for Reagan, gamma would be 1.0. However, gamma is not appropriate to the type of relationship we are examining. One could make an argument for using tau-b or d_{rc} here, but the interpretation would be significantly different than it is for lambda. Remember that the signs of measures of association for nominal variables are not substantively meaningful; in Table 12.9, it would not make sense to call the relationship between race and vote either positive or negative.

Choice of Measures

One of the largest contrasts between predictive measures like lambda and the covariation measures like d and tau is illustrated in Table 12.10. Lambda is zero because knowing the value of the independent variable does not help to predict the dependent variable. Regardless of the category of the independent variable, we always guess that the person voted for a Democrat. However, the covariation measures d and tau show that the two variables vary together moderately. Therefore, one must be careful to specify what type of model relationship is expected. The statistics are often quite similar, but as Table 12.10 shows, they can also be quite different.

Table 12.10   Congressional Vote by Race in 1984

| Vote | Black | | White | | Total |
	Percent	Frequency	Percent	Frequency	
Republican	10%	9	48%	516	525
Democratic	90	86	52	551	637
Total	100%	95	100%	1,067	1,162

$N = 1,162$

tau-b = .214 d_{rc} = .389   gamma = .799   lambda$_{rc}$ = .00

SOURCE: 1984 American National Election Study.

SIGNIFICANCE TESTS

How do researchers judge whether or not a relationship between two variables exists? One possibility is to observe the size of measures of association. If they are different from zero, we might conclude that the two variables are related to one another. However, this approach would ignore the fact that even though two variables are unrelated, a measure of association could be slightly different from zero due to chance. Since most surveys are based upon samples of populations, slight variations in sampling can produce measures of association that are not the same as those for the population as a whole.

To handle this problem, researchers calculate a sample interval around an estimate of a measure of association. This interval specifies the range of values within which the true value of the measure for the population is likely to fall. The size of the interval depends upon the sample size and upon the observed magnitude of the measure of association. Researchers are most concerned about inaccurately claiming there is a relationship between two variables when there is in fact no relationship in the population. The question, then, is whether an observed relationship is statistically significant.

The Chi-Square Test

There are significance tests for most of the measures described in this chapter. We shall use as an example the best known statistical significance testing procedure: the chi-square (χ^2) test. It is used to test the hypothesis that there is no relationship between the variables in the population (for an example of statistical independence, see Table

12.3) and tests whether the observed data justify rejecting this null hypothesis.

Consider again the relationship between education and subjective social class. In 1984, 51 percent of the people considered themselves to be members of the working class, and 49 percent considered themselves to belong to the middle class. If education does not affect class status, 51 percent of each education group would consider themselves to be members of the working class. There were 474 people who did not graduate from high school, so 244 of them would be expected to be working class. However, the observed figure is actually 332 (Table 12.5). Chi-square contrasts the observed and expected values for each combination of education and class. It squares the differences between the expected and observed values, divides by the expected value [$(332 - 243.64)^2/243.64 = 32.05$ for working-class respondents who did not graduate from high school], and sums up the quotients for all the cells in the table. This calculation for Table 12.5 gives a chi-square value of 173, as shown in Table 12.11.

Could this value have occurred by chance? To answer this question, determine the degrees of freedom for the chi-square, defined as $(r - 1) \times (c - 1)$, where r = number of rows of the table and c = number of columns (one less than the number of rows of the table) $\times$ (one less than the number of columns). Table 12.12 shows the chi-square value required for significance for different numbers of degrees of freedom,

Table 12.11   Calculation of Chi-Square for Table 12.5

Category	Observed	Expected	$\dfrac{(Observed—Expected)^2}{Expected}$
Grade school, working class	332	51% of 474 = 243.64	32.05
Grade school, middle class	142	49% of 474 = 230.36	33.89
High school, working class	460	51% of 786 = 404.00	7.76
High school, middle class	326	49% of 786 = 382.00	8.21
College, working class	321	51% of 904 = 464.66	44.42
College, middle class	583	49% of 904 = 439.34	46.98
Total	2164	2164.00	$\chi^2 = 173.3$

Degrees of freedom = (Number of rows − 1) × (Number of columns − 1)
$$= (2 - 1) \times (3 - 1) = 1 \times 2 = 2$$

chi-square $= \sum \dfrac{(Observed—Expected)^2}{Expected} = 173.3$

$p = 0.00001$

Table 12.12 Chi-Square Values Required for Significance (Permitting a 5% Chance of Error)

Degrees of Freedom	Chi-Square	Degrees of Freedom	Chi-Square	Degrees of Freedom	Chi-Square	Degrees of Freedom	Chi-Square	Degrees of Freedom	Chi-Square
1	3.84	6	12.59	11	19.68	16	26.30	30	43.77
2	5.99	7	14.07	12	21.03	17	27.59	40	55.76
3	7.81	8	15.51	13	22.36	18	28.87	50	67.50
4	9.49	9	16.92	14	23.68	19	30.14	60	79.08
5	11.07	10	18.31	15	25.00	20	31.41	70	90.53

Degrees of Freedom	Chi-Square
80	101.88
90	113.14
100	124.34

SOURCE: From E. S. Pearson and H. D. Hartley, Eds., Biometrika Tables for Statisticians, Vol. 1, 3rd ed. (New York: Cambridge University Press, 1966), Table 8. Reprinted by permission of the Biometrika Trustees.

taking no more than a 5 percent chance of concluding that a relationship is significant when it in fact is not.

For the present example, degrees of freedom equal: $(2 - 1) \times (3 - 1) = 1 \times 2 = 2$. With two degrees of freedom, a chi-square value of 6 or more will occur by chance less than 5 times out of 100. Since we found a chi-square value of 173, we can confidently reject the null hypothesis that there is no relationship between the two variables. The relationship is greater than would be expected on the basis of chance and sampling error. Note that chi-square is essentially a test for a predictive relationship at the nominal level; it does not check whether respondents who are higher on one variable are higher on the other.

The level of significance required in a significance test is set arbitrarily. The .05 level was employed in the previous paragraph, taking at most a 5 percent chance that the value is significant when it is not. While .05 is most common, one sometimes sees .1 used (a less stringent test) or .01 (a more stringent test). Since the specification of any of these levels is arbitrary, some researchers prefer to report the probability of obtaining the observed chi-square value if the true relationship is zero. This allows the reader to judge whether that probability is so large as to preclude believing that the two variables are associated with one another.

Computer programs that calculate chi-squares typically also indicate probability. The lower the value, the more likely it is that the two variables are actually related. Thus, if the computer output shows a significance or *p-value* of .00001, then the odds against obtaining the observed results by chance are very high. The larger the relationship, the smaller the probability value. As an example, the chi-square of 173 with 2,164 respondents has a probability of .00001, which indicates that it is highly significant. By contrast, a chi-square of 4.4 has a probability value of .11, showing that it is nearly significant.

Unfortunately, there are problems common to most tests of statistical significance. For one thing, they are based upon the assumption that simple random sampling was employed. When other types of samples are used, the assumptions of these significance tests are not met. Most researchers believe that violation of this assumption does not bias significance tests substantially, so it is rare to see other tests in the literature.

Substantive Criteria

Because significance tests depend in part on the size of the sample involved, with a large sample almost any relation will be statistically significant. Therefore, except for very small samples (100 or less), tests of significance do not help researchers to decide which relationships are strong and which are not. They only help one to decide whether a relationship is different from zero. However, it is always important to assess the *substantive significance* of a relationship between two variables. An association of .09 may be statistically significant, but it is not very important, since it indicates that the independent variable is not of much use in predicting the dependent variable's value. In some cases a weak relationship can be substantively important. For example, if a certain television advertisement increases sales of a soft drink by 1 percent, that can amount to a change of millions of dollars in sales. Therefore, by this standard the relationship is quite substantial. Researchers should always try to judge the substantive significance of relationships in addition to their statistical significance.[2]

In any case, we should not just look through data for strong associations. That strategy would not account for the chance variation in a set of data. If one computes enough measures of association, there will be a few large ones just by chance. Rather than seeking large associations, researchers should choose which associations to examine on the basis of well-justified theories. If those associations turn out to be small, that is a substantively important negative finding.

Finally, it is important to remember that finding a relationship that is substantively important does not mean that one variable caused the other. Association does not prove causation. That two variables covary does not in itself show that a change in one produces a change in the other. There is always the possibility that some other variable or variables are causing both of the original variables to change. In order to speak more definitely about causation, one must examine more than two variables at a time—the subject of the next chapter.

SUMMARY

It is often useful to summarize large cross-tabulations. The measure of association used to summarize a table depends partly on the level of measurement of the variables and partly on the model of association that one has in mind. Tau, *d*, and gamma are frequently used to sum-

---

[2]For further development of the arguments for and against using significance tests, see Denton E. Morrison and Ramon E. Henkel, eds., *The Significance Test Controversy* (Chicago: Aldine-Atherton, 1970).

marize relationships among ordinal variables. Lambda can be used to summarize the relationship among nominal variables. The chi-square test is the most commonly used test of significance to determine whether a relationship in sample data is likely to hold in the greater population of interest. However, in addition to testing the statistical significance of a relationship, it is important to assess its substantive importance.

Questions

How would you interpret the following situations? (Watch for fallacies in the application of the statistics.)
1. The association between race and interest in politics is $-.30$.
2. Tau assessing the relationship between religion and attitude on abortion is .15.
3. Lambda assessing the relationship between region and vote is .20.
4. Gamma assessing the relationship between attitudes on abortion and divorce is .85.
5. Tau assessing the relationship between age and attitudes toward divorce is .05.

13

Control Tables

If a researcher wishes to explain attitudes, beliefs, or behavior, two-variable cross-tab tables and bivariate measures of association do not provide enough information. Those techniques are useful for determining whether two variables are related to one another, but finding a relationship does not document that one variable causes another. Having found that two variables are related, the researcher must test various possible explanations for why they are related.

For example, in Chapter 11 we examined the relationship between race and voter turnout. Having found a weak relationship, with whites slightly more likely to vote than blacks, we may try to explain it. Since there is no genetic difference between whites and blacks that causes blacks to vote less than whites, it seems likely that race and voting behavior are related because of social or psychological processes. A researcher interested in explaining this relationship would construct some possible explanations and attempt to test each of them.

One way to test explanations of causation is to introduce a third variable into a bivariate analysis. For example, in the case of race and voter turnout, we might hypothesize that education is an important determinant of voting behavior, and that blacks were less likely than whites to vote in 1984 because of differences in education. Alternatively, one might argue that the most important determinant of whether a person votes is his or her beliefs about whether the candidate choice will make a meaningful difference. Perhaps, one might speculate, blacks were less likely than whites to vote because of differences in their beliefs about the usefulness of voting. These and other hypotheses for the observed relationship can be tested by controlling for third variables in examining a bivariate relation. Controlling is a method of holding a third variable constant while examining the relationship between two other variables. This chapter explains how this is done.

HOW TO IDENTIFY SPURIOUS RELATIONSHIPS

Consider the bivariate relationship (Table 13.1) between the number of fire trucks sent to a fire and the amount of damage done by the fire (measured in dollars). There is a strong positive relationship between these two variables (tau-b = .57). The more fire trucks are sent to a fire, the more damage is done. Having observed this relationship, we might now wish to explain it. Since fire trucks are sent to fires before damage is assessed, time ordering is consistent with the hypothesis that the number of fire trucks sent causes the amount of damage done. However, we know that fire trucks reduce damage, so this explanation seems unlikely to be valid. We must therefore generate another explanation for the observed relationship.

If we think about it for a moment, we realize that the severity of the fire is related to both the amount of damage and the number of fire trucks at the scene. A fire chief is likely to send more trucks to serious fires, and the more serious the fire, the more damage is likely to be done. We might therefore imagine that the observed relationship is that the severity of the fire causes both the number of trucks sent and the amount of damage done. If this hypothesis is true, we would expect to find that there is no relationship between number of trucks and amount of damage if we examine only fires of the same level of seriousness. To do so, social scientists construct what are called control tables.

Table 13.1   Fire Damage by Number of Fire Trucks at the Scene

Damage	Number of Trucks			
	None	1–2	3–4	5+
$10,000 or less	98%	40%	12%	2%
$10,001 to $100,000	2	39	26	14
$100,001 to $1,000,000	0	21	48	65
More than $1,000,000	0	1	14	19
Total	100%	101%	100%	100%
N (total 943)	(125)	(217)	(341)	(260)

tau-b = .570 d_{rc} = .563   gamma = .750   lambda$_{rc}$ = .288

SOURCE: Hypothetical.

Table 13.2   Fire Damage by Number of Fire Trucks at the Scene for
Minor Fires Only

	Number of Trucks			
Damage	None	1–2	3–4	5+
$10,000 or less	98%	97%	97%	0%
$10,001 to $100,000	2	3	3	0
$100,001 to $1,000,000	0	0	0	0
More than $1,000,000	0	0	0	0
Total	100%	100%	100%	0%
N (total 230)	(125)	(76)	(29)	(0)

tau-*b* = .017 d_{rc} = .005   gamma = .097   lambda$_{rc}$ = .000

SOURCE: Hypothetical.

A control table in this situation would display the relationship between the number of fire trucks and the damage for minor fires only,
the relationship of those same variables for moderately serious fires
only, and the relationship for major fires only. We would expect no
relationship between the number of fire trucks and the damage for any
of these three subtables. Tables 13.2 through 13.4 show what this
might look like. Keep in mind that the data in Tables 13.2 through 13.4
are exactly the same as in Table 13.1. The only thing that has been
done is to divide the cases into three groups depending upon the third
variable (the seriousness of the fire, measured by the number of
alarms). If you add up the cases in Tables 13.2, 13.3, and 13.4, you will
once again have Table 13.1.

For minor fires (Table 13.2), the relationship between the number
of fire trucks sent and the damage has effectively disappeared. Re-

Table 13.3   Fire Damage by Number of Fire Trucks at the Scene for
Moderate Sized Fires Only

	Number of Trucks			
Damage	None	1–2	3–4	5+
$10,000 or less	0%	10%	10%	9%
$10,001 to $100,000	0	70	66	67
$100,001 to $1,000,000	0	20	24	22
More than $1,000,000	0	0	0	2
Total	0%	100%	100%	100%
N (total 304)	(0)	(117)	(133)	(54)

tau-*b* = .042 d_{rc} = .036   gamma = .075   lambda$_{rc}$ = .000

SOURCE: Hypothetical.

Table 13.4   Fire Damage by Number of Fire Trucks at the Scene for
Serious Fires Only

Damage	None	1–2	3–4	5+
$10,000 or less	0%	0%	0%	0%
$10,001 to $100,000	0	0	0	0
$100,001 to $1,000,000	0	75	74	78
More than $1,000,000	0	25	26	22
Total	0%	100%	100%	100%
N (total 409)	(0)	(24)	(179)	(206)

tau-b = −.046 d_{rc} = −.037   gamma = −.102   lambda$_{rc}$ = .000

SOURCE: Hypothetical.

gardless of the number of trucks sent, the damage was almost always
$10,000 or less. Also, all of the correlation measures are zero, indicat-
ing no relationship is present in the table.

Table 13.3 shows that for moderately serious fires, the relationship
between the number of trucks sent and the amount of damage done has
also disappeared. The distribution of cases in damage categories is almost exactly the same for all categories of the independent variable;
hence, no relationship is present. The association between the two
variables is effectively zero.

Table 13.4, for serious fires, is very similar to the previous table except that the cases have moved down to the higher-damage categories.
But again there is no relationship between the independent variable
and the dependent variable because the distributions are essentially
the same for the categories of the independent variable. Also, the measures of association are again all approximately zero, indicating no
relationship.

Not surprisingly, we see that there is no relationship between the
number of trucks and the damage for any of these three tables. Note
that all of the taus are near zero. Thus we conclude that the original relationship between the number of trucks and damage (without controls) is *spurious*. It can be accounted for entirely by controlling for the
seriousness of the fire.

HOW TO INTERPRET CONTROLS

Possible Results

How do we interpret the various patterns of associations in control tables? If the associations are all zero after controlling, as in the

above example, then the bivariate relationship is spurious. The independent variable did not cause the dependent variable; instead, the control variable affected them both and induced an association between them.

If the associations in the separate control tables are considerably reduced but still above approximately .10, it is safe to conclude that some but not all of the bivariate relationship is spurious. On the other hand, if the bivariate relationship remains unchanged after controlling (if the measures of association are just about as high in the control tables as in the original), one would conclude that the control has no effect on the original relationship.

Still another possibility is that the relationship between the two variables is different for the different categories of the control variable. The relationship might (1) be stronger for some category or categories of the control variable, (2) disappear — be zero — for some, or (3) be in opposite directions (the association changes its sign) for others. In these cases we say that the original relationship is *specified* by the control variable. In other words the control variable determines what the relationship is. An example follows:

A common control variable in survey analysis is education; often two variables seem to be related to one another, but both prove to be caused by education. The fact that education is related to both variables creates a spurious relationship between them. Consider an example from the 1972 American National Election Study. In that year a greater proportion of men than women voted; the difference was about 6 percent. That difference is statistically significant, though only barely. Additionally, it is consistent with evidence collected since women won the vote in the United States: all studies showed women voting less than men.

When faced with this association, it is natural to speculate about why it occurs. One possibility is that gender causes turnout, though this is hard to imagine, since there are no obvious genetic differences between men and women that would lead to higher voting rates among men. However, it is reasonable to expect that people with more education vote more than people with less education, since there is a positive association between education and turnout. Furthermore, men in the United States are more likely to have a college education than women; that is, there is an association between sex and education. Thus, since high education is associated both with high turnout and being male, the apparent relationship between sex and turnout might be due to their both being related to education. To see whether this is so, we might look only at men and women who possessed the same amount of

Table 13.5   Turnout Rates by Sex

	Sex	
	Male	Female
Voted	80%	69%
Did not vote	20	31
Total	100%	100%
N (total 1,954)	(883)	(1,071)

tau-b = .12 d_{rc} = .11
gamma = .28   lambda$_{rc}$ = .00

SOURCE: Hypothetical.

education (so there are no educational differences between them). First, we would look at men and women with high levels of education, then at men and women with medium education, and then at those with low education. We would expect to find no turnout differences between men and women in any of these tables.

Table 13.5 displays a hypothetical bivariate relationship between sex and turnout. According to these data, men vote 11 percent more than women. The value of tau-b is .12, which indicates that there is some relationship between sex and turnout. Table 13.6 shows the same hypothetical data broken down into three groups based on education. Controlling for education eliminates the relationship between sex and turnout. Turnout rates of men and women are identical for the college-educated, the high-school-educated, and the grade-school-educated. For each category the percent difference between men and women is zero. The association between sex and turnout within each education category is therefore zero. Since there is no relationship between sex

Table 13.6   Turnout Rates by Sex for Different Educational Levels

	Grade School		High School		College	
	Male	Female	Male	Female	Male	Female
Voted	60%	60%	75%	75%	90%	90%
Did not vote	40	40	25	25	10	10
Total	100%	100%	100%	100%	100%	100%
N (total 1,954)	(150)	(571)	(300)	(350)	(433)	(150)

tau-b = .00   tau-b = .00   tau-b = .00
gamma = .00   gamma = .00   gamma = .00
d_{rc} = .00 d_{rc} = .00 d_{rc} = .00
lambda$_{rc}$ = .00   lambda$_{rc}$ = .00   lambda$_{rc}$ = .00

SOURCE: Hypothetical.

Table 13.7   Reported Turnout by Sex for 1972

	Male	Female
Voted	76%	70%
Did not vote	24	30
Total	100%	100%
N (total 2,283)	(975)	(1,308)

tau-b = .07 d_{rc} = .06   gamma = .16   lambda$_{rc}$ = .00

SOURCE: Center for Political Studies, 1972 American National Election Study.

and turnout once education is controlled, it is appropriate to conclude that the bivariate relationship is spurious.

One might wonder how there could be a turnout difference of 11 percent in the full table but zero differences within each category of education. Those with low education tend to turn out less, and women are overrepresented in the low-education category. Consequently, it appears that women vote less than men when one looks at the composite, Table 13.5. The apparent turnout differences really prove to be educational differences between men and women.

Let us turn from hypothetical data to real data from the CPS 1972 American National Election Study. Real data are seldom as clear or straightforward as hypothetical data. Table 13.7 shows the uncontrolled relationship between sex and turnout for 1972. The following three tables show the relationship controlled for education.

The turnout difference between men and women with low education is 17 percent (Table 13.8); the difference was only 6 percent for Table 13.7. The turnout difference between men and women with high school educations (Table 13.9) more closely resembles the weak relationship in the original table; there are about a 6 percent difference in Tables 13.7 and 13.9. The final control table for those in the high-education

Table 13.8   Reported Turnout by Sex for 1972, Grade-School Education Only

	Male	Female
Voted	67%	50%
Did not vote	33	50
Total	100%	100%
N (total 440)	(199)	(241)

tau-b = .17 d_{rc} = .17   gamma = .34   lambda$_{rc}$ = .00

SOURCE: 1972 Center for Political Studies, 1972 American National Election Study.

Table 13.9   Reported Turnout by Sex for 1972, High School
Education Only

	Male	Female
Voted	74%	68%
Did not vote	26	32
Total	100%	100%
N (total 1,145)	(413)	(732)

tau-b = .06 d_{rc} = .05   gamma = .13   lambda$_{rc}$ = .00

Source: Center for Political Studies, 1972 American National Election Study.

category (Table 13.10) clearly indicates that education specified the relationship between sex and turnout.

The relationship is moderately positive for those with low education, weakly positive for those with medium education, and negative for those with high education. In 1972 women were less likely to vote than men, but this is true only for people with less than a college education and mainly for those with only a grade-school education. College education proved to be the equalizer—college-educated women tended to vote more than college-educated men. College education apparently compensates for sexual biases in political socialization in the United States. Although we still may not know all there is to know about this relationship, we certainly know more than we did from only the bivariate table.

Incidentally, women no longer vote less than men. The above analysis suggests that the lower turnout of women in 1972 was due to their lower educational level. As the educational level of men and women equalized, one would expect the turnout difference to disappear—and that has been the case. Women now go to college nearly as often as men do, so the association between education and gender has declined. As would be expected, the turnout advantage of men disappeared with the

Table 13.10   Reported Turnout by Sex for 1972, College
Education Only

	Male	Female
Voted	85%	89%
Did not vote	15	11
Total	100%	100%
N (total 696)	(362)	(334)

tau-b = $-$.06 d_{rc} = $-$.04   gamma = $-$.16   lambda$_{rc}$ = .00

Source: Center for Political Studies, 1972 American National Election Study.

increased education of women. Indeed, Table 13.10 hints that college-educated women may vote at a higher rate than college-educated men, suggesting that women will eventually vote at higher rates than men — which is exactly what was reported for the first time in 1984 by the Census Bureau.

In this example we examined the effect of sex on turnout while controlling for education. However, if we were interested in studying the relationship of education to turnout, we might instead have examined the bivariate relationship between education and turnout, controlling for sex. Examining only the men in Tables 13.8 through 13.10, we find that men with more education voted more often in 1972 than those with less education. A similar effect holds for women; in fact, education had a greater effect on turnout for women than for men. Again, the relationship has been specified. Which control is employed depends upon our theories and what is being studied, sex differences and conditions that govern them, or education differences and the conditions that govern them.

In some cases an analyst might wish to determine which of a set of independent variables has the greater effect on a dependent variable. The control data in Tables 13.8 through 13.10 need only be reorganized to highlight whether sex or education had a greater effect on turnout. Table 13.11 and Figure 13.1 show the turnout rates for different combinations of sex and education. The number beside each percentage in Table 13.11 is the number of cases on which it is based according to Tables 13.8 through 13.10. Clearly, education differences had greater effects on turnout in 1972 than did sex differences. However, different combinations of sex and education have different effects, with sex having a greater effect on turnout at lower education levels. This is an example of an *interaction*, in which the variables have separate effects on turnout and also have a combined effect.

USING ADDITIONAL CONTROLS

Analysis of social-science data usually involves using more than a single control variable, either trying a variety of controls individually or employing several controls together. If a control for education had not affected the original relationship between sex and turnout, then we might have to think more about why men might turn out more than women. For example, we might think that age is involved: young mothers might turn out less than young fathers, but otherwise there would be no turnout differences between men and women. To test this,

Table 13.11   Reported Turnout by Sex and Education for 1972

Education	Male		Female	
	Percent	Frequency	Percent	Frequency
Grade School	67	199	50	241
High School	74	413	68	732
College	85	362	89	334

SOURCE: Center for Political Studies, 1972 American National Election Study.

we might check whether men and women over thirty turn out in equal proportions. We would be on the right track if they do (and we would then make further tests), but if not, we might look even harder for a third variable explaining the overall turnout differences. We might then hypothesize that women voted less than men because young women are socialized to the attitude that politics is men's work. We could test this by examining men's and women's beliefs about political behavior.

Another consideration is that several variables may be involved in explaining why women vote less than men. Although we have shown examples of one control variable, it is possible to control for more than one variable at a time. For example, we could control the relationship between sex and turnout for both interest in politics and education. If we did so, we would have as many tables as there are pairs of values on

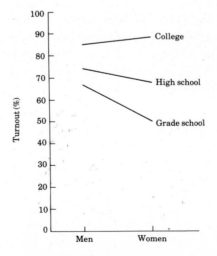

Figure 13.1
1972 Reported Turnout By Sex and Education
(Based on Center for Political Studies, 1972 American National Election Study.)

the two control variables. The logic of this analysis could be extended to any number of simultaneous control variables, and the number of tables that must be constructed increases geometrically.

It is always difficult to decide which variables to control. There are several rules to help with that decision. First, control for only those variables that are related to both independent and dependent variables. Controlling for a variable cannot explain the original association unless it is associated with both. Second, control for only variables that occur before both the independent and dependent variables. If the variable is temporally between the two instead of antecedent to both, it cannot explain the original association. Studying how such *intervening variables* operate can show how a causal relationship works but cannot render the causal relationship spurious. Third, use established theories as much as possible. What variables does theory suggest may be important? In particular, what variables may precede (and therefore be able to cause) the independent variable?

In this chapter we have seen the reason that looking at two-variable relationships is only the beginning of data analysis. The apparent effect of one variable on another can change considerably when other variables are added to specify the causal process more completely.

SUMMARY

Sometimes a relationship between two variables is spurious; both are caused by some third variable. One way to test for spuriousness is to control on a third variable, a potential cause, and see if the relationship in the separate control tables is reduced. Before claiming that one variable causes another, it is important to control on third variables that might render that causal claim spurious.

Table 13.12   Attitudes Toward Women's Role by Age

Role for Women	Under 35	Age 35–55	Over 55
Equal Role	68.3%	62.0%	43.5%
Neutral	19.6	22.6	30.7
Traditional Role	12.0	15.4	25.7
Total	99.9%	100.0%	99.9%
N (total 2,008)	(799)	(669)	(540)

tau-b = .179 d_{rc} = .165   gamma = .387   lambda$_{rc}$ = .000

Source: Center for Political Studies, 1984 American National Election Study.

Table 13.13 Attitudes toward Women's Role by Age, Controlling for Education

Women's Role	Grade School Only			High School Only			Some College		
	<35	35–55	>55	<35	35–55	>55	<35	35–55	>55
Equal	46.3%	39.8%	41.5%	59.7%	52.3%	39.9%	79.5%	76.0%	51.0%
Neutral	27.5	32.0	30.4	25.9	27.8	32.4	13.4	15.8	29.0
Traditional	26.3	28.2	28.1	14.4	19.8	27.7	7.2	8.2	20.0
Total	100.1%	100.0%	100.0%	100.0%	99.9%	100.0%	100.1%	100.0%	100.0%
N (total = 2001)	(80)	(103)	(217)	(313)	(237)	(173)	(404)	(329)	(145)

Grade School Only:
tau-b = .020
d_{rc} = .021
gamma = .031
lambda = .000

High School Only:
tau-b = .147
d_{rc} = .142
gamma = .230
lambda = .000

Some College:
tau-b = .171
d_{rc} = .141
gamma = .316
lambda = .000

SOURCE: Center for Political Studies, 1984 American National Election Study.

Questions

1. Tables 13.8 through 13.10 show the effect of sex on turnout rates, controlling for education. Use those tables (or Table 13.11) to construct control tables showing the effects of education on turnout, controlling for sex.

2. The 1984 National Election Study measured attitudes on the proper role of women. Table 13.12 shows how age affects whether the person tends to favor a traditional role for women or an equal role for women. Education is a particularly useful control when the effects of age are being studied. The younger generation often seems to have different attitudes than the older generation, but this may be at least partly due to their having more education than the older generation. An education control can reveal whether the supposed generation gap is really an education gap. Table 13.13 restates Table 13.12, controlling for education. Interpret the results. Is there a generation gap in attitudes on this topic, or is it an education gap?

14

Correlation and Regression

This chapter describes procedures for analysis of relationships among interval-level variables. These procedures are the analogues of the techniques for analysis of ordinal and nominal variables discussed in previous chapters.

SIMPLE REGRESSION

Interval-level techniques are more powerful than ordinal-level and nominal-level techniques. They can measure how strongly related a pair of variables are and describe the effect of one variable on the others. Such techniques can numerically measure the effect of a change in the independent variable on the dependent variable.

Linear Regression

Figure 14.1 illustrates a hypothetical relationship between education and income. Each point in this graph represents one survey respondent. Note the exact linear relationship: all the points are on a single straight line. It is a positive relationship; those with higher amounts of education make greater incomes.

How can the relationship between education and income in Figure 14.1 be summarized? First we can determine how much of a change in income is associated with a specified change in education. According to

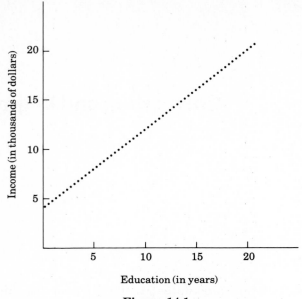

Figure 14.1
Hypothetical Linear Relationship
Between Education and Income

the graph, an increase of a year in education corresponds to a $800 increase in income. For example, those with thirteen years of education make $800 more than those with twelve years. In statistical parlance, the $800 figure is known as the *regression coefficient*—the change in the dependent variable associated with a one-unit change in the independent variable. It is the slope of the line—the increase in height corresponding to a one-unit move to the right in the figure.

We can determine the equation of the straight line. People with zero years of education have an annual income of $4,000, according to the figure. Therefore, the equation of the line is

$$\text{Income} = \$4,000 + \$800 \text{ (years of education)}$$

Thus, the income of those with twelve years of schooling is $4,000 + 12 ($800) = $4,000 + $9,600 = $13,600. Statisticians call the $4,000 figure the intercept of the line—the point at which the value of the dependent variable (income) corresponds to a value of zero for the independent variable (education).

We can summarize how well people's income can be predicted from their education. In Figure 14.1 perfect prediction is possible using a

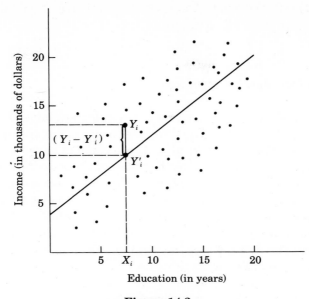

Figure 14.2
Hypothetical Imperfect Relationship
Between Education and Income

linear prediction scheme. Statisticians use a correlation coefficient to summarize the accuracy of prediction. The correlation is perfect (equal to 1.0) for Figure 14.1 because the points are all along the straight line. It would be zero if education did not predict income at all, and it would be negative if greater education led to lower income. The statistic that is used to measure linear correlation is known as Pearson's r. Its square (r^2) indicates the proportion of the variance in the dependent variable explained by the linear prediction from an independent variable. The procedure for calculating of Pearson's r will be described later in this chapter.

Perfect relationships, such as that found in Figure 14.1, are never found in real data. Figure 14.2 illustrates a more realistic example; as education increases, people generally have a higher income. Even though the relationship is not perfectly linear, we can still seek the best-fitting linear prediction rule. This line has been drawn in Figure 14.2. The figure shows that an increase of a year in education is associated with an average increase of $800 in income, so the coefficient of regression is the same as in Figure 14.1. The intercept is also $4,000, so the equation is identical to that in Figure 14.1. However, the correlation between education and income is lower, since the relationship is no longer prefectly linear. There is still a positive relationship, but it is much weaker than that in Figure 14.1.

The Procedure for Regression

The best-fitting linear prediction rule estimates the income value for a person with a given level of education. For example, a person with twelve years of education is predicted to have an income of $13,600. The predictions will not be perfectly accurate. As seen in Figure 14.2, there is a deviation between the actual values and the predicted values. The preferred prediction rule is one that minimizes these deviations so that the predictions are as close to the actual values as possible. One effective means is to minimize the sum of the squared deviations. This is known as the *least squares* criterion for the best-fitting linear relationship.

Notation. Let us call the dependent variable Y and the score of the person i on that variable y_i (read "y-sub-i"). The mean value of Y ($\overline{Y}$, "Y-bar") is obtained by summing the set of Y values and dividing by the number of individuals, N. That is,

$$\overline{Y} = \frac{y_1 + y_2 + \ldots + y_N}{N} = \frac{\sum_{i=1}^{N} y_i}{N}$$

where $\sum_{i=1}^{N} y_i$ is the sum of the N observations on Y. (This is read, "the sum of y-sub-i, where i goes from 1 to N.")

All summations in this chapter are with respect to i, with i ranging from 1 to N (summing over the individuals), so we shall abbreviate this notation to $\sum_i y_i$ (or $\sum Y$). In this system of notation, the mean is

$$\overline{Y} = \sum_i y_i / N$$

and the variance of Y is

$$s^2_Y = \sum_i (y_i - \overline{Y})^2 / N$$

The Least Squares Criterion.   Say that we want to predict person i's score on the dependent variable (y_i) using person i's score on some other variable (X). Let $y_i{}'$ be the value we predict for y_i on the basis of the person's X score (x_i). If we do not predict person i's Y value exactly, there will be some error: ($y_i - y_i{}'$). We want this error to be as small as possible over the set of individuals. The "least squares criterion" minimizes the average squared error:

$$s^2{}_{Y'} = \sum_i (y_i - y_i{}')^2/N$$

The equation for the straight line:

$$y_i{}' = a + bx_i$$

where a is the intercept, the point on the Y axis at which the line crosses it when X equals zero, and b is the regression coefficient, the slope of the line. Algebra or calculus can be used to obtain formulas for the values of a and b that lead to a rule minimizing $s^2{}_{Y'}$.

There are many ways to calculate the regression coefficient (b) and the constant (a). One formula for b:

$$b = \frac{N \sum XY - \sum X \sum Y}{N \sum X^2 - (\sum X)^2}$$

When a person's X value equals the X mean, the best prediction for Y is the Y mean. So:

$$Y' = a + b\overline{X} = \overline{Y}$$

As a result, the estimate for the intercept is as follows:

$$a = \overline{Y} - b\overline{X}.$$

These formulas are illustrated in Table 14.1.

These formulas are fairly complex, and most social scientists use a computer to perform these calculations. Although it is important to understand where the answers came from and how to interpret them, computers spare us the burden of performing the computations.

The Degree of Linear Relationship.   How well does the linear equation fit the data? The residual variance, $s^2{}_{Y'}$, gives one indication. Also, we can determine the degree to which we can predict the Y values better knowing X than without knowing X.

If we had no knowledge of a person's score on predictor variables, our best guess of his or her Y score would be the Y mean, $\overline{Y}$. The prediction error for person i would be $(y_i - \overline{Y})$, and the average squared error over the set of individuals would be:

$$s^2{}_Y = \sum (y_i - \overline{Y})^2/N$$

which is simply the variance of Y. Had we made any guess other than the Y mean, the average squared error would have been larger, so the mean is our best estimate of Y without knowledge of X. If $s^2{}_y$ is the average squared error in predicting Y without knowledge of X, and $s^2{}_y{}'$ is the average squared error in predicting with knowledge of X, then the proportional reduction in error is as follows:

$$r^2 = (s^2{}_Y - s^2{}_Y{}')/s^2{}_Y$$

where r is the correlation between X and Y.

Thus, the square of the correlation coefficient is the proportion of the variance of Y that can be accounted for by linear prediction from X. An r^2 of 1.00 indicates perfect prediction; an r^2 of zero indicates no linear relationship.

Correlation.   In Chapter 12 we presented several measures of association that summarized the degree of relationship between two ordinal variables or between two nominal variables. The comparable measure of association between two interval-level variables is Pearson's r, the correlation coefficient. It follows the same conventions presented in Chapter 12 for interpreting measures of association:

1. The absolute value equals 1.0 if there is a perfect relationship between two variables—here if there is a perfect linear relationship as in Figure 14.1.
2. The absolute value equals 0.0 if there is no relationship—here if the variables are statistically independent.
3. The larger the measure's absolute value, the greater the relationship.
4. A value greater than zero represents a positive relationship.
5. A value less than zero represents a negative relationship.

The formula for calculating the correlation coefficient r is as follows:

$$r = \frac{N \sum XY - \sum X \sum Y}{[N \sum X^2 - (\sum X)^2][N \sum Y^2 - (\sum Y)^2]}$$

This formula is also illustrated in Table 14.1.

As shown in the last section, the square of r indicates the proportion of the variance in Y that is accounted for by X. This provides a useful interpretation of Pearson's r values. For example, if the correlation is above .7, more than half of the variance of the dependent variable is accounted for by the independent variable. If the correlation is below .3, less than 10 percent of the variance of the dependent variable is explained by the independent variable.

Table 14.1 Computation of Correlation and Regression Statistics

Person	Age (X)	X^2	Income (Y)	Y^2	XY
1	6	36	$ 3,800	14,400,000	22,800
2	6	36	9,000	81,000,000	54,000
3	6	36	13,600	184,960,000	81,600
4	12	144	10,300	106,090,000	123,600
5	12	144	13,900	193,210,000	166,800
6	12	144	16,600	275,560,000	199,200
7	16	256	13,800	190,440,000	220,800
8	16	256	16,800	282,240,000	268,800
9	16	256	19,800	392,040,000	316,800
10	20	400	14,900	222,010,000	298,000
11	20	400	20,200	408,040,000	404,000
12	20	400	24,900	620,010,000	498,000
Sum	162	2,508	$177,600	2,970,040,000	2,654,400

$$r = \frac{12(2,654,400) - (162)(177,600)}{\sqrt{12(2,508) - 162^2}\sqrt{12(2,970,040,000) - 177,600^2}} = \frac{3,081,600}{3,973,446} = .776$$

$$r^2 = .776^2 = .601$$

$$b = \frac{12(2,654,400) - (162)(177,600)}{12(2,508) - 162^2} = \frac{3,081,600}{3,852} = 800$$

$$\bar{X} = \frac{162}{12} = 13.5$$

$$\bar{Y} = \frac{\$177,600}{12} = \$14,800$$

$$a = \$14,800 - \$800(13.5) = \$4,000.$$

$$Y' = \$4000 + \$800X$$

SOURCE: Hypothetical.

Regression Residuals. Recall that the regression was designed to minimize the sum of the squared deviations from the regression line. Table 14.2 shows the Y values predicted from the regression equation of Table 14.1 and the deviations between the actual and predicted Y values. These deviations, the $(Y - Y')$ column, are called *residuals.* Table 14.2 gives the $s^2_{Y'}$ value for these data. The r^2 interpretation in terms of the proportional reduction in error gives the same r^2 as in Table 14.1.

The residuals indicate what part of the dependent variable is not explained by linear prediction from the independent variable. If variation in the dependent variable is to be further understood, we must find other independent variables that are correlated with these residuals. For example, if we find that persons 3, 6, 9, and 12 in Table 14.2 were older than the others and that persons 1, 4, 7, and 10 were younger than the others, we would conclude that age is correlated with the residuals. Therefore, age should be included as an explanatory variable. Analysis of *residuals* is useful in deciding whether additional explanatory variables should be included in a model.

Table 14.2 Calculation of Regression Residuals

Person	Age (X)	Income (Y)	Y'	Residual Y − Y'	(Y − Y')²
1	6	$ 3,800	$ 8,800	− $5,000	25,000,000
2	6	9,000	8,800	200	40,000
3	6	13,600	8,800	4,800	23,040,000
4	12	10,300	13,600	− 3,300	10,890,000
5	12	13,900	13,600	300	90,000
6	12	16,600	13,600	3,000	9,000,000
7	16	13,800	16,800	− 3,000	9,000,000
8	16	16,800	16,800	0	0
9	16	19,800	16,800	3,000	9,000,000
10	20	14,900	20,000	− 5,100	26,010,000
11	20	20,200	20,000	200	40,000
12	20	24,900	20,000	4,900	24,010,000
Sum	162	$177,600	$177,600	0	136,120,000

$$Y \text{ variance} = s^2_Y = \frac{12(2,970,040,000) - 177,600^2}{12^2} = 2,846.33$$

$$\text{Residual variance} = s^2_{Y'} = \frac{136,120,000}{12} = 1,134.33$$

$$r^2 = \frac{2,846.33 - 1,134.33}{2,846.33} = .601$$

SOURCE: Hypothetical.

Summary.   The regression coefficient, b, is the rate of change of the dependent variable (Y) with respect to the independent variable (X); the correlation coefficient, r, measures how well the data fit the line described by a and b. The square of the correlation coefficient, r^2, can be interpreted as the proportion of the variance of Y that can be accounted for by X.

Interpretation of Regression

Some Cautions.   It should be emphasized that the coefficients of correlation and regression are based on the linear model. Sometimes there is a strong nonlinear relationship between two variables. Imagine, for example, that people with high levels of education had difficulty in getting jobs because there were more such people looking for jobs than there were jobs suitable for them. The relationship between education and income might then look like the one shown in Figure 14.3. There is a strong predictive relationship, but it is not linear. Pearson's r here would be very small because it measures *linear* corre-

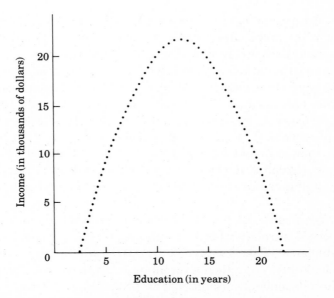

Figure 14.3
Hypothetical Curvilinear Relationship
between Education and Income

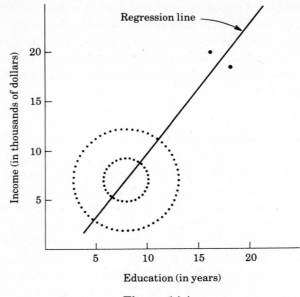

Figure 14.4
The Effect of Outliers on Regression

lation. The possibility of curvilinear relationships makes it important to look at the graph of the relationship between the variables rather than relying exclusively on the correlation coefficient.

Graphing the data can also help detect some undesirable conditions. For example, there may be a strong apparent correlation between the variables only because of one or two measurements. In Figure 14.4 there is no correlation for the main cluster of people. However, two people have unusually high educations and unusually high incomes. This is enough to make the total correlation in Figure 14.4 large. A glance at a graph would be enough to indicate whether an apparently high correlation is caused by a few outliers as in Figure 14.4.

Significance Tests. Researchers often want to know whether an observed correlation between two variables is totally explained by sampling error. This is equivalent to asking whether the correlation coefficient differs significantly from zero. A correlation of zero means that the independent variable does not predict the dependent variable, so we wish to test whether the independent variable has a statistically significant effect on the dependent variable. If we have a simple random sample from a population and we assume that the variables have normal distributions (the bell curve of Figure 10.1), then Table 14.3

Table 14.3 Pearson's r Values Required for Significance
$(p = .05)$

Number of Cases	Nondirectional Test	Directional Test
10	.63	.55
15	.51	.44
20	.44	.38
25	.40	.34
32	.35	.30
42	.30	.26
52	.27	.23
62	.25	.21
72	.23	.195
82	.22	.18
92	.205	.17
102	.195	.16
152	.16	.13
202	.14	.12
302	.11	.095
502	.09	.07
1,002	.06	.05
2,002	.04	.04

can be used to test the significance of the correlation coefficient as a function of the number of respondents on which the correlation is based.[1]

In order to test whether a correlation is significantly different from zero, the nondirectional test column in Table 14.3 shows the minimum correlation value required for significance (taking no more than a 5 percent chance of declaring a correlation significant when the population correlation is actually zero). For example, a correlation of .20 would be significant for a sample size of 102, though a correlation of .19 would not be.

In some situations we have good reason to expect that a correlation is positive. For example, though we may be unsure that education has an effect on income, we expect that any effect of education on income is positive. In that instance the directional test column in Table 14.3 is used to determine if a correlation is significantly greater than zero. This test is less rigorous than the nondirectional or two-tailed test, as can be seen by the fact that a correlation of .19 is now significantly greater than zero for a sample size of 102. The directional or one-tailed

---

[1]For two-variable relationships, the significance test for correlation coefficients given here is equivalent to testing the significance of the regression coefficient b.

test should be used only when one is sure of the sign of the correlation coefficient before looking at it.

Significance tests are not very useful for large samples, such as those used in most surveys. Recall that the square of the correlation coefficient indicates how much of the variance of the dependent variable has been explained statistically. Table 14.3 shows that with large samples a correlation may be statistically significant even though it does not account for much of the variance in the dependent variable. Even when a correlation of .20 is significant, only 4 percent of the variance is being explained! So the researcher should not rely on significance tests but should consider how much variance the independent variable explains. For example, the correlation between the arbitrary sequential number of each interview in the computer file and a person's presidential vote in the 1972 American National Election Study was .037, which will occur by chance with 1,582 cases only about 7 times out of 100. However, the correlation explains a trivial proportion of the variance on the vote (less than 0.2 percent of the variance) and has absolutely no substantive significance. By itself statistical significance is not a good way to evaluate correlations of large surveys.

The significance tests given here are exact only when using simple random sampling, which is not the most common sampling procedure for surveys. In samples using clustering (such as most national surveys), the sampling error is larger than for a simple random sample, so larger correlations than shown in that of Table 14.3 are required for significance.

When a correlation is significant according to Table 14.3, there is no more than a 5 percent chance that the true correlation in the population is actually zero. In other words, if a large number of correlations are examined, 5 percent of them will appear significant by chance alone. Therefore, if a researcher generates a hundred correlations and finds about five to be significant, those significant correlations may be due to chance. This is another reason not to judge the importance of a correlation on the basis of statistical significance alone.

Assumptions. The validity of the results of a regression analysis depends on a number of assumptions about the data. Violating some of these assumptions has little effect on the results, but other assumptions can be critical to an analysis. We describe the key assumptions below.

The most elementary assumption is that the variables must be interval. However, it is increasingly common to see applications of interval statistics to ordinal and nominal data. Nominal variables can be handled routinely with these procedures (see page 243), so the critical question is how great is the risk of faulty conclusions in analyzing ordinal variables with interval statistics. Some authorities claim that too much has been made of the distinction between numeric and ordinal measurement and that there is not much risk in this situation.[2] This point is controversial since there is even some chance of finding a negative correlation when the true correlation is positive, or vice versa.[3] We are uneasy about the increased use of interval-level analysis on ordinal data, although it appears that the practice will not generally lead to faulty conclusions.

The relationship between the variables is assumed to be linear rather than curvilinear. Another basic assumption is that the complete set of explanatory variables must be included in the regression equation. This assumption means that the regression coefficients for a simple regression — with one predictor variable — may be incorrect if other variables that also cause the dependent variable are not included in the regression equation. This is called the *specification* assumption: a regression equation is properly specified only if all relevant predictors are included. This requirement leads researchers to use multiple regression, which we describe below.

The remaining assumptions get more technical. There must be no measurement error in the independent variable, or the estimates of the regression coefficients will be incorrect. In particular, the regression slope will be *attenuated* — closer to zero than it should be.

The regression equation states that the dependent variable Y is a linear function of the independent variable $(a + bX)$ plus an error term (e). The remaining regression assumptions concern that error term, which should have a mean of zero. This assumption is of little practical importance; violating it means that the estimate of the intercept term a is incorrect. However, the focus is usually on the estimate of the slope term b, which is correct even if this assumption is violated.

For each value of the independent variable X, the variance in the error terms is supposed to be identical. If this assumption is violated, it is necessary to use a different form of regression analysis. To determine if this condition of equal variance, *homoscedasticity*, is met, examine scatter plots of the regression error term against the predictor variable.

In addition, the error terms are supposed to be independent from

[2]Sanford Labovitz, "The Assignment of Numbers to Rank Order Categories," *American Sociological Review* 35(1979):515–24.

[3]See, for example, David M. Grether, "Correlations with Ordinal Data," *Journal of Econometrics* 2(1974):241–46.

each other. This assumption is often violated when analyzing time series. For example, if you were analyzing a time series that shows how a variable changed over time, the errors one week would likely depend on the errors the previous week, so this assumption would be violated. In such situations it is necessary to use a different form of regression analysis to correct for this *autocorrelation* problem.

Also, the independent variable is assumed to be independent of the error term. When this is violated, the regression coefficients are incorrect. Generally, this problem is handled by adding more predictors to the regression equation, since the error term becomes independent of the independent variables if all relevant predictors are included. Finally, we must assume that the error term has a normal distribution. This assumption is essential for significance testing but is not critical if the regression equation is being used for descriptive purposes only.

As an example of the use of the one-predictor regression analysis with survey data, we will consider the 1984 American National Election Study question regarding the role of women. The question asked the respondents to indicate their position on a seven-point scale, ranging from favoring an equal role for women (category 1) to favoring a traditional role for women (category 7). This variable could be considered ordinal, but we treat it as interval in order to illustrate regression analysis.

Since the question may reveal a generation gap, the effects of age on attitudes toward the role of women should be examined. The Pearson's r between age and the attitude question is .14. This correlation is very small, but it is statistically significant since it is based on 1,892 respondents. The regression equation is: Attitude = 2.074 + .013 age. In other words, a year of age changes attitudes toward women .013 units on the 7-point scale. This effect may seem small, but it predicts a difference of .52 between 68-year-old people and 18-year-olds. Older people do have a more traditional image of women's role in society than do younger people, but the difference is slight. Age explains only 2 percent of the variance in the attitudes toward women ($r^2 = .0196$). There is a generation gap, but it has a very slight impact on these attitudes.

CORRELATION MATRICES

Often the researcher is interested in the relationship among a whole set of variables. For example, to decide whether different questions on media usage all tap the same thing (Chapter 9), a researcher might examine all the pairwise correlations between questions asking how of-

Table 14.4   Correlation Matrix

	Age	Education	Sex	Women's Role
Age	1.000	.278***	−.019	.140***
Education		1.000	−.042	−.190***
Sex			1.000	.021
Attitudes toward role of women				1.000

N = 1,892

*p < .05
**p < .01
***p < .001

SOURCE: 1984 American National Election Study.

ten respondents follow a political campaign on television, the radio, magazines, and newspapers. To do so, compute the Pearson's *r* between television and radio use, the Pearsons's *r* between television and magazines, between television and newspapers, between radio and magazines, and so on.

The most efficient way to display this set of correlations is in a *correlation matrix* (Table 14.4). The variables are listed in order on the columns and the rows. The cell entries show the correlations between the row and column variables.

The correlation between television and radio may be shown with the cell for television as the row, and radio as the column, or in the cell for radio as the row and television as the column, or both. Usually each correlation is shown only once, so the correlation matrix has the triangular pattern of Table 14.4. Note the diagonal cells have ones in them since the correlation of a variable with itself is perfect.

Finally, we have used a common system to denote which correlations are significant. A single asterisk is used to show a correlation is significant at .05; there is no more chance than five out of a hundred of getting correlations this large by chance alone if the true correlations are zero. Two asterisks are used to show significance at .01, and three asterisks show the correlation is significant at .001.

CONTROLS

Correlation does not prove causation. Two variables may be correlated not because one causes the other but because both are caused by the same third variable. For example, why are education and income cor-

Table 14.5   Spurious Relationship between Education and Income

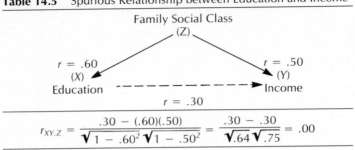

$$r_{XY.Z} = \frac{.30 - (.60)(.50)}{\sqrt{1 - .60^2}\ \sqrt{1 - .50^2}} = \frac{.30 - .30}{\sqrt{.64}\ \sqrt{.75}} = .00$$

SOURCE: Hypothetical.

related? Perhaps both are caused by the social class of the person's parents.[4] People who come from an upper-middle-class background may tend to have more education and greater incomes; people who come from working-class backgrounds may tend to have less education and a lower income. Table 14.5 indicates how family social class could cause the relationship between education and income. To determine whether family social class is the cause of the relationship between education and income, look at the relationship with the effects of family social class statistically removed.

Partial Correlation

How can the effects of a variable be removed from a relationship? The control table procedure in Chapter 13 does so by partitioning the sample into separate groups of respondents with the same value on this variable. The relationship is then examined separately within each group. The regression logic explained in the previous section permits a different approach for numeric data.

If regression is used to predict the person's education from the family's social class, the residuals indicate the variance in the person's education that could not be predicted by the family's social class. Similarly, for predicting the person's income from family social class, the residuals indicate the variance in the person's income that could not be explained by family social class. Having removed the effects of the control variable (family social class) from both variables, we recalculate the correlation between education and income. This correlation between residuals is known as a *partial correlation*.

---

[4]Assume that we have an interval-level measure of parents' social class.

If education is labeled X, income is labeled Y, and family social class is labeled Z, then the partial correlation coefficient of interest is the correlation of X with Y controlling for variable Z, denoted $r_{XY \cdot Z}$. It can be computed from the pairwise correlations:

$$r_{XY \cdot Z} = \frac{r_{XY} - r_{XZ} r_{YZ}}{\sqrt{1 - r_{XZ}^2} \sqrt{1 - r_{YZ}^2}}$$

In an analogous manner *higher-order partials* remove the effects of two or more variables from a relationship, for example, between education and income controlling for family social class and age of the respondent.

Comparison with Control Tables

There are three forms of controls: experimental, physical, and statistical controls. *Experimental controls* are used when a control group is compared against the treatment group to judge the effect of an experimental manipulation. In survey research respondents differ on a third variable that can be *physically controlled* using the control table logic of Chapter 13. The researcher divides the sample into groups, based on their value on a third variable, and then constructs separate cross-tabulations for each control group. However, there are sometimes too few cases in some control groups to produce reliable control tables. The statistical control procedure just described can be used instead: using partial correlations to correct the correlation between two variables for their relationships with control variables. Thus, when the data are interval, controlling by physically separating the cases into groups as in Chapter 13 is not necessary; partial correlations can be computed instead.

Partial correlations are especially useful in determining whether a two-variable relationship is spurious (see Chapter 13). The relationship between education and income would be spurious if it could be explained entirely in terms of the two variables having a common cause. In that case the correlation between education and income would equal the product of the correlations of each of those variables with the third variable, as in Table 14.5. By the formula given above, the partial correlation between education and income controlling for the third variable is zero. Thus, if the original correlation between two variables is large but the partial after controlling on a third variable is zero, the original relationship is shown to be spurious. If the third variable does not fully explain the two-variable relationship, then the partial correlation coefficient indicates how closely related education and income are above and beyond their relationships with the third variable.

The partial-correlation coefficient is less useful when a third variable "specifies" a two-variable relationship (Chapter 13). For example, say that the correlation between education and income was positive for older people but negative for younger people (because young people with college educations are still in school or just starting their careers). The partial-correlation coefficient does not indicate whether a correlation is different in separate control groups. Instead, the partial correlation between education and income controlling on age would be near zero because it is a weighted average of the correlations for the different age groups.

MULTIPLE REGRESSION

The discussion of causal processes in Chapter 8 emphasized the possibility of several independent variables jointly causing a dependent variable. Perhaps income is a function of both education and age. An older person with a college education probably has more job experience and seniority than a younger person with a college education, so the older person is likely to have a higher income. Thus, we require a prediction rule that takes into account a person's education and age. Table 14.6 illustrates this model.

The Procedure for Regression

We cannot merely calculate separate single regressions to determine the effect of education on income and the effect of age on income. (Education and age are likely to be correlated, so part of the apparent

Table 14.6   Income as a Function of Education and Age

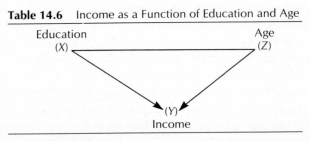

SOURCE: Hypothetical.

effect of education is really an age effect and vice versa.) Instead, we must determine the effect of education on income with age held constant, and the effect of age on income with education held constant.

This can be done by regressing residuals. To determine the effect of education on income with age held constant, predict income from age, then predict education from age, and finally calculate a regression between the two sets of residuals. The resultant partial regression coefficient would give the effect of education on income controlling for age; a similar calculation of the partial regression coefficient shows the effect of age on income controlling for education. The partial regression coefficients show the rate of change of the dependent variable with respect to each of the independent variables, controlling on the other independent variables.

Rather than computing the residuals and regressing them on one another, *multiple linear regression analysis* is usually used to obtain the partial regression coefficients. Its computations are different from those described in the previous paragraph, but they produce identical results. Multiple-regression analysis seeks a linear-prediction rule for the dependent variable Y from the independent variables (label X and Z), so that

$$Y' = a + b_{YX.Z}X + b_{YZ.X}Z$$

The a is an intercept for the regression, and the b's are partial slopes. In each case the first subscript denotes the dependent variable, the second the independent, and control variables are listed after the dot.

As in simple regression, the a's and b's are chosen so that they predict the dependent variable, Y, with a minimum squared error. That is, the least squares procedure seeks to minimize the average squared error:

$$s^2{}_{Y'} = \frac{\Sigma\,(y_i - y_i')^2}{N}$$

We will not derive a and b here, nor will we show their formulas. These calculations are nearly always done on a computer.

As in two-variable regression, we can summarize the extent to which the dependent variable can be predicted from the independent variables with a correlation coefficient. The multiple correlation coefficient is called R, and R^2 gives the proportion of the variance in the dependent variable that can be explained by all the independent variables acting together according to a linear rule. In terms of proportional reduction in error:

$$R^2 = \frac{s^2{}_Y - s^2{}_{Y'}}{s^2{}_Y}$$

Interpretation of Multiple Regression

Comparing Predictors.   A common question in multiple regression analysis is which predictor is more important. This is often difficult to judge from the regression equation. In part this is because the different predictors are sometimes measured in different units. In the present example they are both measured in years, but that would not be true if we were predicting income from education and parent's income. In addition, the different predictors have different amounts of variance. Even though education and age are both measured in years, differences in education (from zero to twenty years) are much less than differences in age (from twenty-five to sixty-five). A year of age may seem to make less difference than a year of education, but forty years of age could have a greater effect than twenty years of education.

A means of comparing the impact of variables measured in different units and with different variances is required. This is done by standardized regression coefficients, often known as beta weights (β). Each variable is given the same variance by subtracting the mean from the variable and dividing by its standard deviation. These standardized variables now have a mean of zero and a variance of one. Once the variables all have the same variance, new regression coefficients are calculated; the resulting beta coefficients indicate the relative importance of the variables. The difference between standardized and unstandardized values depends on the variance of the variables:

$$\beta_{YX.Z} = b_{YX.Z}\frac{s_X}{s_Y}$$

Significance Tests.   Tests of the significance of regression coefficients assume that simple random sampling was used and that the variables are normally distributed. The usual test (taking 5 percent chance of error) is whether the coefficient is at least twice its standard error. This is often expressed in terms of a *t-statistic*, which should generally be at least 2, or an *F-statistic*, which should generally be at least 4. More exact probability statements can be made, but this rule of thumb is very close for regressions with at least sixty cases. If a coefficient is not significantly different from zero, then the variable can be safely dropped from the regression. The multiple correlation coefficient also has a significance test. If it is not significantly above zero, then the regression exercise has not helped to explain the dependent variable.

Some Cautions.   The regression analysis explained here can encounter a variety of problems. Linear regression cannot detect the curvilinear form of the relationship between a pair of variables shown in Figure 14.3. It also does not detect the interactive effects of combinations of independent variables (see page 248), as when education has a greater impact on the income of younger people than older people. It is possible to use more complex regression approaches, which can take even these factors into account. Doing so requires careful statement of theory in advance.

Another problem is that two predictors may be so highly correlated that their separate effects cannot be distinguished. To use our example, the most extreme case would be if age and education were perfectly correlated, so that older people always had more education than younger ones; the effects of age and education could not be separated. We never find perfect correlations, but if two predictors are correlated at more than .70, their regression coefficients become so unstable that we cannot rely on estimates of them. This condition is known as *multicollinearity*.

Dichotomous Variables.   Special problems are created by dichotomous variables. They can be used as predictors by scoring one category 1 and the other 0. This coding produces a *dummy variable*. It is possible to handle nominal variables in a similar way. For example, if there are four categories of region (north, east, south, and west), then three dummy variables can be constructed: (1) north versus (0) rest; (1) east versus (0) rest; and (1) south versus (0) rest. (Why not west versus rest? Because the west is the only region with a score of zero in all the other variables, so its effect is actually the baseline). These dummy variables are included in the regression equation along with the rest of the independent variables.

Unfortunately, a dichotomous variable cannot be a dependent variable in a multiple regression analysis. The problem is that although the regression will predict a large number of values, the dependent variable can obtain only the values of 0 and 1. This will inevitably detract from the quality of the regression. Therefore, one should avoid the usual regression analysis with dichotomous dependent variables.

As an example: Table 14.7 summarizes the analysis of the question regarding attitudes toward the role of women. High scores on the de-

Table 14.7   A Regression Analysis of Attitudes toward the Role of Women

Age

Education → Attitudes toward the role of women

Sex

Unstandardized Regression Equation:
   Attitude = 3.351 + .009 Age − .093 Education + .051 Sex
                  (.002)   (.013)   (.070)

   $R = .211$ $R^2 = .045$ $N = 1,892$

Standardized Regression Equation:
   Attitude = .095 Age − .163 Education + .016 Sex

   $R = .211$ $R^2 = .045$ $N = 1,892$

Revised Regression Equation:
   Attitude = 3.438 + .009 Age − .093 Education
                  (.002)   (.013)

   $R = .211$ $R^2 = .045$ $N = 1,892$

NOTE: Figures in parentheses are the standard errors of the corresponding regression coefficients.
SOURCE: 1984 American National Election Study.

pendent variable indicate support for a traditional role for women. The independent variables are age, years of education, and sex (coded as dummy variable 0 for men and 1 for women). According to the correlations, older people, people with less education, and women are more likely to support a traditional role for women than others.

The effects of age and education are statistically significant when comparing the partial regression coefficients with their standard errors. The respondent's gender does not have a separate significant effect on views toward the proper role of women. The beta weights reveal that education is twice as important as age. There is an education gap as well as a generation gap.

Since sex effects are not significant, Table 14.7 also includes a recalculation of the regression using education and age alone as predictors. According to the prediction equation, sixty-eight-year-old people without any formal education are expected to have an average score of 4.0 (near the center of the scale), while twenty-eight-year-olds with twenty years of education are predicted to have a score of 1.8 (toward the equal-role end). This analysis accounts for only about 4 percent of the variance in the dependent variable. Therefore, other variables must be brought into the analysis if we are to understand the determinants of attitudes toward the role of women.

Causal Modeling

The last complication in this introduction to multiple regression is the notion of the complex causal process, which we mentioned in Chapter 8. If the causal process has several elements, then a series of regressions is required. There are simultaneous equation methods to handle such cases, and causal modeling and path analysis determine *path coefficients*, which show the relative importance of the various causal paths. We shall introduce causal modeling here, though a full description is beyond the scope of this book.

The most important distinction in causal modeling is between *recursive* models such as that of Figure 14.5, in which the causation is all unidirectional, and *nonrecursive* models such as the model in Figure 8.1, in which the possibility of reciprocal causation is allowed. The nonrecursive case is the more complicated, in that the analyst must make sure that there are at least as many equations to solve as unknown path coefficients to estimate — known formally as the *identifi-*

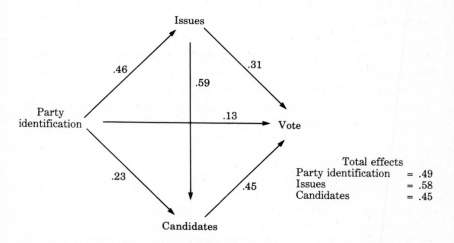

Figure 14.5
A Causal Model of Voting for 1972

(From Arthur H. Miller, Warren E. Miller, Alden S. Raine, and Thad A. Brown, "A Majority Party in Disarray," *American Political Science Review, 70,* 1976, fn. 29, Reprinted with permission of the publisher.)

cation problem. In the simpler recursive model, the path coefficients are similar to standardized regression coefficients.

In regression analysis we had to differentiate only between the dependent variable and the independent variable. In causal modeling several variables may be explained in terms of several other variables. Therefore, we designate the variables being explained by other variables inside the model as *endogenous*. Variables that cause other variables but whose causes are not included in the model are *exogenous*.

In path analysis it is essential to map out the entire hypothesized causal process, with arrows drawn for all plausible causal connections. All variables that affect the endogenous variables are to be included in the model, particularly if they cause more than one of the endogenous variables, so that the errors in the regression equations for different endogenous variables are not correlated with one another. In nonrecursive models it is particularly important to include sufficient exogenous variables that it is possible to solve uniquely the regression equations for the endogenous variables.

An example of this recursive model is shown in Figure 14.5. Candidate orientation had the greatest direct effect on vote for 1972 in this model (.45); however, since it affects the vote both directly and indirectly, position on issues had the greatest total effect (.58).[5]

SUMMARY

Correlations and regression coefficients can be computed to estimate the strength of relations between interval-level variables under a linear model. Simple regression shows the effect of one predictor on a dependent variable, while multiple regression shows the effects of several predictors with the others controlled statistically.

Questions

1. A correlation of .30 means that the independent variable explains _____ percent of the variance in the dependent variable.
2. A correlation of .10 is significant in a large survey. This means:
   a. the relationship between the variables is important enough to study further.

---

[5]For an explanation of the measures used here, see Arthur H. Miller et al., "A Majority Party in Disarray," *American Political Science Review* 70 (1976):769.

b. the true correlation is within .10 of the sample correlation.

c. 10 percent of the variance is explained by the relationship.

d. even if the relationship is too small to be very important, the relationship between the variables in the sample is more than sampling error can explain.

e. none of the above.

3. The regression coefficient (b) in a single-predictor regression equation is found to equal .50. That means:

a. the independent variable explains 25 percent of the variance in the dependent variable.

b. a one-unit change in the independent variable induces a half-unit change in the dependent variable when the effects of the other variables are controlled.

c. the relationship is statistically significant.

d. the correlation between the two variables is less than 1.0.

e. none of the above.

4. Which variable is more important in the regression equation $Y' = 1,200 + 15$ (years of education) $- 9$ (years of age)?

PART III

Survey Guidelines

15

Writing Survey Reports

In this final part of the book, we shall consider some general guidelines for survey research: guidelines as to how to write reports of survey analysis, guidelines as to how to read and evaluate reports of polls, and guidelines as to the ethics of survey research.

The final stage of survey research is writing a report. Reporting research results is important because it permits others to make use of the findings and can suggest the directions that future research should take. There is no single correct way to write a report; different authors use different approaches, all of which are valid. What is important is that the details of the survey procedure and results be clearly communicated to readers. In this chapter, we suggest that when you prepare to write a research report, you think about the scope of the report, its organization, and its style.

SCOPE

A relatively brief report (such as a term paper or a journal article) cannot address every question that can be asked in a field of study. A report that tries to do so inevitably flounders. It is better to limit the *scope* of your work; a complete treatment of a narrow topic succeeds better than an incomplete treatment of a huge topic. Also, a concrete contribution to a field is more useful than a disjointed set of comments.

Choice of Topic

The scope of a report is partly established when the topic is chosen. Suppose it is time to report the results of a survey of religious groups. First one must choose between writing a relatively broad report and writing a relatively narrow one. A broad report might contrast different groups, such as Protestants and Catholics, in terms of their political attitudes. However, such a report would probably find relatively small differences and would not explain them. Instead, a more narrow topic, such as the difference between Protestants and Catholics in terms of their voting behavior in presidential elections, might be indicated, first documenting a relationship and then assessing whether it is affected by a series of controls. This amounts to testing whether the observed relationship can be explained by a series of alternative hypotheses. For example, voting differences between respondents of different religions can possibly be explained by differences in their education and social background. This is likely to produce a more interesting report because the controls permit a detailed analysis of causes and effects.

Generally, an analysis of causes is more interesting than a simple descriptive report. One particularly unsatisfactory effort is a report of the attitudes held by a single group—such as one describing the political attitudes of women. Usually, studying the differences between women and men is the primary motivation for such a study. However, focusing on a single group does not reveal whether their attitudes are distinctive. It may be that the political attitudes of men are identical to those of women. A report that contrasts the attitudes of women and men is better, especially if it examines the reasons for those differences. A report that addresses different causal explanations is of even greater value.

In choosing a topic, make sure it lends itself to statistical analysis. It is most important that there be some differences among people in terms of the variables of interest. For example, it is difficult to study attitudes toward political protest if almost all respondents share the same attitudes. Similarly, there must be differences in the independent variable if it is to explain differences in the dependent variable. Therefore, examine the marginal distribution of the variables before deciding what can be meaningfully studied.

Do not limit the group you are studying so severely that statistical controls are impossible. An in-depth analysis of the political attitudes of American Jews using a single national survey of 1,500 people would be difficult because the sample is likely to include too few Jews for meaningful analysis with controls. Again, check that a meaningful analysis is possible before committing yourself to a topic.

Research Results

Be careful not to overstate your conclusions. In previous chapters we have explained why it is difficult to document that a relationship between two variables represents the effect of one on the other. We have also indicated that the effect of a variable can be gauged accurately only if all relevant predictors are included in the model. Since it is never certain that some predictors have not been omitted from an analysis, any statement of conclusions about causality must be tentative. In addition, it is important to avoid the temptation to overgeneralize from the results of a survey. For example, you might find that people who attended school longer were more likely to vote in the 1984 presidential election. It would be inappropriate to conclude from this that better-educated people always vote more often. Different results might hold for different countries and in different years in the United States. It is therefore important to state conclusions in terms of the population and period being studied.

Finding that two variables are not related to one another does not necessarily mean that the choice of topic was poor and that the results are not worth reporting. Science progresses as much by disproving expected relationships as by discovering powerful relationships. Null findings should be reported candidly; there is no need to change the topic. It is also a mistake to examine a series of relationships and report only the strongest ones. The quality of a research report depends on its coherence, its theoretical importance, and the imaginativeness of the analysis, not on whether it documents strong relationships.

ORGANIZATION

Different research reports have different schemes of organization, but one scheme is very common. A typical report begins with a statement of the problem to be studied, along with an indication of why the problem is important. This is usually followed by a discussion of the results of previous studies in the area, then the author's own theory and the hypotheses that were tested in the research. Sometimes the hypotheses are listed and numbered, but a conversational style is more common, with the hypothesis developed as part of the presentation of the problem and theory.

The next major section in most reports is a description of the methodology. This includes sampling details and sample size, interviewing method, questions used, and methods of analysis. The analysis of the data follows. Some authors restate their first hypothesis, discuss their test of it, then move to their second hypothesis, and so on. More common is a conversational approach in which the discussion flows logically, and hypotheses and results are brought up in a flowing, interwoven fashion.

After the analysis usually come the discussion, conclusions, and summary. These sections review the importance of the results and indicate what future tests would be appropriate. This last point is important. Rarely does any research effort settle all the questions on a given topic. The report summarizes the research that has been conducted, and the author can put those findings in perspective by relating them to previous research on the topic. The author can indicate what other topics should be studied, what other ways of studying the present topic would be useful, how the research design might be improved in the future, and so on. A final paragraph might restate the most important conclusions of the research effort.

STYLE

Finally, it is useful to consider the style to be used in technical writing. Research reports usually include large numbers of tables and data displays. Most readers find it difficult to read a report that has sentence after sentence of numbers. The use of statistics does not provide an excuse for an unreadable writing style. If anything, the writing of research reports requires an especially engaging writing style, since the author must keep the reader's interest while presenting many numbers. The report should be written in a readable style, without permitting the numbers and data displays to detract from the text.

A common error in research reports is trying to impress the reader with too many statistics. It is better to report only necessary and meaningful statistics than to include every one computed in the course of analysis. For example, there is no need to report percentages based on only a small number of cases; random change of a couple of responses would affect the result too much for it to be taken seriously. When reporting percentages, do not be unnecessarily precise. To report that

14.31 percent of the sample has a particular attitude is going overboard. Most survey analysts report only one digit after the decimal point (14.3 percent) and often just report whole percents (14 percent). Do not include every percentage in the text. A few of the more important percentages might be worth mentioning in the text, but it is best to provide only a verbal discussion in the text and report all numbers in tables. Similarly, when reporting correlations, avoid overprecision: a correlation of .5132 is better reported as .51.

Perhaps it goes without saying, but if you are unsure what exactly a statistic means, do not report it. A reader can usually tell when an author does not understand the correlations being reported and has included them only because the author believes that reporting correlations is good. A report that uses simple statistics the author understands is more effective than a report that presents statistics the author does not understand.

One term to use carefully in research reports is *significant*. Significance has a very precise statistical meaning that must be appropriately documented with relevant statistics. If that meaning is not intended, then it is better to say *important* or *consequential*. Reserve the term *significant* for when formal significance tests have been used.

Writing research reports is an art. The author must develop a readable style and must find ways to display data that are easy to understand. Well-planned percentage tables are a good idea, and clear figures and charts can effectively communicate trends and relationships. Do not put a hundred tables in a research report, no matter how fond of them you are. A reader will not have the patience to read them all. Instead of presenting a large number of tables, perhaps one table summarizing the results in each of the separate tables would suffice. Or perhaps a few typical tables might be shown to make the same point that one could make with a dozen tables.

Perhaps the simplest way to develop a good style when writing research reports is to refer to the styles of journal articles that you liked and the styles of articles you found boring, and try to emulate the better-written pieces. There are also good guide books to successful writing. Research costs a lot of money, and analysis can take a long time; given the expense and effort, it is important to communicate the results in an effective manner. The suggestions given above will help you.

SUMMARY

In writing a report on research involving a survey, keep the scope of the project limited, organize the paper tightly, and do not overwhelm the reader with results.

Question

Use one or two pages to write up your analysis of the following table. It is a cross-tabulation of respondents' party identification with whether or not they approve of the president's handling of his job. (Assume the president is a Republican).

Partisanship

President	Republican	Independent	Democrat	Total
Approve	60%	50%	40%	48%
Disapprove	40	50	60	52
Total	100%	100%	100%	100%
Number of cases	(350)	(420)	(630)	(1,400)

Tau-b = .153 d_{rc} = .135   Gamma = .266   Lambda$_{rc}$ = .104
Tau-c = .174

Source: Hypothetical.

16

Evaluating Surveys

Many criticisms have been leveled against surveys. All research techniques have potential problems, and survey research is no exception. Indeed, many people love to hate surveys. Politicians behind in the polls attack them, just as ancient kings turned against messengers who brought them bad news. Two major charges are made of surveys: that they are inaccurate and that they are destructive. These criticisms are discussed in this chapter.

THE ACCURACY OF POLLS

One can often read articles in newspapers describing the results of recent public opinion polls. These polls address such questions as: How is the public evaluating the president's job performance? Who is likely to win the next election? How does the public feel about some current issue? Is public morality changing or remaining stable?

How seriously should one take the results of surveys reported in the news media? Do they accurately describe attitudes, beliefs, and behavior of Americans? Critical readers of poll results should ask themselves these questions each time they read about a new survey. For some polls, the answer to the second question is probably yes, whereas for other polls, the answer is probably no. In this section we describe some problems a critical reader of polls should consider.

HOW POLL WAS CONDUCTED

The latest New York Times/CBS News Poll is based on telephone interviews conducted Aug. 18 through 21 with 1,210 adults around the United States, excluding Alaska and Hawaii.

The sample of telephone exchanges called was selected by a computer from a complete list of exchanges in the country. The exchanges were chosen so as to insure that each region of the country was represented in proportion to its population. For each exchange, the telephone numbers were formed by random digits, thus permitting access to both listed and unlisted residential numbers.

The results have also been weighted to take account of household size and number of residential telephones and to adjust for variations in the sample relating to region, race, sex, age and education.

In theory, in 19 cases out of 20, the results based on such samples will differ by no more than 3 percentage points in either direction from what would have been obtained by interviewing all adult Americans. The error for smaller subgroups is larger. For example, for those 18 through 44 or 45 and older, the margin of sampling error is plus or minus four percentage points.

In addition to sampling error, the practical difficulties of conducting any survey of public opinion may introduce other sources of error into the poll.

Reading Results of Polls

The best reports on polls are those that give you the most information about how the study was done. Compare, for example, the report of the gun poll discussed in Chapter 1 with the above description of the method used for a poll from *The New York Times*. The first says little about the sampling—only that the results are based on a "nationwide telephone poll of 1,251 adult Americans." The sampling error is not even mentioned. By contrast, *The New York Times* reports the sample size and sampling error, the dates of the interviews, an indication of how the phone sample was taken (random-digit-dialing with stratification by region), and a description of their procedure for weighting to correct for demographic variation in samples. *The New York Times* clearly presents its poll as one to be taken seriously as hard news, while the Associated Press treats its gun poll as merely informative.

Reports of polls rarely provide complete information about the study design, sampling, questionnaire construction, data collection, coding, and data analysis. The less information you find about the details of a study, the more suspicious you should be of its results. Do not just read survey reports passively; ask yourself the questions described below.

Study Design.   Who sponsored the study—someone with an ax to grind or an objective organization? Trust the results more if the sponsor seems objective than if the sponsor might want the results to propagandize. If the sponsor might have some bias, examine the report to see whether the procedures used to conduct the study might have biased the results.

When were the interviews taken? It is a mistake to assume that public attitudes are the same for the present as they were in the past. All sorts of events can change public attitudes, so it is important to determine whether the poll was taken before or after a news event focused public attention on the topic of the study. If the dates of the interviews are not given, assume that the study may be older than it looks and try to remember any news events that might have been responsible for the findings of the study.

Sampling.   Sampling is one of the most frequent sources of error in survey research. This is partly due to its complex and technical nature but may also be due to a poor sampling design or to the sloppy execution of a well-prepared sampling design. Many errors at the sampling stage can be traced to a single problem: sampling without knowing the probability that any given individual will be selected from the population about which you want to generalize. For example, questioning people who walk down the street in front of a newspaper office does not yield a valid sample of all people living in a city. Not everyone in the city has an equal chance of being in the sample, since some sets of people may not walk through that part of town. Another example of the same problem is interviewing only Indiana University sophomores when the population of interest is all college students in the country. The sample must reflect the entire population about which you want to generalize.

In reading the results of a poll, ask yourself how the sampling was performed. Was it a random sample? If the sampling appears to be a nonprobability sample, think through how the choice of people to interview might have affected the results.

How many interviews were conducted? Were there enough interviews to produce reliable results? Remember that the size of the population has little effect on the number of interviews needed—taking just 50 interviews in a city of 300,000 people provides results that are just as valid as those based on 50 interviews conducted across the United States.

What was the sampling error? Reputable surveys publicize their sampling errors. If the sampling error is not reported, it may be that the sampling procedure was not a probability procedure and therefore did not permit its calculation. When enough money is spent on a poll to obtain a large sample with a sampling error of 3 percent or less, the sponsors are usually proud of their poll and publicize the sampling error. If they do not mention the sampling error, it may be much higher than 3 percent.

Was the appropriate population sampled? Sometimes one group of people is sampled, while the population of interest is a different group. Always think through whether the sample was of the appropriate group.

Questionnaire Construction.   Unfortunately, respondents answer the questions they are asked rather than the questions that they should have been asked. In evaluating a survey, always check to see whether they were asked the right questions—those that truly represent the objectives of the survey. Also, check to see how the questions were worded. If the wording is not reported, it may mean that the questions were slanted. If the wording is given, is it clear or ambiguous? Is the wording biased to favor one view over others? Would the average citizen have understood it? If the wording seems questionable, do not assume that the results are accurate.

It is very difficult to eliminate errors in questionnaire construction. Even after repeated pretesting, when every question appears to be well written, one can still discover during the actual interviewing that a question is not eliciting the information the investigators expected.

If a report says that attitudes have changed over time, were the same questions asked at both times? If polls conducted by two different polling organizations are being compared, assume the wording differed unless you are told otherwise. Don't believe a report of attitude change if different wording of questions may have been used at different times.

Data Collection.   Obtaining the actual interviews is the next stage in a survey and the next source of error. Often, in spite of a well-designed sampling procedure, the people responsible for executing it do not carry it out in full. For example, a careful sampling of respondents can be undermined if no attempt is made to contact designated respondents who are not at home when the first visit or call is made. The representative nature of the sample will be destroyed as the sample becomes biased in favor of people who are often at home.

A relatively rare but nonetheless serious source of error is faked interviews. A similar problem occurs when the interviewer interviews the wrong person in a household. This usually happens because the interviewer is hurrying and does not exactly follow the instructions for respondent selection. Again, this can introduce error into the survey.

Refusals are another source of error at this stage. People who refuse to be interviewed are probably less cooperative in general than those who agree. Additional biases may result from other differences between those who refuse to be interviewed and those who do not. It is necessary to know the refusal rate of a survey in order to determine how serious the refusal problem is for that survey. The results of a survey with a high refusal rate should not be generalized to the population of interest without extreme caution.

The interviewing process can introduce bias. Generally, expect little interviewing error on surveys conducted by professional interviewers because of their greater experience in dealing with difficult situations and in eliciting cooperation from respondents. Professionals have less difficulty in obtaining interviews, are usually well-trained, and have the skills necessary to communicate to respondents that there are no *correct* answers to attitude questions. When you are deciding how much to rely on a particular survey, ask: Who did the interviewing? How were they trained? How much experience have they had?

In evaluating a poll, ask yourself who did the polling—a fly-by-night little-known operation or a reputable polling organization? Most reputable polling organizations belong to the American Association for Public Opinion Research. When they join, members subscribe to a code of ethical conduct. If the polling organization is inexperienced, it is less likely to conduct the poll correctly.

How were the interviews taken—by mail, by phone, or face-to-face? Good polls can be taken by each of these means, but each has potential problems, especially with the response rate. What is the response rate? Beware of the response rates of mail surveys; they are notoriously low. Simply mailing questionnaires out to a thousand people and tallying the replies that happen to come back is not good polling.

Coding.   The next stage at which errors can arise is the coding process. Coding is a relatively simple process for closed-ended questions and may therefore be boring to execute. As a result, it may be subject to the same kinds of errors that occur in any boring work. On the other hand, coding open-ended questions calls for careful judgment as to the meaning of respondents' answers. Coders often wonder what a respondent's inflection was when answering the question or wish that the respondent had been asked just one more probe question. In these cases it is often difficult to classify responses. Two separate sets of coders sometimes code the same questions; this allows the reliability of the coders' decisions to be assessed. This is costly, but it allows investigators to determine the quality of the coding. If there are too many disagreements between coders, a new coding system must be devised.

The coding is fairly invisible to the reader of poll results. Still, when reading poll results, ask yourself whether the questions were openended. If so, does the coding scheme look clear-cut? Are the categories separate enough to make coding easy, or do they seem to overlap? Can you imagine what type of answers would be coded in each? Are there any likely answers that would be difficult to code?

Data Analysis. Was causation adequately tested? Remember that causation is hard to demonstrate. Ideally, alternative explanations should be tested. If only one explanation is given, think through whether some other explanation could also account for a study's findings.

If the distribution of responses on a question is given, do the results look plausible? How are don't-knows and other missing-data categories handled? Was a filtering question used, or was everyone asked the question? Can you tell what proportion of people gave real answers to the question? Can you tell the intensity of attitudes? Is there any reason to think that people on one side of the issue are more intense than those on the other side, even if they are less numerous?

Are percentages computed in the correct direction? Figure out what the dependent variable and the independent variable are, and be sure that percentages are within categories of the independent variable. If the percentages were calculated in the wrong direction, they may not prove what the author claims they prove.

Are appropriate subgroup comparisons made? If the attitudes of one group of people are being described, check to see if they are different from those of the population as a whole. Reports sometimes focus on one subgroup (such as young people), but the results given for that subgroup may be the same as for the rest of the population.

Is the overall sample demographically representative of the population? If not, perhaps the data should have been weighted to correct for accidentally getting too many of one group in the sample. Is there any clue that the data were already weighted? Weighting can be completely legitimate, but sometimes it is used to cover up serious sampling problems.

Conclusions.   All in all, the best posture for reading reports of polls is suspicion. Don't believe the results just because the author wants you to; consider how good polls are supposed to be conducted, and see if the poll being reported measures up. If it does, the results can be taken seriously, if it does not, or if you cannot tell, treat the report as suggestive but not conclusive. It is possible to conduct a high-quality poll, but don't presume that every poll is of high quality.

In reading a report of a poll, remember the steps involved in conducting a good survey and think through whether you are being told enough to be sure that those steps were followed. Many good polls are reported, but many bad polls are also reported, so don't automatically accept poll reports as scientific truth.

Execution Errors in Surveys

Reports of surveys in the media generally report the study's sampling error. Rather than reassure readers, this often makes them suspicious. Some readers view the sampling error as evidence that poll results are always wrong, while others do not believe that it is possible to know how much error there is in a survey. The truth is that the reported sampling error is just one of the errors that occur in surveys. When a news report says that there is a 3 percent margin of error in a poll, all it means is the error due to having interviewed a sample rather than the full population. Sampling error is reported because it can be calculated, but as we have seen, there are many other errors of execution that cannot be so easily quantified. Sampling error does not take into account the errors in research design, questionnaire construction, interviewing, or coding. As a result, the true level of error in a survey is always above the reported level.

It is useful to separate the errors in surveys into two categories: (1) random errors that do not bias a survey's conclusions, and (2) systematic errors that are likely to bias a survey's conclusions. Random errors result from chance, as when a questionnaire is lost or when a coder accidentally writes 3 on a coding sheet instead of 2. Errors of this type can usually be assumed to cancel one another out and therefore not affect the distribution of responses to questions in any significant way. However, if the survey has been executed in a particularly sloppy manner, random error could be so high as to threaten the results. A survey conducted at an unusually low cost may have skimped on error control and may not give reliable results. Random errors also diminish the apparent relationship of a variable with other variables, so it is important to avoid them as much as possible.

Systematic errors, for example, a high refusal rate among elderly respondents, are even more harmful to a survey's accuracy. Cultural and ethnic biases in a questionnaire are another source of systematic error, as when researchers use a questionnaire that was developed in the United States in another country without modifying the questions to suit the differences in language and culture. When there are systematic biases in a study, all of its conclusions must be suspect. There are no easy ways to detect systematic errors. It is often useful to think through the topic of the study to see if there could be unintentional systematic biases. Also, it is worth finding out who sponsored the study: Did the sponsor have a reason to want particular results? Look carefully for systematic errors.

It is often difficult to gauge how serious these errors are. Since technical details are rarely reported, it is usually impossible to be sure that the sampling, interviewing, coding, and analysis were conducted appropriately. The reader is usually forced to trust, on the basis of the survey organization's reputation, that it performed these procedures professionally so that the random error was kept low and there was no intentional biasing of the results.

With little information about the procedures used in conducting a poll, it is still possible to evaluate its quality by determining whether the results are consistent with relevant evidence from previous high-quality surveys. Do they fit with what we already know? How do the percentages compare with what other surveys have found about the same population? Do the demographic characteristics of the sample resemble what the United States census surveys indicate they should be? Some of the most important errors in survey research have been discovered by a person who said, "That doesn't look right to me," and then investigated to find out why.

THE PROPRIETY OF POLLS

Some critics charge that whatever potential benefits polls have, the costs to society of conducting them are much more significant. According to the critics, reporting the results of polls in the media has adverse effects on the political process. It is important to understand these charges against polls, as well as their benefits.

Morality of Polls

One charge sometimes made against polls is that they interfere with the political process. Some critics claim that polls interfere with elections by creating bandwagon effects. When the public learns that a particular candidate is ahead in the polls, this argument proposes, some undecided voters jump on the bandwagon and support that candidate. If poll results were not reported in the media, the critics claim, these undecided voters would be forced to study the candidates' views and make their own decisions.

Consistent with this argument, evidence suggests that a candidate who looks good in polls and in early primaries has an easier time getting people to contribute money to the campaign and gets more attention from the news media. However, many candidates have won even though they were behind in the early polls. In Britain from the end of World War II through 1980, the party ahead in the polls when the election was called lost support by election day, suggesting more of an underdog effect than a bandwagon effect. Also, George McGovern won the Democratic party's nomination in 1972 after defeating the early poll favorites in the presidential primaries. Similarly, Michael Dukakis won the 1988 Democratic presidential nomination with ease, even though he attracted little attention in the early polls. All of this suggests that candidates often can do well regardless of the polls. Thus, if surveys do have bandwagon effects, they can be counteracted.

Survey results can affect political behavior in other ways as well. For example, polls showing that one candidate is far ahead in a race may deter other potential candidates from mounting campaigns. By many accounts Nelson Rockefeller chose not to run for president in 1960 and in some later years because he was behind in the polls, whereas his active campaigning might have changed public attitudes sufficiently to get him nominated and elected.

Polls can also affect voter perceptions of whether it is worth their time to vote. When a race is portrayed as decided long before election day, some citizens may decide not to vote. Voter turnout in American presidential elections has in fact declined since widespread publication of preelection polls became prevalent.

A related criticism of polls is a charge by Elisabeth Noelle-Neumann that polls lead to a "spiral of silence."[1] She has argued that people change their attitudes on political issues because they want to agree

---

[1]Elisabeth Noelle-Neumann, *The Spiral of Silence* (Chicago: University of Chicago Press, 1984).

with the majority. Consider a survey reported in a newspaper saying that 65 percent of the nation opposes a national health insurance program. According to Noelle-Neumann, when the 35 percent of people who favor it read about the poll, they will feel out of step with others. As a result some of them will change their attitude in order to conform to the majority. Two months later, a new poll in the same newspaper reports that 80 percent of the nation opposes national health insurance. Now the remaining 20 percent of supporters feel even more out of step with the nation, and some of them change their attitudes. This spiraling effect leads, says Noelle-Neumann, to a suppression of minority opinion. If polls were not reported in the media, people might hold more heterogeneous views on political and social issues. Thus, polls may influence processes of public opinion formation and change.

A particularly serious problem occurs when a bad poll affects the course of a political campaign. In 1980 President Jimmy Carter and challenger Ronald Reagan did not agree on terms for a debate until late in the campaign. When the debate finally occurred, the ABC television network ran its own poll. People who felt Carter won were told to call one 900 phone number, while those who felt Reagan won were told to call another 900 phone number. This call-in poll found Reagan won the debate according to two-thirds of those phoning in, while a more conventional CBS News poll showed only a 44 percent to 36 percent margin for Reagan. The ABC poll was probably one of the worst polls in the history of political polling. Since people are charged fifty cents to phone 900 numbers, this polling procedure discriminated against people who will not or cannot pay to register their feelings. Given the time-zone differences across the country, people on the West Coast had more time to phone in their views after the debate than easterners did — and Reagan had more supporters on the West Coast. Finally, the possibility of manipulating the poll by making multiple calls means that the poll may have been rigged. Regardless of these problems, the ABC poll was widely reported and may have affected public perceptions of who won the debate, which in turn could have affected the outcome of the election.

Another criticism of polls is that release of exit poll results during voting hours discourages some people from voting. In 1980 the television networks reported the results of exit polls on the early evening news. The results indicated that Ronald Reagan would win, even though there was still time to vote in most states. Jimmy Carter conceded defeat while West Coast voting booths were still open. This caused some people in western states to stay at home instead of going to vote. Even if the presidential race was decided, this may have affected some close House and Senate races in the West. Several losing Democratic candidates claimed that most of the people who stayed at home would have voted for them, so they might have won had this not happened. In part, the fault was Carter's; he need not have conceded while voting was still going on. But it was also irresponsible for the media to report exit polls while people were still voting. The networks appeared to put their desire to be the first to report the election results ahead of the consideration that their behavior might effect the outcome of the election itself.

The 1980 early report led to public pressure on the media to withhold results until the polls close. Because of this pressure, the networks now withhold reports in a state until its polling places officially close. However, it is often easy to tell the results of the exit polls from the network coverage. For example, Dan Rather began the CBS coverage of the 1984 election day returns at 7:30 p.m. Eastern Standard Time, saying "Good evening, everyone. Can Ronald Reagan make it a fifty-state sweep?" He next summarized the electoral vote totals at that moment: 136 for Reagan, while Mondale had "zero, none, zip, nada." Then he added: "Walter Mondale has seen the light at the end of the tunnel—and it's out." Switching metaphors, Rather summarized the situation: "If today were a fish, Walter Mondale would throw it back in."[2] People who had not voted yet certainly could have guessed from this performance that network exit polls showed Reagan winning by a landslide, so their votes would not matter. CBS News used projections for states in which polls had closed to declare President Reagan reelected at 8:01, two hours before voting ended on the West Coast. Thus, ethical questions remain about such tampering with the basis of democracy.

These problems lead to frequent calls for laws limiting the publication of poll results. Whenever election results seem to have been affected by poll results, some legislators urge restrictions on publication. One common suggestion is to bar publication of poll results during the week or two prior to an election. Another is to outlaw broadcasting of poll results on election day before all the polls have closed. However, these suggestions raise some serious questions about the right of the press to freedom of speech. Even if laws were adopted, they could lead to serious abuse if high-quality polls conducted by respectable polling organizations were not published while candidates leaked their own lower-quality polls. Perhaps the real value of the continuing calls for

---

[2]John Corry, "TV: The Coverage on Election Night," *The New York Times*, 8 November 1984, p. A24.

official regulation is to make pollsters somewhat more responsible, since they realize they could hurt themselves if they act too irresponsibly.

It is worth pointing out that problems with publication are not limited to political polls. Reports on other surveys can also have undesirable consequences. For example, publication of a poll documenting the extent of drug use on a college campus could adversely affect public perceptions (and alumni support) of that college. Suppression of such a poll might violate freedom of speech, but publication of the poll might not be necessary. A researcher does not have to seek publication of poll results in local newspapers to gain publicity, particularly if the real purpose of the survey is scientific. Indeed, doing so may be unnecessarily damaging.

Another problem is that media reports of poll results are often misleading. A survey can document current public attitudes on an issue, but the results may be meaningless if the public has really reported nonattitudes. A poll might make it seem that a large proportion of the public supports a particular government action, when in fact the public does not care one way or another about it. The ethical question is how much attention should the media pay to polls on topics on which the public does not have well-established attitudes. Polls are often meaningless, and misleading publicity for such polls could have adverse effects on the government's decision making.

A final charge against the morality of polls is Benjamin Ginsberg's accusation that polls weaken the role of public opinion rather than strengthen it.[3] Because polling can be scientific, it now dominates other means of expressing opinions, such as protests, writing letters to public officials, and working through interest groups. However, Ginsberg argues, polls provide government officials a greater chance to manipulate and shape attitudes than do those other forms of expressing opinions. Ginsberg concludes that polling has decreased the importance of public views in our democracy.

Ginsberg's arguments are provocative, but we wonder if our democracy would be better off without polls. Polls allow manipulation of public opinion, but they do answer conflicting claims as to what majority opinion is. It is too easy for leaders to claim to speak for a majority when their position is actually a minority viewpoint, and polls help prevent that. We may not always be happy about what the public thinks about an issue, but it is appropriate to know what the public's opinion is—if there is a real opinion.

---

[3]Benjamin Ginsberg, *The Captive Public* (New York: Basic Books, 1986).

Importance of Polls

From this discussion it should be clear that surveys can have a number of undesirable social consequences. Most people would probably argue that the risks involved in collecting survey data should only be taken if the benefits of these data are sufficiently large. Indeed, some people argue that they are not. For example, critics argue that poll data on public opinion are unimportant because public opinion doesn't influence anything. Surveys may measure attitudes, these individuals say, but attitudes have no effects. However, this criticism seems clearly to be wrong, since an accumulating body of evidence shows that public opinion does influence what government does. Indeed, surveys are tools that allow social scientists to study the nature and extent of the relationship between public attitudes and government policy.[4]

A related criticism of polls is that they are not worth conducting because they only confirm common sense. On the contrary, academic surveys have been used to gain insights into voters' psychology, to build theories of voting behavior, to test such theories, to study public attitudes toward wars and presidents, and to gain information about such topics as human fertility, religious views, race relations, and the urban community.

Public attitudes are much more complex than one might guess. For example, given that dissent against the Vietnam war was centered on college campuses, support for the war might have been expected to be least among the college educated — but the opposite was the case. Similarly, one might have expected those who felt the war was a mistake to favor withdrawal from Vietnam, but instead they were more likely to favor escalation. These findings are not illogical, but they were unexpected, and they were important because they suggested strategies to opponents of American involvement in the war for persuading others to oppose the war. Since public attitudes are complex, and survey findings often do not confirm common sense, polls certainly seem worth doing.

At the most general level, a democracy must be concerned with what the public thinks, and polls are a good way to measure public attitudes. One might argue that polls should not reign supreme since the public is not fully informed about every issue. Still, it is appropriate for government decision makers to know the shape of public opinion when they

---

[4]Benjamin I. Page and Robert Y. Shapiro, "Effects of Public Opinion on Policy," *American Political Science Review*, 77(March 1983):175–90.

make policy decisions. One encouraging development in recent years has been a growth of polling in some East European nations as Communist leaders became interested in monitoring public attitudes. The point is that public attitudes should be important to the decision makers, and polls are a good means of measuring those attitudes. Thus, polls serve extremely important social functions and are beneficial to society, so it is worth guarding against abuse of polls so that we can enjoy their benefits.

SUMMARY

Surveys have been criticized over the years on a variety of counts. It is important to understand the limitations of surveys as well as their advantages. Surveys can be inaccurate, but at least there are clear guidelines as to how to conduct high-quality surveys. In reading the results of a poll, think through its sampling and other factors that could have affected the results. Some errors are random, but systematic errors distort the results. The misuse of polls can distort the political process, which means that it is particularly important for polls to be reported appropriately. The importance of surveys can be debated, but we contend that they provide useful information without overly distorting the political process.

Questions

1. Find an article reporting on a poll in the news section of your local newspaper. How complete is the description of the survey procedures? Is the sampling clearly described? Is it obvious what questions were asked? What more detail would you want in order to evaluate the poll?
2. Find an article reporting on a poll in the features (such as entertainment or sports) sections of your local newspaper. How does the level of reporting on survey procedures compare to that in the article you found for question 1?

17

The Ethics of Polls

Concern with the ethics of scientific research has grown in recent years. There is considerable potential for abuse in scientific research in general and in survey research in particular, so it is important to guard against that abuse. Safeguards need not hinder the research process; indeed they protect researchers who might otherwise not think about the potential for abuse of their work.

Some guidelines have been established to help focus attention on issues of ethics. For example, the federal government imposes limits on the human subjects research it sponsors. Universities must comply with these federal rules, since they receive federal funds. As a result, university research on human subjects must be approved in advance by a review committee. Ethical guidelines have also been established by several professional organizations, including the American Sociological Association and the American Association for Public Opinion Research (AAPOR). The AAPOR Code of Professional Ethics and Practices is especially important, since pollsters wishing to join that society must sign a statement subscribing to its code; most prominent survey organizations are represented in the AAPOR membership. In this chapter we discuss two broad ethical issues: the rights of respondents and professional practices.

THE RIGHTS OF RESPONDENTS

People who contribute their time to talk to interviewers have the right to expect that they will not be personally injured by participation in the project. The injury question is more severe in medical research than in survey research, and it is in medical research that the need for regulation of research practices first became apparent. Ill people are often willing to participate in an experiment in the hope that they will feel better, without realizing that the experimental drug could worsen their condition. In a few notorious cases so-called medical research was performed without the consent of the subjects, such as the inmates of Nazi concentration camps in World War II and the black Alabama prisoners in the 1950s who were not told that treatment of syphilis was being withheld. Reflection on such abuses has led some people to argue that participation in all research should be meaningfully voluntary, where *meaningful* means that the person understands the risks involved in the project before agreeing to participate.

Informed Consent

If participation in surveys is to be meaningfully voluntary, respondents must consent to be interviewed after being apprised of the topic of the research. Thus, survey respondents should give their informed consent before being interviewed.

Survey researchers often believe that compliance with the informed consent rule hinders their research. There are two reasons for this belief. First, stressing the voluntary character of participation in a survey can lower the response rate. The more one reminds people that they need not participate, the less likely they are to do so. The resulting lower response rate makes it more difficult to generalize the survey results to the population of interest. As a result, researchers typically want to underemphasize the voluntary character of participation, mentioning it only briefly while attempting to secure a potential respondent's cooperation. Interviewers generally handle this problem by giving a brief description of the project and asking the person if he or she is willing to be interviewed. If the respondent grunts anything that sounds like "OK," the interviewer quickly begins the interview before the respondent can think much more about it.

Informed consent is also problematic because telling respondents about the topic of the survey might lead them to answer questions differently than they would have had they not known the topic. For example, researchers doing a study of American attitudes toward other countries may not want respondents to be alerted to that focus from the beginning. They may prefer to ask people many general questions to see how often the topic arises spontaneously. The interviewer may be instructed to say that the interview is about public affairs generally, without focusing the respondent's attention on world affairs. Stating the purposes of a study in general rather than specific terms is a common way to handle this trade-off of ethical and practical concerns.

Serious ethical problems can arise in research that conceals its purpose from respondents. Using surveys as a guise for observation is especially repugnant. For example, it would be unethical for researchers to claim to interview people about their political opinions when the real purpose is to make observations of people's houses or living arrangements. Similarly, it would be unethical to claim that a survey is intended to measure attitudes on one topic when the real focus of the research is on a different topic. People are suspicious enough of interviewers already these days, so deceiving respondents would only cause more problems for the polling industry. If mild deception seems to be essential, respondents should at least be told the true purpose of the interview when it is over, but it is better to avoid the deception totally.

One topic of frequent controversy is whether respondents have a right to know who is sponsoring a survey. Again, this can influence whether or not a person is willing to participate in the survey. For example, Democrats might not be willing to participate in a survey sponsored by the Republican party. If they do agree to participate, they might try to answer so as to mess up the results of the survey. In such a situation the sponsor is reluctant to have its identity disclosed at the beginning of an interview. Yet one can reasonably argue that people have a right to know who is going to use their opinions before they decide whether to share those opinions.

Academic researchers generally favor disclosure of the sponsor as part of the introduction and the voluntary consent process, but other survey organizations often avoid such disclosure. The interviewer may be instructed to give the name of the research operation (usually an innocuous sounding company, like Opinion Research Company) rather than name the financial sponsor if the respondent asks who is conducting the survey.

The ethical guidelines of government and professional organizations differ in how they handle the informed consent issue. Survey research is largely exempt from the federal government's guidelines for research on human subjects, but that exemption would not hold if the subjects were deceived as part of the research. The American Political Science Association has not issued any ethics rulings on informed consent of respondents, nor are such rulings included in the American Sociological Association's code of ethics. The AAPOR Code states only that members must "strive to avoid the use of practices or methods that may . . . seriously mislead survey respondents," possibly because many polling organizations represented in the AAPOR membership do not want to limit what their interviewers can say to induce the cooperation of respondents.

This lack of emphasis on informed consent in ethical guidelines for survey research makes it especially important that surveys be conducted so as to minimize the potential risks to respondents. In particular the confidentiality of the responses and treatment of sensitive topics are points of concern.

Confidentiality of Interviews

In many situations respondents are willing to be interviewed only if they are guaranteed that they will not be quoted directly. One way to ensure this is to keep the interviews totally *anonymous*, meaning that even the researcher does not know the names of the respondents. Such anonymity can be achieved in some surveys, as when an instructor distributes a questionnaire to a class and tells students not to put their names on the forms.

Unfortunately, anonymity often conflicts with other goals of the researcher. In mail surveys, for example, the response rate is typically low at first, so researchers want to prompt those who did not send back the questionnaires. However, sending follow-up prompts requires knowing who did and who did not send back the forms. Researchers generally handle this by putting an identifying number on each questionnaire so they can tell which have not been returned, but that destroys anonymity. Even in phone and home interviews researchers often want the names of respondents so they can check to be sure the interviews took place to avoid cheating by interviewers. Also, names are necessary if the researcher wants to do follow-up interviewing with the same respondents in the future.

Thus, researchers often do not want to provide complete anonymity to their respondents. Instead researchers generally guarantee *confidentiality* by promising not to identify who made a particular statement, even if the researcher knows who was interviewed. Most survey researchers are willing to assure confidentiality, since they want to use their survey to describe the overall opinions of the public rather than those of specific respondents.

Interviews are frequently kept confidential by removing identifying materials (names, addresses, phone numbers) from interview schedules and just identifying them by a unique number. The research office will also maintain a secret file that records which respondents have which identification numbers, so the researcher can get back to the correct interview if it is necessary to check some information. Access to the confidential identification file is usually strictly limited, though its existence could still pose problems, as we describe below.

The rights of respondents to confidentiality extend to publication of the survey results. Most survey reports are intended to describe general tendencies rather than to describe particular respondents. However, the description of results can sometimes accidentally identify the respondent. For example, a report on interviews with state legislators quoted a "five term majority-party legislator from a western suburb of Pittsburgh who is a lawyer with a degree from a prominent Massachusetts law school." By providing so much information, researchers identified the respondent as fully as if the lawmaker's name were given. Similarly, publication of survey data in such a way that an analyst can locate the attitudes of the one young black doctor in a northern suburb of Philadelphia who has three children violates the right to confidentiality.

Care should be taken to preclude such identification. In the case of the state legislative interviews, for example, the report could modify nonessential aspects of the person's background so as to camouflage identity. Data should not be published at so low a level of aggregation that individual respondents can be identified. The Census Bureau does not release its results on small areas that would permit such identifications, and surveys often do not include census tract numbers in their data files even if such information is known so as to make identification of individual respondents more difficult.

The ethical guidelines for survey research emphasize the importance of anonymity and confidentiality. The federal guidelines for research with human subjects stress anonymity but exempt most surveys if the responses are recorded in such a manner that the respondents cannot be identified directly or indirectly. Both the American Sociological Association and AAPOR require confidentiality unless it is waived by the respondents. Thus signatories to the AAPOR code agree that: "Unless the respondent waives confidentiality for specified uses, we shall hold as privileged and confidential all information that might identify a respondent with his or her responses. We shall also not disclose or use the names of respondents for nonresearch purposes unless the respondents grant us permission to do so."

Sensitive Topics

Some survey topics, such as asking people about their sexual behavior, use of alcohol and drugs, and illegal conduct, are inherently sensitive. Respondents are not reluctant to discuss such topics; researchers have consistently found that people are astonishingly open about them. People apparently enjoy talking to others who genuinely want to listen to their ideas and experiences, and so respondents are willing to open up about most subjects when they meet an interviewer who is a trained listener. This tendency has permitted studies of several sensitive topics, such as Kinsey's interviews in the 1950s with volunteers about their sexual behavior and interviews with jailed prisoners during the race riots of the 1960s.

Despite people's willingness to be interviewed on sensitive topics, there remains a question of the ethics of asking questions that may disquiet people. For example, questions about various forms of sexual behavior distress many people with traditional values. There is no way to avoid this problem completely, since even what appears to be an innocent question may distress some respondents. However, the researcher should take care not to distress respondents unduly. Unless they are essential to the purposes of the research, risky questions should not be asked. Indeed, some questions are better not asked even if they are essential to the purposes of the research.

A major problem with interviewing on sensitive topics is that respondents might be injured if their responses became public. Imagine that a newspaper publishes a survey detailing the extent of drug use on a campus, after which the local police subpoena the questionnaires in order to identify respondents who admitted illegal drug use. The investigators might not want to release their interviews, but ignoring the subpoena would lead to legal action, possibly including imprisonment.

If information on sensitive topics must be gathered, the researcher should attempt to maintain the confidentiality of the interviews by removing identifying materials from the interview schedules. If an identification file is necessary, access to it should be limited, and that file should be destroyed when it is no longer essential. Even this strategy would not fully protect the respondent or the researcher, since there is no legal protection for the interviewer-respondent relationship to parallel the protections accorded to lawyer-client and doctor-patient relationships. Just as some journalists have gone to jail rather than identify their sources, so some survey researchers have had legal problems when their interviews have been subpoenaed, and destruction of evidence is certainly not a complete defense in such cases. One political scientist has served time in jail because he refused to supply his interview data involving the Vietnam War.

It is useful to see how these problems have been handled in the various research guidelines and ethical codes. In the 1970s the federal government's requirements for voluntary participation, informed consent, and minimization of risks in human subjects research included survey research. To comply, researchers had to defend any potential harm to respondents in their surveys on the basis of the value of the knowledge to be gained. Universities established human-subjects review panels, and these panels would examine survey questionnaires and procedures before the study could go into the field.

It soon became apparent that these requirements were delaying surveys from going into the field even though surveys generally posed no serious harm, and the federal guidelines were revised in the 1980s to exempt interviews from these rules. Exceptions are surveys on sensitive topics when confidentiality is not assured, surveys involving minors, and surveys involving prisoners. Whether such exemption is fully satisfactory on ethical grounds remains debatable. Intriguingly, surveys of public officials and candidates for office are totally exempt from review, regardless of the topic of the research. The federal government still requires approval of questionnaires before the interviews are conducted for surveys conducted under federal contract, which is an extreme form of prior clearance.

The American Sociological Association guidelines emphasize that "research should avoid causing personal harm to subjects used in research." Those guidelines also illustrate the complexity of the dilemma involved in the confidentiality rule for sensitive topics: "Even though research information is not privileged communication under the law, the sociologist must, as far as possible, protect subjects and informants. Any promises made to such persons must be honored. However, provided that he respects the assurances he has given his subjects, the sociologist has no obligation to withhold information of misconduct of individuals or organizations." The AAPOR code seeks to avoid procedures that may harm or humiliate survey respondents, but that does not fully address the question of surveying on sensitive topics.

PROFESSIONAL PRACTICE

The history of science is littered with occasional instances of fraud. The faked fossil skull of Piltdown man planted by a hoaxer in 1918, the apparent forgery starting in 1955 by psychologist Cyril Burt of IQ data on twins, and the alleged 1981 falsification by John Darsee of data on the effect of drugs on limiting damage after heart attacks in dogs are but three well-known examples.

While the perpetrators of these frauds were usually motivated by a desire for personal prestige, they often used their faked data to bolster their side of scientific arguments. For example, Burt claimed high correlations of intelligence scores for twins who grew up separately in order to argue that intelligence is inherited—an argument that often has been used to bolster the theory of genetic inferiority of some races and peoples. Given the possibility that scientific fraud can be used to advance particular arguments and theories, it is important that science be conducted with professionalism, with sufficient information reported about procedures employed in the study, so that other investigators can conduct independent replications to confirm the results claimed.

Polls should be conducted with professionalism in accordance with serious concern for data quality, reliability, and validity. However, even when a poll has been conducted in a completely professional manner, the reporting of the results may not be neutral. Analysis procedures should not be chosen so as to lead to a desired conclusion. Interpretations of the data should be consistent with the findings and should acknowledge the limits of confidence for the data.

Fortunately, the public seems to be aware that it is possible to lie with statistics, which limits the ability to distort poll results. The burden of proof should be on the poll: if it does not report its procedures and does not test alternative explanations of its results, its credibility is in question. In the 1970s, concern about press reporting of polls began to mount, partly because some of the reports seemed inaccurate and partly because some of the polls seemed poor. The public clearly required more information in order to evaluate press reports of polls, and that led to the polling industry adopting some disclosure rules.

Disclosure Rules

As emphasized in Chapter 16, when poll results are published, it is important that sufficient information is disclosed so that readers can decide for themselves how seriously to take the results. AAPOR has developed voluntary guidelines for reporting of polls. These guidelines require that news reports of polls include such information as the name of the sponsoring organization, the date of the interviewing, the sampling procedure along with sample size and sampling error, and the exact questions asked. These guidelines are policed by the National Council on Public Polls (NCPP). Conformity to these guidelines is voluntary and at best extends only to news reports of polls, but the NCPP does investigate charges against polls and has on occasion negated the validity of a poll.

Sponsored Research

A special set of ethical issues is involved in sponsored research. One important issue involves the right to publish from the survey. Sponsors have the right to keep confidential any proprietary data they have collected by a private polling firm, and polling firms respect that right. On the other hand, openness should be a criterion for research in universities, so that grantors should not restrict publication of sponsored research in university settings. Prepublication clearance by the sponsor is considered a particularly unacceptable practice in academic research. Many universities and professional associations try to insist that surveys conducted for the government be unclassified.

Serious problems also occur when the sponsor tries to affect the conclusions and when the sponsor tries to conceal its identity. The public has a right to know the identity of the sponsor of a study whose results have been published, in order to judge whether the sponsorship explicitly or implicitly affected the findings. If a private sponsor insists on anonymity, at the very least the nature of the sponsor should be described in general terms so that the reader can tell whether the research was sponsored by a business, a union, a political candidate, or some other.

Limits to Surveys

A final ethical issue is whether the public has the right to know —or not to know—some information that can be obtained only from surveys. In taking the census, the government claims that it has a right to know the number of people living in an area, and most people accept that claim. Yet the census also includes questions on many other topics such as whether the person is a citizen of the country, the person's education, the quality of housing, and so on. It can reasonably be argued that such questions are beyond the proper concern of the government. The larger issues here are which matters the government has a right to know about and whether these matters extend beyond facts to public attitudes. Does society have a right not to know about certain matters? The fact that information can be collected does not mean that the public should know it, but what matters fall into each domain is a topic of disagreement.

SUMMARY

There are ethical problems involved in all research, including surveys. The survey researcher is not necessarily the best neutral adjudicator of these ethical problems, but inevitably the researcher must make ethical decisions. Minimally, it is important that the rights of the respondents and the rights of the public be consciously considered in planning a survey and in publishing its results. Some would argue that these rights are so important that external imposition of rules for survey conduct and reporting are necessary, though others feel that such rules would infringe on the rights of the researchers and the press. Like all ethical issues, these problems are likely to be debated without easy answers.

Questions

1. Have you ever been the respondent in a survey? If so, do you remember how the interviewer obtained your consent to participate? Were you given a choice, or was your participation assumed? Did you have a clear idea of who sponsored the survey? Did any of the questions bother you as inappropriate or nosey? Were you guaranteed that your answers would be kept confidential? Afterwards, did you feel good about having participated in the interview, or did you feel you were taken advantage of in some way? If you have never been a respondent in a survey, ask one of your parents if they have ever been interviewed in a survey and ask about their recollections of the experience.
2. Do you feel there should be legal limits on surveys? For example, should surveys not be permitted on certain topics, or should certain intrusions on a person's privacy not be permitted? Or, would you like to see limitation placed on survey research as a protection of the right of free speech guaranteed by the First Amendment?

Further Readings

Research Design

Campbell, Donald T., and Stanley, Julian C. *Experimental and Quasi-Experimental Designs for Research*. Chicago: Rand McNally, 1963.

Webb, Eugene, J., et al. *Nonreactive Measures in the Social Sciences*, 2nd ed. Boston: Houghton Mifflin, 1981.

Sampling

Hess, Irene. *Sampling for Social Research Surveys, 1947–1980*. Ann Arbor, Mich.: Institute for Social Research, 1985.

Kalton, Graham. *Introduction to Survey Sampling*. Beverly Hills: Sage Publications, Inc., 1983.

Kish, Leslie. *Survey Sampling*. New York: John Wiley & Sons, Inc., 1965.

Survey Research Methods

Babbie, Earl R. *Survey Research Methods*. Belmont, Calif.: Wadsworth Publishing Co., 1973.

Backstrom, Charles H., and Hursh-Cesar, Gerald. *Survey Research*, 2nd ed. New York: John Wiley & Sons, Inc., 1981.

Warwick, Donald P., and Lininger, Charles A. *The Sample Survey: Theory and Practice*. New York: McGraw-Hill, 1975.

Telephone Polls

Frey, James H. *Survey Research by Telephone*. Newbury Park, Calif.: Sage Publications, Inc., 1983.

Groves, Robert M., and Kahn, Robert L. *Surveys by Telephone: A National Comparison with Personal Interviews.* New York: Academic Press, Inc., 1979.

Lavrakas, Paul J. *Telephone Survey Methods: Sampling, Selection, and Supervision.* Newbury Park, Calif.: Sage Publications, Inc., 1987.

Questionnaire Design

Bradburn, Norman M., Sudman, Seymour, et al. *Improving Interview Method and Questionnaire Design.* San Francisco: Jossey-Bass Inc., 1981.

Converse, Jean M., and Presser, Stanley. *Survey Questions: Handcrafting the Standardized Questionnaire.* Beverly Hills: Sage Publications, Inc., 1986.

Schuman, Howard, and Presser, Stanley. *Questions and Answers in Attitude Surveys.* New York: Academic Press Inc., 1981.

Interviewing

Converse, Jean M., and Schuman, Howard. *Conversations at Random.* New York: John Wiley & Sons, Inc., 1974.

Dexter, Lewis A. *Elite and Specialized Interviewing.* Evanston, Ill.: Northwestern University Press, 1970.

Kahn, Robert L., and Cannell, Charles F. *The Dynamics of Interviewing.* New York: John Wiley & Sons, 1967.

Survey Research Center Field Office. Interviewer's Manual, revised ed. Ann Arbor, Mich.: Institute for Social Research, 1976.

Poll Results

Converse, Philip E., et al. *American Social Attitudes Data Sourcebook, 1947–1978.* Cambridge, Mass.: Harvard University Press, 1980.

Gallup, George H. (ed.). *The Gallup Poll: Public Opinion.* Wilmington, Del.: Scholarly Resources, various years.

Miller, Warren E., Miller, Arthur H., and Schneider, Edward J. *American National Election Studies Data Sourcebook: 1952–1978.* Cambridge, Mass.: Harvard University Press, 1980.

Robinson, John P., Rusk, Jerrold G., and Head, Kendra B. *Measures of Political Attitudes.* Ann Arbor, Mich.: University of Michigan, 1968.

Schuman, Howard (ed.). *Public Opinion Quarterly.* Chicago, Ill.: University of Chicago Press.

Public Opinion Magazine, American Enterprise Institute, Washington, D. C.

Advanced Topics in Survey Research

Rossi, Peter H., Wright, James D., and Anderson, Andy B. (eds.). *Handbook of Survey Research.* New York: Academic Press Inc., 1983.

Turner, Charles F., and Martin, Elizabeth (eds.). *Surveying Subjective Phenomena*. 2 vols. New York: Russell Sage Foundation, 1984.

Secondary Analysis

Hyman, Herbert H. *Secondary Analysis of Sample Surveys: Principles, Procedures, and Potentialities*. New York: John Wiley & Sons, 1972.
Kiecolt, K. Jill, and Nathan, Laura E. *Secondary Analysis of Survey Data*. Beverly Hills: Sage Publications, Inc., 1985.

Basic Statistics

Blalock, Hubert, M., Jr. *Social Statistics*, rev. 2nd ed. New York: McGraw–Hill, 1979.
Hays, William L. *Statistics for the Social Sciences*, 2nd ed. New York: Holt, Rinehart and Winston, 1973.

Advanced Statistics

Hanushek, Eric A., and Jackson, John E. *Statistical Methods for Social Scientists*. New York: Academic Press, Inc., 1977.
Berry, William D., and Lewis-Beck, Michael S. *New Tools for Social Scientists*. Beverly Hills: Sage Publications, Inc., 1986.

Measurement

Zeller, Richard A., and Carmines, Edward G. *Measurement in the Social Sciences: The Link Between Theory and Data*. Cambridge: Cambridge University Press, 1980.

Statistical Inference

Morrison, Denton E., and Henkel, Ramon E. (eds.). *The Significance Test Controversy*. Chicago: Aldine–Atherton, 1970.

Measures of Association

Costner, Herbert L. "Criteria for Measures of Association," *American Sociological Review*, 30(June 1965):341–53.
Freeman, Linton C. *Elementary Applied Statistics for Students in Behavioral Science*. New York: John Wiley & Sons, Inc., 1965.
Liebetrau, Albert M. *Measures of Association*. Newbury Park, Calif.: Sage Publications, Inc. 1983.

Siegel, Sidney. *Nonparametric Statistics for the Behavioral Sciences*. New York: McGraw-Hill, 1956.

Weisberg, Herbert F. "Models of Statistical Relationship," *American Political Science Review*, 68(December 1974):1638–55.

Statistical Controls

Rosenberg, Morris. *The Logic of Survey Analysis*. New York: Basic Books, 1968.

Scaling

Maranell, Gary M. (ed.). *Scaling: A Sourcebook for Behavioral Scientists*. Chicago: Aldine Publishing Co., 1974.

Regression Analysis

Draper, Norman R., and Smith, Harry. *Applied Regression Analysis*. New York: John Wiley & Sons, Inc., 1966.

Edwards, Allen L. *An Introduction to Linear Regression and Correlation*. San Francisco: W.H. Freeman, 1976.

Tufte, Edward R. *Data Analysis for Politics and Policy*. Englewood Cliffs: Prentice–Hall, 1974.

Causal Modeling

Blalock, Hubert M., Jr. *Causal Inferences in Nonexperimental Research*. (Chapel Hill), N.C.: University of North Carolina Press, 1964.

Blalock, Hubert M., Jr. (ed.). *Causal Models in the Social Sciences*, 2nd ed. New York: Adline Publishing Co., 1985.

Research Reports

Becker, Howard S. *Writing for Social Scientists*. Chicago: University of Chicago Press, 1986.

Strunk, William, and White, E. B. *The Elements of Style*, 3rd ed. New York: Macmillan Publishing Company, 1979.

Evaluation of Polls

Asher, Herbert B. *Polling and the Public*. Washington, D.C.: Congressional Quarterly, 1987.

Gallup, George H. *The Sophisticated Poll Watcher's Guide*. Princeton: Princeton Opinion Press, 1972.

Roll, Charles W., Jr., and Cantril, Albert H. *Polls: Their Use and Misuse in Politics*. New York: Basic Books Inc., 1972.

Answers

Chapter 2

While there are no "correct" answers to these questions, it might be worth considering the answers given by one study of this topic.* A survey of men was used, presumably because men are more likely to be violent than women. The sample included rural residents and urban residents, thus allowing comparisons between those groups. Questions on different types of violence were included so that the uniqueness of interracial violence could be studied. Violence was broadly defined to include lawful acts by police (such as shooting looters) as well as criminal acts by rioters (which ranged from burning a draft card to burning a person). The main differences found in attitudes centered on who was committing the violence — some people approving violence on the part of authorities and other people approving violence that was intended to yield social change. That is, public attitudes were determined more by who committed the acts than by the degree of violence.

Justifying Violence (Ann Arbor: Institute for Social Research, 1972).

Chapter 3

1. b
2. Nothing — no conclusions should be based on only eight respondents.
3. c
4. b
5. d (This is the definition of sampling error.)
6. 3

Chapter 4

1. A person's education includes the number of years of school completed, the degrees the person earned, and the type of post-high-school education the person had. (This includes vocational schools and business colleges. And it suggests we may want to differentiate between types of colleges, since people who went to private or small colleges may have different attitudes from those who went to public or large universities.) There is no single correct way to ask all of this, but it is important to get as much information as possible from the person for later use in the analysis. (Note that you can find information about the person's college yourself if you get its name, so there is no reason to ask the person its size, quality, or other information of that type.) Below is shown the wording of the questions used by the Center for Political Studies to measure education. This is only one of many ways to ask the question, but the series illustrates the complexity of obtaining even factual data.

    a.   How many grades of school did you finish?
    a-1. (If less than 12) Do you have a high-school equivalency diploma or certificate?
    b.   Have you had any other schooling? (What was that?) (Any other?)
    c.   (If attended college) Do you have a college degree?
    c-1. (If yes) What degree(s) have you received? From which college(s)? Where (is that/are they) located?
    c-2. (If no college degree) What was the last college you attended? Where is that located?

2. Again, there are many possible ways to phrase a question on this topic. Some major distinctions are between permitting abortion (a) under no circumstances, (b) only for medical reasons, and (c) under all circumstances. Below is a good wording that is used in the National Election Studies. What is most important is to avoid emotionally charged phrases such as "killing fetuses" and "a woman should control her own body" so the question does not bias the answer.

    There has been some discussion about abortion during recent years. Which one of the opinions on this card best agrees with your view?

    a. By law, abortion should never be permitted.
    b. The law should permit abortion *only* in cases of rape, incest, or when the woman's life is in danger.
    c. The law should permit abortion for reasons *other than* rape, incest or danger to a woman's life, but only after the need for the abortion has been clearly established.
    d. By law, a woman should always be able to obtain an abortion as a matter of personal choice.

Chapter 5

1. The interviewer should probe to find out what is on the respondent's mind. Is R worried about the possibility of war, upset about our attempts for accommodation with Russia, or some other issue? The response could mean anything. Asking "How do you mean that?" can provide clarification. Also, the question asked what the most important problems were. After R's initial answer (and probes for clarification), the interviewer should ask, "What do you think are some other important problems facing this country?" or, "Anything else?"

2. The interviewer should repeat the second question or probe in some other way to give the respondent another chance to say more. R's answer so far sounds very much like he or she is just giving the question a moment's thought before answering.

3. As for occupation, the interviewer should probe to find out exactly what the person does. *Engineer* could mean anything from janitor to spacecraft designer. Probes are essential for finding out precisely what a person's occupation is.

Chapter 6

There is no single correct answer, but an answer should take into account a large variety of possible replies to the question as well as a variety of different possible analyses of the question. One possible approach would be to use several short codes on traits of the person named plus a large general code. An example of a short code for sex would be:

1. Male
2. Female

7. Don't know
8. Not a person (e.g., Mickey Mouse)
9. Question not asked

The large code would have some general code ranges (for Democrats, Republicans, and so on) and several detailed codes. For example:

000-099. Democrat	
001. Joe Biden	011. Ted Kennedy
002. Jesse Jackson	012. Jimmy Carter
003. Michael Dukakis	013. Walter Mondale
004. Bruce Babbitt	014. Mario Cuomo
005. Richard Gephardt	015. Gary Hart
006. Paul Simon	098. Any Democrat
007. Albert Gore	099. Some Democrat other
008. Bill Bradley	than named above
100–199. Republican	
101. George Bush	197. Ronald Reagan
102. Robert Dole	198. Any Republican
103. Pat Robertson	199. Some Republican not
104. Jack Kemp	named above

105. Paul Laxalt
106. Pete DuPont
107. Alexander Haig
200–299. Nonpolitician
  (nationally known)
201. Ralph Nader   290. Anybody but a politician
202. Lee Iacocca   291. Nationally prominent
202. Dan Rather   businessman, named
203. William Rehnquist   292. Other television figure
204. Billy Graham   293. Other religious figure
                                          299. Other nonpolitician

300–399. Personal
  Acquaintance
301. Me (Respondent)   305. R's minister, priest, or rabbi
302. Respondent's spouse
303. Member of R's family
304. Friend or neighbor
400–499. Fictitious person
401. Mickey Mouse   499. Other fictitious person
402. Donald Duck
900–999. Miscellaneous
  answers and
  categories
900. No one
990. Someone in other than
  above categories
998. Don't know
999. Question not asked

Chapter 7

1. First, you cannot generalize about young people when the sample is of high-school seniors. In particular, dropouts have been omitted from the study. At best, conclusions can be drawn about high-school seniors. Also, answers about drug use may not be candid. Some students would not be willing to admit drug use, and many would be unwilling to admit they have not tried drugs. Finally, *drugs* is a very broad term that could include anything from marijuana to heroin (and some would say anything from aspirin to alcohol). The meaning of the question "Have you experimented with drugs?" is not clear.

2. The survey gave members of Congress a very abstract choice. It is very easy for them to claim they follow their constituents' wishes like good public servants. Their answers are not likely to be predictive of how they behave in the case of a real conflict. Presenting the legislators with an actual conflict would yield more meaningful answers.

3. It is probably difficult to code how ideological a given goal is. The intercoder reliability should be checked before believing this result.

4. a. Interval (or ratio)—this is a real number, the units are meaningful, and there is a meaningful zero point.

Chapter 8

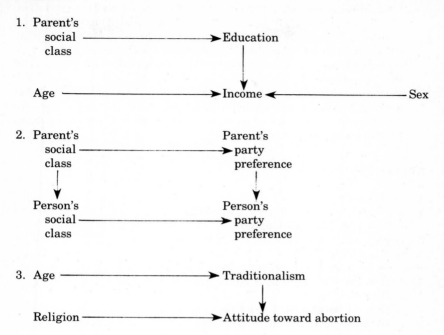

1. Parent's social class ——————→ Education

   Age ——————————→ Income ←—————————— Sex

2. Parent's social class ——————→ Parent's party preference

   Person's social class ——————→ Person's party preference

3. Age ——————————→ Traditionalism

   Religion ——————————→ Attitude toward abortion

   b. Nominal—these are discrete categories, not in any systematic progression.
   c. Ordinal—these are ordered categories, without meaningful units.

Chapter 9

1. 1,000
2. 25.0 percent
3. 40.0 percent
4. 35.0 percent
5. "Other party," "not ascertained," and "don't know what parties are."
6. Mode: Democratic; median: independent, assuming that independent is in between Republican and Democrat.
7. $\overline{X} = 80$ $s^2 = 100$ $s = 10$
8. Recode old categories 0, 1, 5, and 6 into new category 2. Recode old categories 2, 3, 4 into new category 1.
9. New category 1 = 1 on both presidential and congressional vote, or
                 = 2 on both presidential and congressional vote.
   New category 2 = 1 on presidential vote and 2 on congressional vote, or
                 = 2 on presidential vote and 1 on congressional vote.
   New category 3 = 3 on either presidential or congressional vote.
10. Add up the three items so that 3 means three campaign activities, 2 means

two campaign activities, 1 means one campaign activity, and 0 means none. Missing data are a problem here. One solution would be to give a person a score of 9 for missing data if the person has a 9 on any of the three questions (thus this is not strictly an additive process). Another possibility would be to count the number of campaign activities that the person performed and give the score 9 only if the person had missing data on all three questions.

11. Performed all three activities; attended meetings and did party work, but gave no contributions; attended meetings, but did no party work and gave no contributions; performed none of the three activities. No other pattern fits this scale perfectly.

Chapter 10

1. 30.85 percent.
2. a. $z = (95 - 75)/10 = 20/10 = 2$, so 0.0228.
   b. $75 \pm 1.96\,(10) = 55.4$ to 94.6.
3. a. $10/\sqrt{101 - 1} = 10/\sqrt{100} = 10/10 = 1.0$.
   b. Yes. $z = (78.5 - 75)/1 = 3.5 > 2.58$.
   c. $78.5 \pm 2.58\,(1) = 75.92$ to 81.08.
4. a. $10/\sqrt{26 - 1} = 10/\sqrt{25} = 10/5 = 2.0$.
   b. No. $z = (78.5 - 75)/2 = 1.75 < 1.96$.
   c. $78.5 \pm 1.96\,(2) = 74.58$ to 82.42.
5. a. $10/\sqrt{26 - 1} = 10/\sqrt{25} = 10/5 = 2.0$.
   b. No. $t = (78.5 - 75)/2 = 1.75 < 2.060$, with 25 degrees of freedom.
   c. $78.5 \pm 2.06\,(2) = 74.38$ to 82.62.

Chapter 11

1. Education.
2. Position on relations with Russia.
3. Yes. The percentages are within categories of the independent variable.
4. c
5. More militant.
6. Small.
7. The number of cases in each educational category.

Chapter 12

1. Race is dichotomous (assuming that races other than white and black are set aside because there are too few cases for analysis), and the sign of a correlation between dichotomous variables is essentially meaningless. Therefore, the minus sign does not mean there is a negative relationship between a person's race and interest in politics. It may mean there is some relationship between race and interest in politics. However, the most useful statement would be one that describes the relationship, as by saying which race has (or claims) the greater interest.
2. Religion is a nominal variable (Protestant, Catholic, Jewish, other, none),

so a tau correlation should not be calculated. This correlation would make sense only if the correlation were computed only on the basis of Protestants versus Catholics (or Christians versus Jews, or some religion versus no religion). Otherwise, lambda should be used to match the nominal character of religion.

3. Knowledge of the region a person lives in yields a 20 percent reduction in error in guessing the person's vote. A statement of exactly how the regions differ would probably be of more value than this summary statistic.

4. There is a strong tendency for attitudes on abortion and divorce to scale. Yet gammas can be much larger than taus, so there is no proof of high covariance between these variables.

5. This correlation is very small. Unless the sample is very large, it is not likely to be statistically significant. Even if it is, the correlation is not of major importance. One might believe this correlation if it fit with other known data, but age differences have only a minor effect on attitudes toward divorce according to this result. One possibility to explore is whether age has a steady effect on the attitude. Perhaps the correlation is so small because young people are more tolerant of divorce than middle-aged people, but middle-aged people are less tolerant of divorce than older people. A lambda correlation might test such a possibility.

Chapter 13

1. Reported Turnout in 1972 by Education, Controlling on Sex

	Males			Females		
	Grade School	High School	College	Grade School	High School	College
Voted	67%	74%	85%	50%	68%	89%
Did not vote	33	26	15	50	32	11
Total	100%	100%	100%	100%	100%	100%
N (total 2,281)	(199)	(413)	(362)	(241)	(732)	(334)

SOURCE: 1972 Center for Political Studies American National Election Study.

2. There are age differences in Table 13.12, with young and middle-aged people being more in favor of an equal role for women than are older people. Table 13.13 shows these age differences remain among college- and high-school-educated people, but nearly vanish among the grade-school- educated. Note also that education has a considerable effect on the views of young people and middle-aged people but has less affect on those of older people. A careful inspection of Table 13.13 would show that educational differences surpass age differences but that generational differences do exist.

Chapter 14

1. $r^2 = 9$ percent.
2. d. Statistical significance does not imply substantive significance.

3. e. It means that a one-unit change in the independent variable induces a half-unit change in the dependent variable when the effects of other variables are *not* controlled.
4. It is impossible to tell from this information. Standardized regression coefficients (beta weights) are required to tell which variable is more important.

Chapter 15

Your answer should point out that, on balance, a majority of Americans do not approve of the president's performance, but that the difference is slight and about the size of sampling error. Furthermore, the difference seems mainly to result from (a) greater support for the president among Republicans than Democrats and (b) the fact that there are many more Democrats than Republicans.

You should indicate that the effect of partisanship on approval of the president is slight. There is an effect, but it is not very large. You might want to quote the tau value, but you can probably make the point more effectively by indicating that there is a 20 percent difference in support for the president between Republicans and Democrats.

You might also suggest some control variables that would help test this relationship. Region is one of the most likely control variables. For example, support for the president might be well above 40 percent for Southern Democrats though well below 40 percent for Northern Democrats. Thus, partisanship might have a much greater effect on approval of the president for Northerners than for Southerners.

Index to Notation and Statistics: Terms and Symbols

Level of Measurement

Other Statistics

Other Notation

INDEX